Suffer
the Future

Africa below the Equator

Suffer
the Future
Policy Choices in
Southern Africa

Robert I. Rotberg

HARVARD UNIVERSITY PRESS
Cambridge, Massachusetts
and
London, England
1980

Library of Congress Cataloging in Publication Data

Rotberg, Robert I
   Suffer the future, policy choices
   in southern Africa.

   Includes bibliographical references and index.
   1.   Africa, Southern — Politics and government —
1975-   2.   Africa, Southern — Economic conditions.
3.   Africa, Southern — Social conditions.   4.   Africa,
Southern — Race relations.   5.   National liberation
movements — Africa — Southern.   I.   Title.
DT746.R67   968.06   79-25845
ISBN 0-674-85401-2

For all those who accept the message of Isaiah 61:11–
that righteousness and praise can be caused to
"spring forth before all the nations"

Contents

SOUTHERN AFRICA

Maps

(*prepared by Vaughn Gray*)

Preface

SOUTHERN AFRICA has long been embroiled in conflict. South Africa, the dominant country in the region, is no longer impregnable; there bitterness between white and black takes increasingly hostile forms at the same time as the government gropes for ways of conceding social and economic betterment without sharing political power. To the north and west, in Zimbabwe and Namibia, long-standing contests for control continue. In all three countries, the heart of the region that makes up the southern third of the continent, there is no ignoring fundamental differences over answers to the basic question: Who is to rule?

Words like *chaos* and *turmoil* have categorized popular reporting of the current circumstances of southern Africa, and hint at a contemporary analysis and an expectation of the future that may or may not be accurate. It is especially because southern Africa is so troubled in ways not readily explicable to most Americans and Europeans that this book has been written. It offers readers an interpretation of today's and tomorrow's headlines as well as an examination of the enduring complexities of three countries the fates of which will long affect citizens of the West. This book tries to provide readers with the basis for making their own dispassionate judgments. It may also permit future positions to be assessed and surveyed.

The peculiar problems of southern Africa will not readily go away. Nor will they be solved easily or conveniently by repression, bloodshed, or outside intervention. It is among the purposes of this book to give substance to such statements, and to provide the framework for the decisions that will be made in the West as well as in southern Africa if the troubled, prosperous nations of southern Africa are to reconcile the interests of their majorities and minorities.

The futures of South Africa, Zimbabwe (formerly Rhodesia), and Namibia (formerly South-West Africa) are of concern to Americans and to all others in the West. "The problem of the twentieth century is the problem of the color line," said William Edward Burghardt Du Bois long ago in *The Souls of Black Folk* (Chicago, 1903). One laudable aim of policymakers in the West is to prevent the problem of the color line from bedeviling the twenty-first century as well. But resolving that problem is not only a matter of the simplistically conceived shift from minority to majority rule in the last African redoubt of white control. Even more, it is the creation of conditions under which the benefits of such a transformation, massive in its implications, can be maximized for all of the inhabitants of southern Africa, for Africa as a whole, and for the West. Is it possible for nations to bring about such a transformation without being consumed by violence? Are there intermediate goals and routes to those goals that it is in the interest of the West, and of the United States, to encourage? Are outsiders capable of exerting an influence on the formulation of policy that is sufficient to generate internal reassessments and an acceptance of hitherto rejected alternative goals and policies for attaining those goals?

Answers to greater and lesser questions of this sort are ideally preceded by a critical examination of the relevant historical, social, economic, strategic, and political forces that have contributed to and exacerbated the conflicts in southern Africa.

This book discusses the strengths and weaknesses of the three problem areas of southern Africa. South Africa is the long-standing focus of primary concern and, like Namibia and Zimbabwe, a nation for which no single solution is either inherently likely to be devised or capable alone of remedying all of its myriad outstanding human disparities. The chapter on South Africa's physical and social fundamentals is followed by two chapters on its current politics, two on its economy (including nuclear issues), and a chapter which suggests lessons for the future. The same broad topics are discussed in the two chapters each on Namibia and Zimbabwe. The final chapter takes these analyses to their logical conclusions, especially for policymaking.

There are many reasons, some already mentioned, for writing a book that attempts to make the problems of a critical region more comprehensible to American and European readers — and even to southern Africans themselves. The major one is my affection, concern, and anxiety for the peoples of the three countries on which this book is focused, for their destinies, and for the fates of those who — unasked — will inherit the whirlwind. That affection and anxiety are based on an acquaintance that has endured for more than twenty years and on an involvement that has intensified more recently. For someone whose professional life has been concerned with the emergence of the Third World, especially with that of the peoples of Africa and the Caribbean, there can be no subject more worthy of attention in the 1980s than southern Africa, a region of which South Africa is the obvious fulcrum.

As a person actively concerned with the future development of an area critical to Americans, I have often been asked to recommend a book which is at once current and knowledgeable about the past, which covers all of southern Africa and not just a part of the troubled region, which is informed about the quality of black as well as white politics, which deals with resources and other economic issues, which is realistic and not romantic, which eschews the kinds of dogma which have long hindered objective discussions of southern Africa, and which informs without preaching. I have been asked for a book that is accessible to all — one not burdened excessively by footnotes and other academic apparatus. What is wanted is a book which will be read comfortably on trains and airplanes and in company boardrooms as well as in the classroom and in professional studies.

Suffer the Future strives to fulfill those needs without sacrificing the care of scholarship. To do so has meant compromises. Many of the conclusions of this book are controversial. Some of the data are in dispute. Yet I have included few citations which discuss the complexities of the controversies or explicitly describe disputed data. I have tried to let this book go to press with up-to-date, reliable figures for mineral production, petroleum, imports, military numbers, and so on. Yet the statistics on which I rely are not always public; many reflect personal investigation, educated inference, or the piecing together of published accounts.

The generosity of the Edward W. Hazen Foundation and the Ford Foundation made possible most of the travel and research on which this book is based. In addition, my participation in a meeting in South Africa sponsored by the World Peace Foundation of Boston (at which the germ of chapter 6 was first presented) and another sponsored by the 1820 Settlers Foundation of Grahamstown provided opportunities for travel and for consultation and discussion with southern Africans and colleagues from the West. Some of the ideas advanced here were first introduced at seminars in the United States arranged by the Seven Springs Conference Center of Mount Kisco, New York, or in articles written over several years for the *Christian Science Monitor* and other newspapers. Many years ago a fellowship from the Guggenheim Memorial Foundation made possible a long, formative visit to South Africa. Years before, too, the combined resources of the Rhodes Trust of Oxford and the Rockefeller Foundation enabled me to make my initial contact with southern Africa and its peoples.

None of these philanthropic bodies bears responsibility for what follows; each, in differing but always welcome measure, has encouraged the kind of intellectual and human process of unfettered discovery without which the ideas contained here — long collated only in the shorthand of the mind — might not so readily have been transferred to the printed page.

Individuals as well as the eleemosynary institutions already mentioned contributed greatly to the research, the travel, the understanding, the writing, and every other conceivable component of this book. It is a pleasure to acknowledge their very great influence. Several individuals — William Bowdler, William Bradley, William Carmichael, John Clingerman, Harvey Nelson, Sir David Scott, and C. Thomas Thorne — provided welcome encouragement and insight during the several years over which this book was transferred from a collection of impressions to the discipline of the printed page. Patrick Bowen, Richard Pendleton, James Rawlings, and Robert Ward helpfully developed information on important problems of detail. Ann Bernstein, Jeffrey Butler, William E. Griffith, Thomas L. Neff, and Richard Ullman were careful and thoughtful critics of crucial sections of various drafts of the book.

Philip Christenson was a mine of knowledge and an assiduous reader on more than one occasion of two central chapters. Helen Kitchen read the whole with her usual eye for precision and clarity and contributed significantly to the reformulation of more than one version of this book. Carrie Hunter undertook the original research for what has since emerged as the chapter on the economy of South Africa. Part of an earlier version of chapter 6 appeared in Helen Kitchen (ed.), *Options for U.S. Policy toward Africa*, a special issue of *AEI Foreign Policy and Defense Review*, I (1978), 41-44. In the battle to develop current statistics and make sense of a welter of often contradictory research, the assistance of Mari Borstelmann proved invaluable. Nicola S. Rotberg, my daughter, drew the first sketches of the maps; the final versions were prepared with his usual professional precision by Vaughn Gray. Ruth Cross prepared the index with flair and speed. Donna L. Rogers presided efficiently over the laborious process of drafting and regular redrafting that was an unusual characteristic of this book's long period of gestation.

Just as it is with lasting gratitude that I acknowledge the assistance and support of those Americans and Britons who have greatly facilitated and shaped my own thinking and work, so it is the greater, and the more painful, part of prudence to refrain from thanking by name the many southern Africans who shared with me their homes, their tables, their ideas, and their friendship, who instructed and criticized, and who greatly influenced the shape of this book while affording me enormous pleasure. Fortunately, most know who they are, and will accept this silent tribute. They include black and white politicians (cabinet ministers as well as leaders of the opposition) and officials of differing persuasions, journalists, academic colleagues, students, diplomats, businessmen, trade unionists, physicians, courageous campaigners for civil liberties, lawyers, chiefs, commoners—some or all members of those hardy, difficult-to-categorize groups that seek reconciliation instead of conflict and cling to a vision of a future in which harmony replaces violence.

Joanna Rotberg, my wife, has always been the best of critics.

The preparation of this book has in part consumed her as well. It has taken a father too much from his children, but the result is presented here for them to read and—like the children of southern Africa—to build upon later.

R. I. R.
18 December 1979

Suffer
the Future

A Note to the Reader

CURRENCY IS GIVEN in the units of the original sources. In terms of United States currency, the South African rand (R) was valued at $1.19 in 1979 and $1.15 in 1978; the Rhodesian dollar (R$) was equivalent to $1.44 in 1979 and $1.30 in 1978.

With a few exceptions that will be clear in the text, measurements have been converted to the English system according to the following standard equivalences: 1 millimeter = 0.0394 inches; 1 kilometer = 0.622 miles; 1 kilogram = 2.205 pounds; 1 hectare = 2.471 acres.

South Africa accepts the independence of Transkei, Bophuthatswana, and Venda, and in many cases excludes those areas from its national statistical reporting. This book includes the homelands as part of South Africa statistically and otherwise.

South Africa

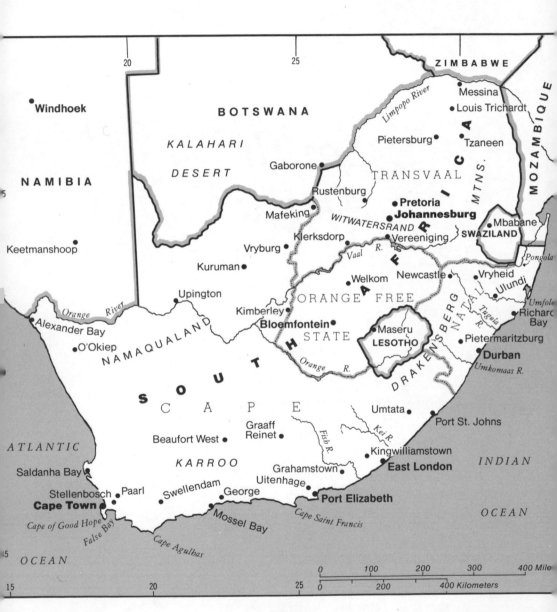

South Africa

1 | The Grounding
of Politics

SOUTH AFRICA is a complex of contradictions. A state that has divided itself along lines of color, it cannot escape the interdependence of all the strands of a single people bound together by geography, history, economic realities, and the cement of circumstance. Although South Africa's rulers have with determination, craft, and ingenuity persisted in denying that interdependence, in attempting to unravel the tangled skein of their inheritance, and in putting asunder the consequences of a collective objectivity, their failure is as patent in reality as it is studiously ignored by official policy. As interdependence intensifies, almost day by day, so the rulers cling with increasing fervor to the comfort of anachronism. They apotheosize the impossible and fiddle with the consequences of that apotheosis. Policymakers still espouse a separation that never existed, chasing a social chimera that, if it could be captured, would modify, if not destroy, the modernity of which South Africans are so rightly proud.

Industrially, South Africa is powerful, innovative, and energetic. Yet the expansion of the industrial base is restricted by social and political shibboleths that are economically irrational and that testify to the endurance of anachronism. Similarly, security and privilege are defined by refuge in the same anachronism, by emphasizing privilege amid poverty and denial and repression alongside opportunity and freedom, by marching squalor in lockstep with splendor, and by the celebration of a pigmental binomialism from which there is no escape. South Africans officially nurture the notion of two separated nations and

3

define that separation strictly, rigidly, and, in theory, irreversibly, by the immutable taint of color. (In the popular parlance this peculiar South African system is known as *apartheid*.) No other state in history has so recklessly risked its own survival and that of its ideals, its rulers, and much of its actual and potential riches for political premises that can only be perpetuated against enormous demographic, social, and economic odds.

The Body Politic

South Africa consists of about 27 million people, only about 4.5 million of whom are classified white. The remainder are black, including 2.5 million Coloureds (persons of mixed descent) and about 0.8 million Asians. By the year 2000 these numbers will swell to about 50 million. The African population will be 37 million and the white population only 6 million; Coloureds will approach 5 million and Asians more than a million. Whites were 20 percent of the total in 1914; they will represent 14 percent in 2000. In the cities, where whites are now outnumbered two to one by blacks, Africans alone will be four times more numerous than whites. These figures, and others presented later in this chapter, are the ingredients of a demographic time bomb that South African policy, as presently conceived, seems determined to detonate.

The people of South Africa inhabit a land of many mineral and few other natural resources. In fact, most of the country consists of a poorly watered, high, temperate plateau of marginal soils. Surrounding the plateau are massive mountain chains, two deserts, a narrow zone of fertile foothills and coastal plains, and, at the perimeter, a long seacoast with numerous ports on two of the world's major oceans. Together this is a mixed endowment, but of its differences and distinctions South Africans have made much—so much, in fact, that South Africa dominates the statistical lists of the African continent and much of the Third World. It boasts more road and rail miles and a higher consumption of electricity per capita, higher levels of literacy, and more hospital beds per capita—to choose only five from a number of standard indicators of development—than all other African and most Asian countries. But the undoubted prosperity and the elevated standard of living of the country, compared with that of other states, masks undeniable internal disparities that are deep, divisive, and increasing in absolute if not in relative terms.

There is the land. A people long wedded to the soil still depend for sustenance and livelihood on the products of a stubborn inheritance. Considering physiography together with climate and rainfall, the land comes in three varieties. The first, the lush, tropical plain between the Indian Ocean and the foothills of the Drakensberg Mountains, and a few other scattered pockets, has high rainfall, rich soil, and generally rewarding conditions for agriculture. Up from the coast is the Highveld, most of which is suitable for grazing and, under careful management, the growing of grain. Underneath the soils of the Highveld, however, are the country's greatest sources of wealth—its minerals in profusion. The third zone, on the western and northern perimeter of the Highveld, is mineral-and water-poor, with a climate and a soil structure that permit arid land grazing and tentative subsistence cropping only. It is an area subject to periodic drought. Over the years, whites have appropriated the better portions of the first and second zones to themselves, leaving only the least attractive part of the first and nearly all of the third to Africans. In terms of total land area, too, the numerically preponderant Africans can farm and reside in only 13 percent of South Africa.

The Distribution of Resources

The homelands, subordinate geopolitical divisions of South Africa, which comprise the 13 percent and in the 1970s held about half of the black population of the country, are supposed to be the places to which Africans have a right. Yet they are situated in what is on average the least favored section of South Africa: the homelands are less well watered and have poorer soils, fewer natural resources, and—compared to the white-dominated parts of the country—a sparse and deficient infrastructure. As long ago as the 1920s, white investigators realized that Africans had been systematically deprived of the more arable lands of their fathers and pushed onto the soils and into the areas least suitable for the kinds of intensive agriculture without which crowded populations could not support themselves.[1] One result was predictable: the African population on the land grew more numerous; its cattle, sheep, and goats grazed the land more as-

---

1. Jeffrey Butler, Robert I. Rotberg, and John Adams, *The Black Homelands of South Africa* (Berkeley, 1977), 10-11.

siduously; and the result was increased overcrowding, poor husbandry, erosion, and a spiral of destruction that made the homelands far less able to support their largely rural populations in the
1970s than they had been one or many decades before.

With some exceptions, the distribution of natural endow-
ments and resources and a series of frontier wars in the nineteenth century have imposed a settlement pattern upon South Africa that has scattered the concentrations of white population
along the coast and in a few, largely gold-determined centers in
the interior. Development has taken place in these white settled
areas and in the small towns dispersed as commercial centers
throughout the vast countryside. Long ago this pattern, and the
restrictions imposed upon African cash cropping by white-controlled governments, forced Africans to support themselves by
selling their labor, often as migrants to the urban areas, or as
subsistence farmers in the homelands.

Well before the middle of this century, the unnatural division of South Africa into two peoples was fixed. The first farmed
the good lands on which rain usually fell, employed black labor
enticed from or compelled to leave the homelands, and was
linked to the cities with their industrial enterprises and their
armies of skilled and unskilled black labor. The second scratched
a bare living from the soil and sent its young men to the cities and
white-owned farms, rarely to return home permanently until they
had exhausted their productivity in the service of whites. Obviously the white sector had the good roads, water, and communications facilities. It had access to lending facilities and to governmental assistance in time of need. The black sector had not, and
still — even in the era of so-called independent homelands — lags
far behind. Educationally and medically the good facilities were
and still are part of the first sector. The second makes do. It is
only where the homelands have declared their independence that
air links have been forged with Johannesburg and new roads and
medical and educational arrangements been explored. Yet even
in the era of showpiece separate development, differences — physical and economic — between the two peoples remain. Only a vast
unscrambling of the map of South Africa could begin to integrate
the two and distribute the benefits of development more equita-
bly.

Yet whites cannot maintain themselves without the labor of blacks. Two-thirds of all economically active African labor is employed in the white economic heartland (some workers commute from nearby homelands), or by whites in rural areas adjacent to the homelands. Urban sections of KwaZulu, Bophuthatswana, and Ciskei are located near Durban, Newcastle, Pretoria, and East London; areas within these homelands have become dormitories in much the same way as Soweto houses and supplies much of the labor force of Johannesburg.

A politically salient product of urbanization, with the concomitant attraction of Africans into the cities, has been the rise of a panethnic consciousness — a stimulation of the bonds of a brotherhood of color. Yet, white South Africans deny — for obvious political reasons — that Africans are one people. (They also deny that whites can be subdivided ethnically.) Historically, their case has merit; if Africans had remained exclusively rural, they might have remained alien from one another, speaking diverse languages, cultivating different crops, and tending cattle and sheep in distinct ways. In Africa or elsewhere, it is not possible completely to escape the entrapment of language, the cultural differences that follow, and the xenophobia that is often a by-product. There were and are undeniable ethnic differences among Africans. But the urban environment and white rule have crowded peoples of many backgrounds together, encouraged them to communicate with one another in common tongues, socialized them to a new culture or at least created a cultural amalgam, and effectively given Africans a sense of common bonds that cut across and sometimes supersede ethnic identities.

The Heritage of Ethnicity

Africans have thus been politicized, and that factor is central to the South African paradox. Today the government emphasizes ethnicity and tries to revert to a preindustrial age by emphasizing primordial differences, separate development, and sectionalism. The demographic dominance of Africans is obviously less threatening if each of the African nations can be dealt with separately by whites. But the ticking of the demographic time bomb, and the location of that bomb — in terms of African numbers, in the cities — makes it unlikely that separate development can reverse the implications of the policy of industrial growth that long ago made whites wealthy and transformed Africans from rural people living at a subsistence level into acculturated entrepreneurs, professionals, skilled workers, and an industrial proletariat.

Because whites do not predominate numerically within South Africa, they often justify separate development on tenuous historical as well as racial grounds. The land was empty when they arrived in 1652, they have long said. Whites from Holland landed in the southwest, at Cape Town, and Africans—the Bantu-speaking forefathers of nearly all blacks resident in today's South Africa—were invading across the Limpopo River in the north. Only Khoi (Hottentots) and San (Bushmen), the whites try to aver, lived in what is now South Africa. A struggle between two colonizers occurred, the whites won, and want to remain in charge.

That is one version of history. Another, supported by archaeological as well as by written and oral evidence, is that the ancestors of today's black population had long resided in South Africa, but for ecological reasons had not farmed or grazed as far southwest as the Cape peninsula. Khoi and San lived in scattered settlements in the western Cape, much as they did when the whites arrived. But they had not been forced back into that area at any recent time. If Africans swarmed southward—and there is no strong evidence of immigrations from the north after A.D. 1000, if before—they did not so much displace Khoi and San as displace other Africans, presumably also Bantu-speakers. Whatever the etiology of settlement, Africans were in place centuries before the arrival of whites. Moreover, the whites essentially stayed at the Cape, interbreeding with Khoi, and with Malays imported from Indonesia, throughout the seventeenth century. Only in the later eighteenth and even more in the nineteenth century did whites begin to compete with Africans for territory far outside of the Cape peninsula.

In the later seventeenth century, the stragglers and victuallers who had earlier been settled at the Cape by the Dutch East India Company were joined by French-speaking Huguenots, fellow Calvinists fleeing the persecutions of Europe. They came in several waves, doubling the population of the Dutch outpost and infusing its people with an especially inflexible theological perspective. In the nineteenth century, Britain, which took control of the Cape Colony from the Dutch in 1795, encouraged British settlement in the Cape and also in the Indian Ocean frontier colony of Natal. Immigration became more important throughout that century than ever before; a wide range of settlers from Europe were attracted to the area, some fleeing pogroms in their own lands. Called by industry, a trickle of European immigrants came to South Africa throughout the twentieth century. Beginning in 1860 south Indians were induced to settle on the sugar plantations of Natal as indentured servants. They stayed on, being preceded and joined by north Indian merchants from Bombay and Gujerat. A few Chinese merchants also came. Classified as Asian, they now number 8,500. There also is a new group of expatriate Japanese and Chinese businessmen who are classified as white.

Coloureds have ancestors who are white, black, and brown. They, as much as Africans and whites, are the indigenous South Africans. The products of both legal and illegal miscegenation during the first centuries of white settlement, they lost the remainder of their political rights, and hence much of their status, only after 1948. During the first century of contact between blacks and whites, especially when Malays were imported as a domestic servant class, miscegenation was assumed and tolerated. After the Huguenot influx, especially in the more narrow-minded Victorian era, with its greater abundance of white women, marriage and liaisons across the line of color were increasingly regarded as illicit.

What is often forgotten is that in the Cape Province the Coloured population is long established, uses Afrikaans as its mother tongue, and has its own culture and its own literature. Coloureds are for the most part urbanized and Westernized. Until the 1950s they saw their destiny as bound up inextricably with that of whites. They are a people within a nation: they fish, farm, raise livestock, and work in industry in the Cape. Only since 1948 has the new order in South Africa — the Afrikaner ascendancy — made of the Coloureds a collection of human tragedies; with families being divided and long-established relationships sundered only because of shades of pigmentation.

The Coloureds — as a political and human problem — are a microcosm of South Africa. In them — although too little will be made of it in this book — is encapsulated the peculiar suffering of a beautiful, developed country with its still unrealized potential. They, like Africans, are a part of the suffering of the past, and they will suffer in its future; but, because of the relationship of demography and resources to power, the confrontation of southern Africa has already bypassed the Coloureds and Asians, both of whom by governmental edict have been divided from whites by color.

The confrontation that will occupy the 1980s and 1990s in South Africa is essentially between Afrikaners, with their grip on power and their monopoly of resources, and Africans, with their numbers and their labor. The stakes, as this chapter and chapter 4 demonstrate, are massive.

The People: Demographic Realities

Of the 26.1 million people who lived in South Africa in mid-1976, 18.7 million (including de facto residents of Transkei, a homeland the independence of which was recognized only by South Africa) were African; 4.3 million, white; 2.4 million, Coloured; and 0.7 million, of Asian descent. Roughly 60 percent of the whites were of Afrikaner and 40 percent of English, Scottish, and Jewish background. The Africans included 5 million Zulu, 4.9 million Xhosa, 2.1 million Tswana, 2 million northern Sotho or Pedi, 1.6 million southern Sotho, 0.8 million Shangaan, 0.6 million Swazi, 0.4 million Venda, 0.6 million miscellaneous others, and 0.4 million "foreign" Africans, many of whom were from Botswana, Zimbabwe, Namibia, and Mozambique. The Zulu, Xhosa, and Swazi languages are closely related, mutually intelligible, and collectively called Nguni. Together the Nguni-speaking population was nearly 11 million in 1976; the Zulu alone, or the Nguni together, will remain the largest single population cluster in South Africa.

The largest cities in 1978 were Johannesburg, with at least 1.3 million Africans (nearly all in Soweto, its African dormitory complex) and about 600,000 whites; Cape Town, with 700,000 Coloureds, 400,000 whites, and 200,000 Africans; Durban, with 350,000 Asians, 300,000 Africans, and 275,000 whites; Pretoria (exclusive of Winterveld and similar African townships), with about 381,000 whites and 306,000 Africans (plus 29,000 Asians and Coloureds); Port Elizabeth, with 250,000 Africans, 175,000 whites, and 150,000 Coloureds; and Bloemfontein, with 120,000 Africans and 80,000 whites. Mdantsane — in the Ciskei, near East London — with nearly 300,000 people, was the largest African city after Soweto and Umlazi, an African suburb of Durban located within KwaZulu.

The African rural population of South Africa consisted of two blocs — the 9 million who resided in homelands, independent or not independent, and the 3 million who worked on white-owned farms. The de facto populations of the homelands in 1977 were KwaZulu, 2.8 million; Transkei, 2.4 million; Lebowa, 1.4 million; Bophuthatswana, 1.2 million; Ciskei, 530,000; Venda, 348,000; Gazankulu, 344,000; KaNgwane, 213,000; and Qwa-Qwa, 92,000. (The Ndebele homeland was established in late 1977.) According to a recent examination of rural magisterial districts, only a few in the western half of the Cape Province could claim a majority of whites. In most of the others in the Cape, either Coloureds or blacks predominated.

These statistics have important political consequences. In 1978 about half of the total black population of South Africa lived in the so-called white heartland of the country. African populations were only marginally larger than whites in the urban areas in the 1970s. Yet in the year 2000 more than half of all Africans will live in urban and other areas now controlled by whites; there they will far outnumber whites. However the government of South Africa attempts to exclude them from the major conurbations, the location of industry and the patterns of employment and settlement that have characterized the twentieth century are expected by all cautious observers to carry over into the twenty-first century. Another way of expressing the implication of the numbers is that although the homelands, independent and not independent, will grow absolutely in population, they are likely to show an absolute decline in the proportion of the total African population resident within their borders. This pattern is accentuated if the urban centers of KwaZulu and Bophuthatswana are excluded from any calculation. There is no way — in other words — that South Africa, as presently conceived, can confidently expect the relative salience of Africans in its urban areas to diminish.

Natural Factors: Benefits and Constraints

South Africa's location astride the southern extremity of Africa at the crossroads of the southern oceans occasioned its settlement from Europe and has influenced its development throughout the succeeding three centuries. A subtropical country on a continent largely tropical; a resource-rich zone amid the resource-poverty of much of the rest of the continent; and a transportation and industrial hub because of its early settlement and location; South Africa has never exhausted the limits of its comparative regional advantage. Its distance and long isolation from the developed nations of the northern hemisphere have also been important, both constraining economic and political development and providing a buffer against many of the modernizing ravages of the twentieth century. Today, South Africa knows that distance no longer shields; as the world has grown smaller, so the economic and political growth of the new nations of Africa has diminished South Africa's prominence. Once South Africa's future was as an outpost of the northern hemisphere; now it lies with Africa and, possibly, within an even more narrowly circumscribed zone called southern Africa.

Encompassing nearly 500,000 square miles, South Africa's territorial extent approximates that of Spain, France, and West Germany combined, two Texases, or four Californias. Along its east-west axis it stretches nearly 1,000 miles; from southwest to northeast (from Cape Town to Messina) it reaches about the same distance; and due north to south the longest distance is about 700 miles. Of prime political and economic, as well as geographical, importance is South Africa's 1,836-mile coastline, with its six major and dozen minor ports, girding one of the busiest long-distance trading routes on the globe.

In African terms, South Africa is geographically unique and privileged. Its access both to the Indian and the Atlantic Oceans, the number and quality of its harbors, and the variety of its climates, topographical zones, soil types, rainfall patterns, and underground resources have long given the peoples of the Republic a natural endowment unparalleled in breadth and diversity on the African continent. Although mixed in quality, it has provided the setting for steady, and in recent decades striking, increments in economic development and the achievement of remarkable, if unequally distributed, levels of national income and industrial growth.

Geographical Regions

The central plateau, which dominates the physiography of South Africa, consists of five subregions. In the far northwest is the southernmost extension of the Kalahari basin, an area of sand-covered parched lands without significant surface drainage. It lies about 2,000 to 4,000 feet above sea level, is thinly populated, and is suitable for marginal grazing only. Of somewhat greater agricultural significance is the Cape Middleveld, at the farthest western range of the plateau between Kimberley and the Namib Desert, with its surface water draining toward the Orange River. Nearly all of the remainder of the plateau, from the bounds of the Karroo in the south to the Limpopo valley in the north, is Highveld, rising from 4,000 to 6,000 feet. Essentially rolling grasslands bisected by the upper Orange River and its tributaries, this is the area that attracted African and white cattlemen, and over which Africans and whites fought bitterly in the nineteenth century. The Highveld is interrupted by the Lesotho lava plateau, with elevations from 8,000 to 11,000 feet.

Johannesburg, at 6,000 feet, guards the northern reaches of the Highveld. The Witwatersrand, on which the city stands, is a ridge or dyke of gold-bearing rock about 62 miles long and 23 miles wide. North of the Witwatersrand lies the Transvaal Bushveld, characterized by open grassland and elevations of only 2,000 to 3,000 feet—about the same height as the Cape Middleveld. To the north, again, there is Highveld—the Pietersburg plain—and then the land falls off toward the Limpopo valley. Near the border of Mozambique the elevation is less than 1,000 feet.

The central plateau, which comprises about two-thirds of the total land mass of the country, is surrounded on three sides by the great escarpment, a continuous chain of mountains and hills dividing the plateau from the coast and, on one interior side, from the sands of the Kalahari Desert. The escarpment attains its greatest heights and most majestic form as the Drakensberg Mountains between the province of Natal and Lesotho. The highest point is 11,425 feet, and most of the other peaks are in the 10,000-foot range. To the north the mountains gradually diminish in height and therefore present less of a barrier to road and rail routes from the interior. To the south, the crestline ranges from 7,000 to 3,000 feet, yet in the western Cape Province the escarpment long barred routes to the north except through a narrow gap near Beaufort West now used by the main rail line from Cape Town to Johannesburg.

On the coastal side of the escarpment are what are variously called the marginal or coastal lands. This general category includes the fertile, steeply stepped foothills of the Drakensberg. The last of the steps takes the eastern foothills down from 2,000 feet to sea level. All are cut dramatically by rivers and streams capable of coming down in torrents. But to the south and west the foothills flatten out into the drylands of the Karroo, a succession of desiccated plains about 1,500 to 2,500 feet above sea level. Farther south and west, mountain ranges—with peaks to 7,600 feet—collide, creating a very narrow coastal plain to the south and demarcating the other coastal plain that stretches from Paarl to the Cape peninsula, which was the first area settled by whites in the seventeenth century and from which the first trekkers moved northward.

The Climate, Water, and Soils

Because of its geographical location, the height of much of its land mass, especially the interior plateau, its long oceanic perimeter, and the interplay of tropical and subtropical atmospheric pressure systems, South Africa is affected by several climates. The sum of these different climates, however, is a remarkably uniform temperature pattern characterized by warm days and cool nights —giving a mean annual temperature of about 60°F. The Highveld, and therefore the major portion of the Republic, has a climate that can be characterized as warm-temperate. The winters are dry, rain falling only in the summer months from November through March. Yet the western Cape has a predominantly Mediterranean climate, with cold, wet winters; the Karroo, the Cape Middleveld, the Kalahari basin and Namib subregions have desertlike climates; and low-lying eastern Natal is warm, humid, and predominantly subtropical. Excessive cold and lasting snow are features reserved for the mountain peaks of the Cape and the Drakensberg; scorching heat is a feature of the Limpopo valley, but the cold waters of the Benguela Current often moderate the equally trying heat of the Namib Desert.

South Africa's scarcest resource is water. Because it is nowhere evenly distributed during the year, and because about 90 percent of the country receives less than 30 inches a year and 65 percent less than 20 inches, South Africa as a whole can be considered arid or semiarid. Twenty inches is usually regarded as a minimum for successful dryland farming. On average less than 3 inches falls annually in the northwestern Cape. This amount generally increases from west to east and south to north, with the heaviest concentrations of rainfall along the eastern slopes of the Drakensberg; Durban often records more than 45 inches. Port Elizabeth, Cape Town, and Pretoria rarely receive as much as 30 inches, and towns such as Kimberley, Graaff Reinet, and Kuruman, between 10 and 20 inches a year.

The closer to Botswana and Namibia and the farther inland one moves in South Africa, the drier and more drought-prone the climate becomes and the less suitable the land is for anything other than extensive stock grazing. There are local exceptions, but, for the most part, average rainfalls are insufficient for intensive agriculture except in the easternmost and southwesternmost extremities of the country. Moreover, these rainfall figures are averages: they mask unreliability, and much local variation. Drought is as frequent as flash flooding caused by cloudbursts. High rates of evaporation are also a hazard, because rain usually falls intensely in the few hottest months on hard, unyielding soil. The amount of standing water evaporated often exceeds the annual rainfall, and, in the center of the Highveld, may reach ten times the amount of annual rainfall.

Irrigation is always a possibility, but the expense of drilling and pumping from 1,000-foot deep artesian wells (locally called boreholes) combines with the saline quality of much of South Africa's subsurface water and the prevalent soil deficiencies to limit most irrigation to that derived from naturally flowing rivers and streams. The northern part of the interior plateau drains westward and northward to the great sweep of the Limpopo River. The remainder of the Highveld drains into the Vaal and Caledon Rivers and thence into the 1,400-mile-long Orange River. Below the confluence of the Vaal and the Orange, however, there are few tributaries bringing substantial water and much demand for irrigation supplies. The other drainage pattern is toward the Indian Ocean off the great escarpment. The Tugela, Umfolozi, and Pongola Rivers bisect the eastern coastal plain, and the Kei and Fish Rivers cut through what is now the eastern part of the Cape Province.

Because of the dearth of surface water (South Africa has only one natural lake, a small one), the shortage of perennial flowing streams, and the cost of damming and piping potable water as well as supplies for irrigation, the settlement of the interior of the country was made possible only by the successful search for underground water. The early railways and the mining industry on the Witwatersrand were developed only with the assistance of borehole water. Even in the 1970s more than half of all white farms rely upon deeply drilled boreholes. Yet South Africa lacks large artesian basins and is undergirded with lava-derived rock intrusions sufficient to interrupt normal underground water flows. Thus borehole water ordinarily depends on percolated rainfall. In some areas, too, underground water is so contaminated with chloride-sulphate solids that its consumption is dangerous both to humans and, over years, to cattle and other live-stock. Government-subsidized boreholes and the use of water from major rivers for drinking or irrigation have almost exclusively benefited whites. Where one sees wind-assisted borehole pumps, water furrows, or ditches carrying water to crops, the beneficiaries are almost always white.

By the mid-1970s, the government had constructed more than twenty dams across the country's major rivers. These river basins supplied water both for human consumption and for nourishing stock and crops. In 1973 wells supplied one-ninth of the water needed in South Africa. But planners were well aware that the potential for future enlargement of the country's water supplies through similar methods was limited. In 1979 water was being supplied to the Johannesburg area from the mountains of Lesothó and from distant Natal. Lack of water, in fact, was the most severe natural hindrance to continued industrial expansion.

Nearly 70 percent of South Africa's terrain is either too mountainous or too arid to be cultivated. Prime arable land made up only about 15 percent of the total, nearly all of which was in white hands. The 30 percent of the country that is neither mountain nor desert includes one zone of rich soil, in eastern Natal. In most of the other areas soils are thin, with inadequate organic content, and are deficient in essential nutrients like nitrogen and phosphorus. Structurally, the soils compact too easily under cultivation; some are severely leached, and all form and reform much more slowly than in the very different conditions of the northern hemisphere. Taken as a whole, the soil is very vulnerable to erosion. Moreover, the processes that deprive the soils of South Africa of organic material and minerals and contribute to the ease of their compaction also make improving their overall quality with fertilizer (especially in the case of lateritic soils) difficult and unlikely.

Improvements on Nature: The Infrastructure

South Africa has developed the most extensive transportation and communications network on the continent. Its roads, railways, harbors, air system, power grid, and telecommunications facilities are the envy of its neighbors and of countries of comparable size and wealth elsewhere in the world. A response initially to the needs of an expanding economy in the nineteenth and twentieth centuries, the strategic significance of a widespread, smooth functioning, modern infrastructure has in recent years been well understood by the government. State control of all infrastructural needs, aimed less at efficiency than at responsiveness to political factors, has since 1910 been exercised through tightly controlled, but nominally quasi-independent, bureaucratic establishments. South African Railways and Harbours, which also administers the state-owned South African Airways, is the largest employer in the Republic outside the civil service and the military; it employed 250,000 workers in 1976. The Post Office is responsible for telephonic and telegraphic communications, as in most European nations, and all broadcasting and television is controlled by a state corporation. Electricity is delivered by a statutory commission. So is petroleum, which is refined by another state corporation. Water supplies are regulated by a cabinet department.

The state has made itself responsible for the provision of many of the kinds of services that are in the hands of private enterprise in the United States and parts of Europe. The result is that over a fourth of all workers are employed by the government; the bureaucracy is correspondingly swollen, and bureaucratic methods have been extended beyond the ordinary reaches of the civil service into nearly all corners of the economy. The tentacles of the state reach far and grasp tightly, affecting whites and blacks in innumerable daily ways. By the norms of Africa and the Third World, this is hardly unusual. Yet by African (not European) standards, the delivery of services reaches relatively high levels of efficiency and is carried out with a minimum of monetary corruption. Whether or not the whole, strictly speaking, is cost-effective is another question, since for several decades South Africa's infrastructure has been developed in accord with militarily derived strategic expectations as well as the interests of consumers. Indeed, the influence of users and interest groups upon infrastructural policy is almost nil in South Africa; in the name of planning and security, the state has systematically stifled dissent in this as in so many other areas.

Railways, Roads, Ports, and Air Services

South Africa began to build railways in 1859. Without navigable rivers, the export of cash crops and, especially, of the mineral resources of the interior, necessitated the construction of long-distance lines. Diamonds and gold summoned railway builders from Europe and opened up a hinterland that had previously been traversed largely by wagons laboriously drawn by spans of plodding oxen. By the end of the 1890s, rails tied the

Cape to the Witwatersrand, the new economic epicenter of the country, and the Witwatersrand to Port Elizabeth, East London, and Durban, the emerging region's other main ports. For political as much as economic reasons a line also went eastward, along an easier route, from the Witwatersrand to Lourenço Marques (now Maputo), the capital of Mozambique. By 1897 a line through Bechuanaland (now Botswana) linked Rhodesia (now Zimbabwe) to South Africa. In 1910, with the amalgamation of the Union of South Africa's four provinces, and the consequent centralization of control over railways, track miles totaled 7,500. Virtually all were of the narrow 3'6" gauge, subsequently the standard width northward to the borders between Zambia and Tanzania.

As the Union prospered from its mineral, agricultural, and, eventually, industrial undertakings, rails continued to be constructed along the coast, and from more and more interior points to major centers of traffic. Beginning in 1921, when South Africa took over the administration of South West Africa (now Namibia), railways were extended there and connected to the South African grid. By 1979, at the completion of the rail extensions from Vryheid to Richards Bay and from Sishen to Saldanha Bay, the South African system was 13,130 miles long (Namibia's rail network was 1,460 miles long); more than two-thirds of the rail mileage in all of Africa was South African. By 1979 nearly a third of the total South African track length had been electrified, and a further 1,500 miles were scheduled to be electrified by 1983; a third of all traffic was hauled by diesel-powered locomotives. (In 1978 the South African Railways owned 1,802 steam engines, 1,698 electric-powered locomotives, and 1,208 powered by diesel fuel. Although many had been mothballed, the steam engines were still available in the event of petroleum shortages.) As late as the 1970s, the railway system's narrow gauge and its many traverses of the great escarpment — which early encouraged the use of the narrow gauge — were necessitating costly new construction and the rebuilding of heavily traveled lines from the Transvaal to the sea.

South African Railways also runs an extensive highway transport system for passenger and freight traffic. Encompassing

32,000 route miles, it benefits from a well-constructed web of more than twenty national motorways (including urban freeways in Cape Town and Johannesburg) and highways, plus—again by African standards—a well-maintained combination of asphalt-surfaced feeder roads that connect all towns to the national routes. In 1977 there were 895 miles of national highway, 115,000 miles of provincial highway, 39,000 additional miles of gravel roads, and about 150,000 miles of unsurfaced minor arteries. In 1976 South Africa had about 2.9 million motor vehicles in use, roughly half of the continental total. In 1970 about 90 percent of those vehicles (then 2 million) were owned by whites, a proportion that has probably since diminished. (Between 1961 and 1971 the rate of motor vehicle ownership by nonwhites increased from 5 per 1,000 to 12 per 1,000; in 1971 the white rate of ownership was 500 per 1,000, second only to the United States worldwide.[2]

South African Railways and Harbours has administered ports along with railways since 1910. Together, the six main ocean terminals handle more cargo collectively than any other in Africa, as does Durban individually. In 1974 the four main ports loaded and unloaded 55 million tons of cargo from and to 17,000 ships. Of the six, however, only Saldanha Bay and Richards Bay, both opened in 1976, are natural harbors; Saldanha Bay's transformation into a port was delayed for three centuries by the absence of locally available supplies of potable water and, in more modern times, by the absence of any economic imperative. All of South Africa's older ports have been modernized despite their poor natural settings.

Durban, the largest of the ports of South Africa, handled about 60 percent of the total cargo, or 32 million metric tons, in 1974. Port Elizabeth lifted 10 million metric tons; Cape Town, 9 million, and East London, 2 million in 1974. In 1976 Walvis Bay—a distant part of South Africa—handled 2 million metric tons of cargo. In addition, tankers of up to 230,000 tons can be accommodated at deepwater moorings off Durban. Cape Town has the largest drydock in the southern hemisphere, a basin

2. Republic of South Africa, Department of Information, *South Africa, 1975* (Johannesburg, 1976), 423.

nearly 400 yards long, and two smaller repair facilities; Durban also has two repair docks. Port Elizabeth has special ore-handling and container facilities. Richards Bay and Saldanha Bay were both designed for the export of coal and, in the latter case, iron ore as well.

Since World War II, when South Africa began to develop its own merchant marine, Safmarine has acquired and staffed nearly seventy ships; it now has a diversified fleet of tankers, ships, sugar and other dry-bulk carriers, refrigerated vessels (for citrus exports), container ships, general cargo ships, and seagoing tugs. Since the late 1960s, South Africa has also subsidized and rationalized shipbuilding, with three yards near Durban forming the mainstay of the industry in the 1970s.

Since 1934 South African Railways has run South African Airways, which has been built up in response to commercial as well as political and strategic imperatives; today it regularly flies the largest passenger aircraft in the world on some of the world's longest nonstop routes. Within the Republic, South African Airways has a virtual monopoly on all air travel in a country where the long distance between major centers has made travel by air increasingly routine. In 1976 South African Airways carried nearly 2.9 million passengers on separate journeys, compared with 460,000 in 1963, and handled 27 million tons of freight, compared with 5 million; it flew 71,000 hours compared with roughly half that number ten years before. In 1979, because of the refusal of most African nations to permit South African Airways to land in or fly over their territory, South African jumbo jets flew nonstop from South Africa to London, Paris, Frankfurt, Madrid, Buenos Aires, and Rio de Janeiro, around all of Africa to Tel Aviv, and to New York, Hong Kong, and Perth with one stop. Among the independent nations of Africa, only the Republic of Cape Verde, Botswana, Malawi, and Mozambique permitted South African scheduled aircraft to overfly and land.

Within southern Africa itself, using the most advanced jet aircraft, South African Airways connected Cape Town and Johannesburg to Windhoek, the capital of Namibia; Salisbury and Bulawayo, Zimbabwe Rhodesia's major cities; Francistown and Gaborone, the principal towns of Botswana; Blantyre in

Malawi; and Maputo in Mozambique. Both Blantyre and Francistown are gateways to Lusaka, Zambia. All the major cities within the Republic were served by South African Airways, as were many smaller towns and remote tourist facilities. For strategic purposes the airport at Upington, along the Orange River in the lowlying Cape Middleveld, has also benefited from unusually long runway extensions. Since most large modern jets cannot fly from the high plateau of Johannesburg with enough fuel to reach Europe nonstop, Upington, at a much lower elevation, is a useful staging point; the same is true for Windhoek and Cape Town. Together, the nation's fleet of modern aircraft, its four international airports and scattered subsidiary sites (South Africa has 331 licensed civil airports), its advanced system of aviation control, and its burgeoning aircraft-maintenance facilities give South Africa a highly developed capacity to conduct the economic skirmishes of peace as well as the military battles of war. Only the necessity to import aviation fuel and spare parts from the United States prevent the country from achieving virtual self-sufficiency in air transport.

Communications and Power

Postal communications between the then independent states of South Africa were regularized in 1883 and again in 1898. After Union new legislation was introduced in 1911 and superseded in 1958. The Republic, which succeeded the Union in 1961, had more than 3,000 post offices in 1964 and only 2,800 in 1974. In the 1970s South Africa exchanged air mail directly with 42 countries and surface mail with 82. The telegraphic side of the post office operations began completely in Morse code, the last signal being exchanged over land circuits in 1971. Today nearly 200 countries can be reached from South Africa by telex either automatically or manually. In 1978 the country had nearly 2.4 million telephones (half the total for all of Africa) and 466 automatic exchanges. By 1979 most of the major cities of the northern hemisphere could be dialed directly from the cities of South Africa. In terms of size, the South African telephone system ranked twenty-first in the world.

About 90 percent of all electricity consumed in South Africa is supplied by the state-run Electricity Supply Commission

(Escom); nearly all of the remaining needs are met in the major cities by municipally owned plants that are being gradually taken over by Escom. Only 2 percent of the total will not be supplied by Escom by 1990. Most of Escom's power is generated by 18 thermal stations, located for the most part near the easily mined coal deposits of the eastern Transvaal, northern Natal, and the western Orange Free State. The availability of water for cooling has also been a feature of the location of the largest plants in the Transvaal. Escom obtains 9 percent of its total electrical needs from the 1,500-megawatt Cabora Bassa hydroelectric facility in Mozambique and a further 2 percent from water-generated plants on the Orange River. Two small gas-generated plants are also in operation. (In the 1980s, South Africa also expects to begin generating power commercially from nuclear reactors being built north of Cape Town.)

The first street lights were lit in Kimberley in 1882, and other towns subsequently followed the lead of the diamond town. Supplying power on a national basis was first seriously planned shortly before Union. In the Witwatersrand area, this was a reality on a regional basis in the 1930s, but it was only after 1948 that Escom began working toward an economical national grid. Not until 1972 was the grid fully established; it supplied about 78 billion kilowatt hours of the Republic's total consumption of 86 billion kilowatt hours in 1978. The grid did not extend into Namibia or Rhodesia, nor did it reach effectively into any of the African homelands or cities (except Transkei).

In 1978, on a per capita basis, South Africa delivered almost as much electricity as France and Italy and considerably more than Spain or Yugoslavia. In 1978 South Africa generated 60 percent of all the electricity consumed on the continent. South Africa supplies power to Namibia, Swaziland, Mozambique, Lesotho, and Zimbabwe. Thanks to inexpensively mined and transported coal, South Africa's electricity is among the least costly (under 2 cents a kilowatt hour) in the world.

Broadcasting and the Press

The South African Broadcasting Corporation (SABC) was established in 1936 after a decade of poorly financed private and municipal attempts to make commercial radio viable. Since then the SABC has offered programs in English, Afrikaans, Sotho, Zulu, Xhosa, Tswana, Venda, Tsonga, Ovambo, and other indigenous languages and, since 1966, an external service in the major languages of Africa and the world. Television was introduced only in 1976, primarily for white audiences. Until then the government had been worried about the impact of foreign influences upon impressionable whites and blacks. The inauguration of a channel for blacks, originally scheduled for 1980, has been postponed. Africans have little role in the existing television system either on camera or off. In 1978 there were about 2.5 million licensed radio households and 1.3 million television sets. Nearly all of the latter were in white hands.

South African television and radio carefully coordinates its news and public-affairs programs with prevailing trends in existing governmental policy. In 1978, for example, both radio and television were well behind even Afrikaans-language newspapers in recognizing and publicizing the existence of the so-called Muldergate scandal that engulfed the Department of Information (see chapter 2 for a fuller discussion of the scandal). Throughout the year radio and television ignored press reports. Finally, when a distinguished jurist released hard evidence of the scandal, his comments made headlines in the press, but the SABC excluded his statements from its television and radio newscasts. In 1977, when testimony about Stephen Biko's death in police custody was making the front page of all local newspapers, television news gave the inquest lower priority than a British firefighter's strike. "News and public affairs programming is blatantly biased," said one investigator, "not only toward white perspectives, but also toward the ruling National Party." During the 1977 election campaign, "government candidates received more than twice as much news time as the three opposition parties combined."[3]

South Africa has not wanted the mass of its people to be exposed to news and features capable of eroding their loyalty to the state. The offerings of the SABC's noncommercial and commercial services have thus been carefully controlled. So has the

3. Jane Burns, "South African TV Network," *Boston Globe,* January 1, 1979.

potential audience for externally originated shortwave broadcasts. In 1977 the SABC switched its main broadcasts from shortwave to frequency modulation, thereby minimizing the local market for radios capable of hearing the shortwave signals of Zambia, Tanzania, Britain, the United States, the Soviet Union, and China. Few inexpensive broadband shortwave sets are now available for the largely African market inside the country. One more potential information loophole has hence been plugged, if not fully or permanently (medium-wave and frequency-modulation broadcasts from black Africa do intermittently penetrate South Africa's black areas).

Newspapers are still a significant, sometimes the only uncontrolled, source of information for most blacks as well as whites. For a comparatively poor, undereducated country, South Africa has a remarkable number of daily newspapers. For an estimated market of about 10 million readers (the size of metropolitan New York City), there are twenty-three dailies, five nationally circulating Sunday papers, and a number of twice-weekly and weekly small-town newssheets.[4] Johannesburg has three English and two Afrikaans dailies and four Sunday papers, one in Afrikaans. Cape Town reads two English dailies and one in Afrikaans. Durban has three English dailies and one on Sunday. Pretoria has an English and an Afrikaans daily, as does Bloemfontein. Port Elizabeth prints two English dailies and East London, one.

Historically, the South African press has been assertive, has done careful investigative as well as vituperative muckraking work, and has gathered the news with as much care as provincial American and British newspapers. After 1948, however, with the Afrikaner ascendancy, the position of the press has steadily been eroded. Hampered by legal restrictions that have been tested and confirmed in the courts, the press has found it more and more

---

4. Actual newspaper readership, estimated by normal market-research survey techniques, was 4.1 million in 1978. Raymond Louw, general manager of South African Associated Newspapers, discussed newspaper readership questions with the author. Average daily newspaper circulation, as distinguished from readership, was 1.3 million for all dailies in the last six months of 1978. The Audit Bureau of Circulation figures for the first half of 1979 were reported in *Financial Mail,* August 3, 1979.

difficult to maintain the vigor of its traditional role as critic and
commentator. The Prisons Act of 1959 effectively ended reporting about prisons and prisoners. The Official Secrets Act of 1956
(amended in 1972) prohibited the communication of what the
government regards as sensitive information relating to police and
security matters. The Defence Act of 1957 shut off all unauthorized reporting on the army, navy, and air force. In 1975, when
South Africa invaded Angola, the press could report little. The
Riotous Assemblies Act (1956) and Internal Security Act (1976)
authorized the minister of justice to ban (prohibit the appearance
of) or punish newspapers that created hostility between the races
or endangered the security of the state, broadly defined.[5] Several
newspapers have been banned and many journalists silenced
under the provisions of these and other laws, the full range of
which is discussed in the next chapter.

Censorship exists (for books, movies, periodicals, handbills,
and so on) through the Publications Control Board, under the
jurisdiction of the minister of the interior. The press can be ordered to omit specific items (sometimes newspapers run blank
spaces) and, because of the peculiar character of South African
libel law, can easily be sued for heavy damages. In 1977 and
again in 1978, the government threatened to pass legislation
curbing the press. As a result the press accepted a new regulatory
code and a press council. The council can suspend newspapers
and fine editors and journalists who violate the provisions of
the code, particularly the sections that require newspapers to refrain from giving offense to racial, ethnic, religious, or cultural
groups, from inciting persons to break the law, or from damaging
the country's standing overseas.

The most far-reaching single attempt to curb the press is
embodied in the Police Amendment Act of 1979, which provides
heavy penalties for anyone who publishes "untruths" about the
police; the onus for demonstrating the veracity of the allegation
rests on the newspaper. In practice, the law forces newspapers to
check their information, even in routine matters, with police

5. John Dugard, *Human Rights and the South African Legal Order* (Princeton, 1978),
181-186.

spokesmen. The same session of parliament made it an offense (in the Inquests Amendment Bill) to anticipate or prejudice the findings of an inquest by premature reporting; anything being investigated by the police would therefore be immune from journalistic scrutiny. In defending the first bill, the minister of justice said that "the work of the South African police is too important to let any Tom, Dick, or Harry write what he likes."[6]

On the whole, the press is comparatively tightly shackled by legislation and restricted by its self-imposed fetters. Investigative journalism still can be pursued, but at great risk. Facts that if revealed, could embarrass the government or its leaders, are treated circumspectly. For example, most editors were aware of the details of the massive information scandal six months or more before they dared to begin to publish even a portion of what they knew. A simple conclusion that was reasonable a few years ago is equally, if not more, apt today: "The liberal Press has been reduced to insecurity and near impotence, and the great English dailies are impeded from discovering and reporting the worst evils of apartheid and are under great pressure to refrain from fundamental criticisms of the Government."[7] An experienced, battle-scarred veteran of many editorial conflicts with the government put the problem in a broader perspective. Although the press has been the immediate casualty, he said, "the real victim is the public and the tragedy here is that in common with attitudes expressed in other parts of the West, the public shows only a slight awareness of the need for a free and vigilant press. The public at large seems apathetic about the implications for itself and government should the free press disappear."[8]

6. Quoted in *New York Times*, April 7, 1979.
7. Leonard Thompson, *Politics in the Republic of South Africa* (Boston, 1966), 129.
8. Louw, also former editor of the *Rand Daily Mail,* speaking at the International Press Institute's Twenty-Eighth General Assembly in Athens; quoted in *Boston Globe,* June 26, 1979.

2 | The Ascendancy of Afrikanerdom

T HE INTERVENTION OF BRITAIN at the end of the eighteenth century intensified the already bitter struggle for dominance in South Africa. The descendants of the seventeenth-century Dutch colonists and their Huguenot coreligionists were both antagonistic to the less fundamentalistic religious and more tolerant political postures of Britain. They clashed with British governors and with the English-speaking missionaries who followed the British to the Cape Colony. As a frontier society intent upon exploiting the harsh but seemingly limitless opportunities of a largely unexplored interior, the descendants of the Dutch and the Huguenots (who were known by 1800 as Afrikaners) resented missionary and colonial protection of blacks, British restraints upon white attempts to subjugate blacks and thus extend the borders of the Cape Colony, and British subordination of local to imperial needs and designs. Thus to the incipient conflict between whites and blacks was added an antagonism between Dutch, or Afrikaner, and British. Both themes dominated the nineteeth as they do the twentieth century.

Boer and Briton

In the nineteenth century Boers—the frontiersmen of Afrikaner society—showed their antipathy to British governance and British attitudes toward Africans by trekking beyond the control of their colonial masters. There they fought Africans, began to hunt, grow crops, and graze animals, and established rurally based, fiercely independent, theocratically dominated states.

28

Their guns and superior fighting skills helped to assure their ascendance over the far more numerous Bantu-speaking Africans of the interior. In one form or another these ongoing battles of the nineteenth century continue, in ostensibly different circumstances — but with equal violence — today.

The nineteeth century witnessed major military clashes between the growing might of the Boers and increasingly apprehensive Africans and between the Boers and their nominal British overlords. Within the cities of the Cape Colony itself, however, colonists who spoke English and those who spoke Dutch cooperated, for the most part, against the representatives of a distant crown. Two traditions grew side by side: that of the interior, where white animus toward Africans was nurtured in conditions of continual conflict, and that of the western Cape, where whites had known Africans as slaves and servants, and where their numbers and their military significance were far less threatening than on the frontier. These two approaches and their adherents might have remained distinct for far longer than they did; it was the discovery first of dry-land diamonds in 1870 and then of the Transvaal gold reef in 1886 that hastened the clash between the Colony and the frontiersmen and exacerbated the conflict between pastoral Africans and pastoral Boers. The mineral discoveries also heightened the demand for labor — for platoons of unskilled workers rather than artisans, herdsmen, or domestic servants. Without its diamonds and gold South Africa would inevitably have developed differently: blacks would not have been enticed into the industrial web so early; there might today be fewer cities, less dependent upon African labor; the attitudes of the Cape and the frontier republics might have remained apart for far longer than they did. Whatever the "ifs" of history, it was the presence of gold and diamonds that ultimately transformed the pastoral and agrarian societies of nineteenth-century South Africa into the industrial, highly urbanized, bitterly divided nation of the twentieth century.

On the eve of the Anglo-Boer War of 1899-1902, South Africa was composed of the long-established Cape Colony, which had emerged from the control of the Dutch East India Company to become a British-governed dependency with local autonomy and a franchise based on income and property; a newly organized, self-governing Natal, where blacks had been subjugated by military might only toward the end of the century; and two Boer republics—the Orange Free State and the Transvaal Republic—where suffrage was limited to white males approved by the elders of the Dutch Reformed Church.

The Cape Colony had evolved a pattern of segregation based initially on custom and later—as the Colony extended its borders beyond the Kei River to encompass Africans whose numbers would overwhelm whites—on demographic imbalance. Property qualifications were imposed in order to limit the percentage of Africans to a small proportion of the Colony electorate. During the last quarter of the nineteenth century the franchise was regularly manipulated in order to keep the number of African voters low, but neither British governors nor the ruling Anglo-Dutch coalition denied (despite the underlying message of the Glen Grey Act of 1894) that blacks had a legitimate, if minor, role to play in the political emergence of the colony and hence, of the greater South Africa. Immediately before the Anglo-Boer War, the political premise of the Colony was strikingly different from that of the other territories, where the idea of a broad suffrage was anathema.

Socially, too, the four polities were organized on different models. In the Transvaal Republic and the Orange Free State, Africans were effectively nonpeople. They had been conquered, and, except where their labor was needed, they were to remain subject to the demands of whites. In British-ruled Natal, there were areas of indigenous control—like Zululand—and rigid segregation in the cities. In the Cape, Africans and Coloureds had worked and lived alongside whites for generations. Patterns of segregation were thus less harsh, but nevertheless real, in the Cape than in the newer entities. The whites there were no more altruistic than their northern relatives, but their early contact had been with Coloureds, their own offspring, and with Africans with whom there had only recently been a struggle over land. Moreover, the whites in the Cape had long been conscious of the need to maintain and foster reasonably stable labor relations. Their economy was based less on consumption than on the husbandry

of indigenous labor. Fruit farms, vineyards, and cash crops of
grain made demands upon workers rather different than those
made by mines and pastoralism.

There was a further difference between the Boer republics
and the Cape. Before the discovery of diamonds, the Colony had
been organized and run as an agriculturally self-sufficient, only
modestly prosperous, outpost of Europe. At least until the middle
of the nineteenth century, the might of Africans had constituted
a severe threat to the Colony's achievements. Whites had made
compromises with Africans, had negotiated with them, and had
never sought to eliminate that which could by no apocalyptic
miracle be eliminated. The influence of missionaries was also
strong in the Cape throughout the nineteenth century. Together
with the oversight of the British Parliament and that of an easily
aroused British public opinion, the influence of the missionaries
helped maintain a standard of official conduct and a Colony-wide
tolerance toward people of color that was foreign to the trekkers
of the frontier. Indeed, the local government of the Cape had
long been led by English-speakers and Anglicized Dutchmen. As
a class they were loyal to values that had been assimilated from
their rulers. In that sense they were linked far more tightly to
modern Europe than their increasingly isolated brethren in the
north. Moreover, the Dutch in the Cape were burghers, not frontiersmen. The northerners thought of themselves as pioneers
whose values were no less worthy, and indeed were more robust,
than those of the citified and effete Cape.

The Anglo-Boer War was the culmination of a longstanding
clash between Imperial Britain and Boer independence, between
differing attitudes toward Africans, and for control of the rich
mineral resources that had been exploited with increasing vigor
toward the end of the century. To the victor in the war presumably went the spoils and the authority to organize South Africa in
the image of socially responsive late Victorian Britain. But if the
treatment of Africans were the hidden agenda in the war, their
well-being was largely forgotten by the victors. This was true of
Britons in official capacities on the spot in South Africa, and in
Britain itself, where South Africa became one of the dominant
issues of the 1906 election campaign. The Liberal party, the

leaders of which were known for their sympathy for the brave but defeated Boers and for their desire to restore political rights to the defeated, won resoundingly. Theirs was a misplaced but genuine altruism: The British from 1906 to 1909 also thought that they could socialize Afrikaners to British and European values, that the denial of African rights in the northern territories would gradually be superseded — that the good by some kind of inverse Gresham's law would drive out the bad.

The Legacy of Union

The retreating British colonial masters were prepared to permit the Union of South Africa to come into existence in 1910 with two distinct political organizing principles, one based on a denial of freedom to Africans, the other based on a presumption of at least partial political rights. There were two varieties of franchise and land tenure and strikingly different customs. The assumption was that British notions (as embodied in the Cape Colony compromise) would continue to prevail because of the superiority of (1) British methods, (2) the English language, (3) the power of assimilation, and (4) the continued impact of world public opinion. But the British architects of the Union of South Africa made three fundamental errors. First, they failed to anticipate the kinds of political compromises that would inevitably be made by a new government wishing to satisfy a disparate, but overwhelmingly white, electorate. Second, they left to later a resolution of the differences between the franchise assumptions of the four constituent parts of the new Union. And, third, they failed to appreciate that Afrikaners, then a minority among whites, would prove more fecund, more wily, more singleminded, more chauvinistic, and more contemptuous of overseas public opinion than the English. Furthermore, the sponsors of the Union failed to appreciate that the economic focus of the new country had already moved decisively from the Cape, with its more European orientation, to Johannesburg and thus into an orbit more thoroughly dominated by Afrikaners. Whatever the reason, the new Union quickly began, even under its ruling Anglo-Dutch coalition, to diminish the influence of Africans. As one example, parliament passed the Natives Land Act of 1913 in order to limit

economic competition between whites and blacks on the Cape
frontier and in the Transvaal, to minimize the political power of
Africans, and to establish a legal basis for territorial segregation;
that law forms the basis of today's homelands.

The Natives Land Act was the first of a number of significant discriminatory initiatives taken by parliament. They paral-
leled a general rejection by ruling whites of attempts by educated
Africans to play a substantial role in the affairs of the Union. In
the 1920s and 1930s, Westernized, skilled Africans became more
prominent. There were lawyers, physicians, newspapermen, writers, and educators in increasing quantity. Yet, despite their ac-
complishments overseas, these assimilated Africans were rebuffed. Whites feared them, as they feared the power of the
black-led Industrial and Commercial Workers' Union, with its
membership of about 60,000, in the 1920s. They ignored the
reformist-minded African National Congress of the 1920s and
1930s (see chapter 3). Indeed, at a time when some British African colonies were beginning to recognize African political aspirations, the white parliament of South Africa in 1936 emasculated
its representation of Africans. In the same year it strengthened
the apparatus of territorial segregation. It had already passed
laws designed to extend that segregation to the urban areas, to
prevent blacks and whites from intermarrying, to prohibit Africans from leaving their employers without permission, and to
make Africans carry identification certificates. Yet, even for Africans, South Africa before 1948 was not a police state. Given what
came later, the apparatus of security was limited, enforcement of
legal segregation was not all-encompassing: Africans were not
prohibited from many kinds of social intercourse with whites;
from being educated with whites; from assembling, protesting,
and airing grievances; from writing and publishing; or from joining political groups of all kinds. Aside from the denial of franchise, there was no abridgement of fundamental human rights.
Even when the Afrikaner-led predecessors of the National party
were in power, they sponsored no massive retreats from the principles of representative democracy. Opposition, moreover, was
healthy. Not only were there the regular prospects of changes in
policy as a result of swings in the mood of the electorate, but on

several occasions, power shifted from the Anglo-Dutch to the Afrikaner party, and back again. The overall health of the parliamentary system was therefore good even though it had failed to make black rights secure. During these years the pulse of white representative democracy was beating, if hesitantly.

The Triumph of Afrikanerdom

The triumph of the National party in the 1948 elections proved revolutionary in its impact on the politics of South Africa. Not only had Afrikaners, including many who had been interned in World War II for their pro-Nazi sympathies, successfully appealed to fears of black advancement and competition, but they had also promised to rewrite the statute book in order to guarantee permanent white dominance. Their 70 seats (of a total of 153) were sufficient, when allied with the Afrikaner party's 9 seats, to oust the United party of General Jan Christiaan Smuts and Jan Hofmeyr (which won 65 seats); they thus had a parliamentary majority large enough to undermine the system of representative democracy that had until then followed the British model. (The Labour party had won 6 of the remaining seats.) The hard-line Afrikaners who were the architects of the unexpected National party victory, and who controlled the party, lacked the inherited shared values of the Cape Dutch and the British. Instead, they took their triumph as a mandate to alter the social, economic, and particularly the political structure of the country. Most of all — as a cardinal dictum to which all else was secondary — the new governing class viewed its victory in ethnic-specific terms. Afrikaners had ousted the hated English and had thus reversed the military result of the Anglo-Boer War. Having done so, Afrikaners were determined never to risk being again ousted from power. Loss of power could threaten white hegemony and, more directly, the opportunity for Afrikaners to redress the humiliations of the past.

A student of modern Afrikanerdom says that "Afrikaners have always been less interested in dialectics than in survival." The electoral victory of 1948 was, he asserts, "secured by a decisive measure of Afrikaner unity . . . identification with the promotion of sectional economic interests and [their] championing of the Afrikaans culture." He writes of the 1970s: "It has become much clearer that apartheid is chiefly a means to maintain white power, wealth, and privileges."[1]

The Mechanisms of Control

In 1949 the leaders of the National party began to behave in a manner that is not uncommon on the African continent. In order to entrench themselves in power forever, Nationalists early used legal and extralegal means to increase their own majority and to hinder the effectiveness of opposition groups inside and outside parliament, to eliminate dissent, and to emphasize conformity. Within their own party there has been an unusual emphasis upon rigid obedience and loyalty to decisions made by the hierarchy and confirmed by the caucus; the influence of a cohesive, shadowy secret society, the Broederbond (Band of Brothers), has been used to exert pressure on those who would break rank and seek rewards outside of the party or Afrikanerdom. Continued disproportionate representation of rural areas and some gerrymandering buttressed the dominance of the party. So has the ruthless elimination of dissent and the equation of most forms of dissent with communism, and of communism with treason.

The ability of the courts to interfere with the supremacy of parliament and to review and overturn legislation had to be curtailed. Constitutional provisions protecting the Coloured vote in the Cape and basic rights such as habeas corpus had to be rescinded. Once the unassailability of the ruling cadre of Afrikanerdom had been assured through deft and deliberate subversion of the rule of law and of representative democracy, the passage of legislation implementing and further safeguarding Afrikaner and National party dominance was easy and inexorable.

Color was the emotive factor. The National party leadership has always made its way politically by playing upon the electorate's fears of black power. Dread of the loss of privilege is real

1. Hermann Giliomee, "Afrikanerdom Today: Ideology and Interests," unpub. paper presented to a conference at the Seven Springs Center, Mt. Kisco, N.Y., 1978. A fuller statement, published after this book was in press, is contained in Hermann Giliomee, "The Growth of Afrikaner Identity," in Heribert Adam and Hermann Giliomee, *Ethnic Power Mobilized: Can South Africa Change?* (New Haven, 1979), 114-122.

among the white community, but it has also been exacerbated
and inflamed for political ends. In the wake of the mismanagement of independent African countries, and of disasters like the
Congo and Idi Amin's Uganda, Afrikaners have had no lack of
horrors on which to dilate. At the highest political levels, however, racial and color-based exclusiveness have been less ends in
themselves than means capable of helping to ensure perpetual
Afrikaner rule. It is power, and what power means, and not race
as such, or at least not race primarily, that explains the Afrikaner
political imperative.

Whatever the motive, the National party had campaigned
on a platform of racial exclusion. Immediately after its electoral
victory in 1948 the party extended the existing legislative prohibition against mixed marriages and private immorality to all kinds
of transracial intercourse involving whites (and not just that between whites and Africans). It introduced the Population
Registration Act to assign all persons to racial categories and the
Group Areas Act to extend residential and commercial segregation to Coloureds and Asians (Africans were already affected by
the Urban Areas Act of 1923). Under the Prevention of Illegal
Squatting Act of 1951, the minister of native affairs could remove
Africans from public and private land and send them to resettlement camps. The Native Laws Amendment Act of 1952 eliminated home ownership and other long-held rights of urban
blacks; it restricted permanent residence in the urban areas to
those who could prove that they had been born in the cities, who
had lived there continuously for fifteen years, or who had worked
continuously for the same employer for ten years. In 1952, parliament also passed the carefully named Natives (Abolition of Passes
and Coordination of Documents) Act so as to require all Africans
previously exempted from the pass laws, including women, to
carry so-called reference books listing their places of origin,
employment history, tax payments, and brushes with the police,
and a photograph on their persons at all times. By enforcing this
act, the government sought tightly to control the movement of
Africans in and out of the urban areas; together with the Native
Laws Amendment Act, the legislation was intended to stem the
growth of the black population in the cities.

By 1979 about 10 million Africans were carrying reference books. In 1978 about 273,000 blacks (only 174,000 in 1977) were arrested for reference book and influx control offenses — an average of 747 a day. In Johannesburg alone during the same period 55,000 were arrested for the same offenses — 151 every day. Another 17,000 were arrested nationally in fiscal 1977-78 under urban curfew laws. Estimates of the total direct yearly cost to the state of pass laws and their enforcement was 112 million rands (R 112 million).[2]

In 1953 the Native Resettlement Act empowered the government to move African residents of Johannesburg to a new location twelve miles from the city. In 1956 and 1957 Sophiatown, the black freehold section outside Johannesburg, was rezoned for whites; Coloureds and Africans were forcibly removed. A similar implementation of the Group Areas Act enabled the government to begin to remove Coloureds from District Six in Cape Town in 1966 (a process that continued as late as 1979) and from Simonstown on False Bay. In another ten cities, and in numerous towns, the same procedure eliminated Africans, Coloureds, and Asians from commercial and residential competition with whites. A total of about 500,000 people have been removed from their homes under the Group Areas Act.

The Elimination of Dissent

Since Africans, Coloureds, Asians, and some brave whites protested the rewriting of South African laws and the denial of both civil rights and civil liberties that was intended by the new legislation, the government increased the number and power of its legal weapons to minimize and eliminate dissent. The Suppression of Communism Act of 1950 made the Communist party illegal. In addition, it permitted the minister of justice to declare kindred groups — that is, groups the aims of which were similar to those of communism — unlawful. Such construction might have had only a limited effect, but the law defined communism not only as Marxism-Leninism, but also as any related form of such a doctrine that attempted to bring about political, industrial,

2. *Star*, March 17, 1979; ibid., April 28, 1979.

social, or economic change within South Africa by promoting disorder or by encouraging hostility between whites and non-whites. Thus the minister of justice could, without effective immediate judicial review, decide that almost any organization opposing the government was communist, and thus unlawful. The act further gave the minister the right to "name" and then to restrict the movements of members and supporters of the bodies that he had declared unlawful. He could prohibit gatherings that he considered to be designed to further the ends of communism, broadly defined. However, the bill did not give the government the right to hamper the activities of persons who had renounced their membership in communist organizations. In 1951, therefore, the 1950 law was applied retroactively to anyone who had ever been a communist.

In 1953, to add to its arsenal, the government, assisted by the votes of six members added on questionable legal grounds from South-West Africa (a lapsed mandate never legally incorporated into South Africa), passed two additional pieces of legislation. The Public Safety Act permitted the governor-general to proclaim emergencies of up to a year, during which summary arrests could be made and detentions without trials or judicial review could be authorized. The Criminal Law Amendment Act permitted imposition of heavy fines, long prison sentences, and corporal punishment of individuals convicted of inciting others to violence or threatening breaches of the peace.

Neither the rhetoric of Afrikanerdom in power nor the translation of that rhetoric into legislation seemed unduly to alarm the bulk of the white electorate. African hostility and fear was obvious, and some whites, and many Coloureds and Asians, protested what was seen as the perversion of South African practice and intent. Yet the United party opposed neither the Public Safety Act nor the Criminal Law Amendment Act. Nor did it speak out against the passage of the Reservation of Separate Amenities Act of 1953, which eliminated the requirement that separate facilities be equal and which thereby intensified the impact of all forms of segregation. The white electorate, aroused by the National party and encouraged to fear creeping communism and black power (and to equate the one with the other) apparently accepted that the party's ends justified any means, even the callous manipulation of the country's political processes. In 1953 the electorate increased the Nationalist majority to 94 of 159 seats. The United party won 57 seats and the Labour party, 5.

Succeeding elections swelled the parliamentary strength of the Nationalists. In 1958 they captured 103 seats; in 1961, 105; in 1966, 126 (of 166); in 1970, 118; in 1974, 123 (of 171); and in 1977, 132 (of 165). As it lost seats, so the United party lost its will. By the middle of the 1950s, it had ceased to present a viable political alternative to the National party in parliament. In the 1960s it generally followed the National party's lead — so much so that Helen Suzman, the lone survivor in the 1960s of 11 Progressives who had defected from the United party in 1959, single-handedly carried the banner of serious opposition to National party policy until she was joined by seven fellow Progressives in 1974 (two won by-elections) and four further refugees from the United party in 1975. By 1977 the renamed Progressive Federal party had won 17 seats (it won an eighteenth in 1979) and had become the official opposition.

Their electoral victories enabled the Nationalists to continue to rewrite the statute book in order to extend their parliamentary power, their control over all aspects of African, Coloured, and Asian life, and their insulation of the security apparatus from the normal (and hitherto expected) processes of judicial review. In 1955, for example, the government concluded a process begun in 1951. Defying the constitution, it enlarged the Senate from 48 to 89 members by giving some provinces more seats than others and by electing senators by a full majority vote of the party that controlled each province. The result was an unassailable two-thirds Nationalist majority of both houses of parliament. Earlier it had enlarged and packed the appellate division of the Supreme Court. Together, these actions, and the passage of the South African Amendment Act of 1956, brought about the removal of Coloureds from the voters rolls in the Cape, eliminating a right that had been entrenched in the Act of Union. The 1956 law also provided that no court could henceforth rule on the validity of a law passed by parliament.

Missionary societies had educated Africans from the begin-

nings of South Africa. In 1953 control over the content and administration of the education of Africans was transferred to the
government. The State-Aided Institutions Act of 1957 gave the
government the right (and the responsibility) to decide who could
visit a library or any place of entertainment. Also in 1957, another Native Laws Amendment Act permitted the government to
prohibit the holding of classes, any kind of entertainment, and
church services if they were attended by Africans in an area that
had been proclaimed "white" under the Group Areas Act. Thus
Africans (domestic servants, for example) could not worship in
white suburbs or attend night schools outside of urban locations.
The curiously named Extension of University Education Bill, introduced in 1957 and finally approved in 1959, made it almost
impossible for nonwhites to continue to attend universities, such
as Cape Town and Witwatersrand, which had for decades opened
their doors to all students. Instead, the state established ethnic
universities, thereby compelling nearly all Coloureds to be educated only with Coloureds, Asians with Asians, and — for Africans
— Zulu with Zulu (at the new University of Zululand), Xhosa with
Xhosa (at the University of Fort Hare, opened originally as a multiethnic college in 1916), and Tswana, Venda, Pedi, Sotho, and
others only with members of the same groups at the new University of the North. The act also made it a criminal offense for
whites to attend the universities for nonwhites.

Throughout the 1950s and 1960s, there were many other
legislative abridgements of freedom. Each was explained by the
need to maintain security in the face of the perceived perils posed
by black defiance or communist subversion. The result was the
construction of a formidable security system, innumerable arrests, the employment of methods of detention and interrogation
that were new to South Africa, major show trials, and — after the
Sharpeville massacre of 1960 — the overwhelming subordination
of ordinary human rights to the declared political imperatives of
the state (as interpreted by the oligarchy that had come to direct
the fortunes of the National party). In 1962, for example, after
B. Johannes Vorster had become minister of justice and Africans
were for the first time resorting to urban sabotage and rural assaults, the police were empowered to detain subjects without

charge, and in solitary confinement, for 12, then 90, then 180 days, and, eventually, for an unlimited period if authorized by a judge; after 1976, such suspects could be detained indefinitely, even without authorization. In 1962 sabotage was made a statutory offence. According to the General Law Amendment act, the so-called Sabotage Act, the definition of sabotage was construed to cover the illegal possession of weapons as well as willful destruction, tampering with property, and unlawful entry. In 1967 terrorism was defined by the legislature to include training for what could be defined loosely as activity harmful to the interests of the state, furthering the objects of communism, and sabotage as defined in the previous act. House arrest was legalized in 1962. The Prisons Act of 1959 had made the unauthorized reporting of conditions in prisons illegal; it also gave the state the power to hold suspects incommunicado. These provisions made it virtually impossible for allegations of mistreatment by prisoners to be proved.

The Structure of Domination

When fitted together, this skillfully devised and carefully arranged mosaic of legislation amounted to a formidable, solid structure of domination. The structure has long depended on: (1) The control and distortion of the institutions of a state that remained outwardly democratic and ostensibly subject to common principles of a Western-oriented rule of law. Yet, in a manner not unknown on the African continent, doing so has meant gaining unassailable authority in parliament, using that authority to subvert the national constitution and the basic legal framework of the state (including the subordination of the judiciary), equating the personal leadership of individuals with the state, and, in practice, making criticism of the actions of the leaders the equivalent of treason. And (2) on rigidifying the enforcement of separation in order to prevent the numerically superior Africans from combining easily against whites, from taking concerted industrial action, or from having the kind of urban standing that could constitute a physical challenge to white-run industries or a psychological challenge to white security. Thus the regime has regulated African employment, movement, residence, sport, sexual relations, and other activities, with draconian rigor. Such regulation has been a response to the racial ambivalence of Afrikaners and to their political fears that Africans would somehow join the English in attempting to destroy the dominance of a majority within a minority. The government has also emphasized ethnic apartness and separate development in an attempt to fracture the solidarity of the African majority. Homeland independence and the banning of urban-based political organizations has provided a means to that political end.

Since the early 1960s the state has employed the many instruments of its arsenal of domination with striking effect. The 1979 military budget was R 1.7 billion (20 percent of the total budget), up 25 percent over 1978. A regular army of 20,000 professionals (500 African, 1,084 Coloured, and 132 Asian), and 35,000 conscripts (15,000 drafted in the 1979 call-up) is buttressed by 150,000 active reservists. The air force, which totals 9,000 servicemen, and the navy, with 5,000, also include reservists. The air force has 345 combat aircraft (more than Italy or Canada or most combinations of African airpower); the navy, three submarines and many surface craft. Of the 35,000 ordinary police, 19,000 are white and 16,000 African, Coloured, and Indian; they are backed up by 13,000 reservists, 4,000 of whom were "active" in 1979. The police are superseded for political operations by the security police, under the minister of police and justice, and the Department of National Security (formerly the Bureau of State Security) directly under the prime minister. The security police, the department, and military intelligence have separate networks of informers, white and black. The state censors and controls publications and films (administering the Publications Act in fiscal 1977-78 cost R 235,000). It also opens mail, taps telephone conversations, has threatened and compelled the press to impose a degree of self-censorship, and uses the state-run television and radio services to disseminate propaganda. In the 1970s, too, state funds were used covertly to influence public opinion within South Africa and to attempt to manipulate the country's image overseas (the Muldergate scandal). Another mechanism of indoctrination is the state-run educational system, which is especially effective in the white sector.

Most of the time this control over information enables the political apparatus to hide and distort its real aims. The press is severely constrained by the Police Amendment Act and other legislation discussed earlier. In criminal cases the defense is often unable to learn the charge against its clients until trial, since discovery motions are usually thwarted on security grounds. In 1978, too, the prime minister attempted to hinder the public disclosure of information by a judicial commission appointed by the president. But more than anything else it is the apparatus of security that undergirds the structure of domination: pass laws and influx control hamper the movement of Africans; police sweeps without judicial sanction are an ever-present possibility; the ability of the various law-enforcement agencies to detain, question, and physically intimidate anyone without effective judicial review or press surveillance obviously has a chilling effect on dissent. In South Africa a legal method akin to a writ of mandamus can be used to compel an official to remedy a wrongful state of affairs and/or to do something that he is legally obliged to do; this is one of several kinds of interdicts (similar to injunctions in the United States). A court-ordered interdict protects individuals against the unlawful deprivation of their rights. However, as a result of the Bantu (Prohibition of Interdicts) Act of 1956, injunctive relief is denied by law in many of the most important areas concerning the involuntary removal of Africans from their homes or their enforced transfer from one area to another.

Although less random and therefore less an instrument of terror than the state-licensed violence of Idi Amin's Uganda or François Duvalier's Haiti, the ability of the South African security apparatus to instill fear has become almost unlimited. In the five years before 1979, 45 Africans had died in police custody while undergoing interrogation. The death of Stephen Biko in 1977 was only the most notorious of these incidents. From 1950 through 1978, 1,385 whites, Coloureds, Indians, and Africans were the subjects of banning orders of varying severity under the Internal Security Act. Being banned, they were prevented from talking or being with more than one other person at a time (while saving the state the costs of their room and board in prison). They

also had to report regularly to the police. By early 1979, a quarter
of the total had fled the country. In the cases of others who had
died, the banning orders continue and prevent them from being
quoted; Robert Sobukwe is an example.

Including 21 Africans released from preventive detention
toward the end of 1978 and immediately served with banning
orders, 168 blacks and whites were banned and alive in South
Africa in February 1979. Among their number were trade unionists; black-consciousness leaders; former members of the African
National Congress, the Pan-Africanist Congress, and the Congress of Democrats; former officers of the Christian Institute;
journalists; and students. Some could not find jobs as professionals, despite their training. Others were prohibited from working
in their own professions; three recently banned black writers were
forbidden in early 1979, for instance, to resume their former
occupations as journalists. In March 1979 a former student
leader was forbidden to attend her own wedding celebration. A
black churchman likes to play tennis but is restricted by the terms
of his banning order to singles: to play doubles would be to take
part in an illegal gathering. Most banning orders apply for five
years and are renewable.

In 1977, in the aftermath of the Soweto disturbances, as
many as 800 persons were being detained without trial; in early
1979, however, the security police were holding only 64, all Africans, in prisons without benefit of counsel or access to relatives.
(An additional 447 prisoners were serving long sentences on
Robben Island, South Africa's Alcatraz, for offences against the
state; nine were under eighteen years of age.) Forty-five were
being detained according to the provisions of section 6 of the
Terrorism Act of 1967; it permits the police to detain suspected
terrorists, or those who are presumed to have information about
terrorism, broadly defined, for questioning indefinitely (if necessary, they may keep the detainees, uncharged, in solitary confinement). The police are not obligated to admit to holding a
detainee, to inform his family of his detention, or ever to bring
him before a court. The Internal Security Act of 1976 (the
revamped Suppression of Communism Act) sanctions preventive
detention of anyone whose activities are thought to endanger the

security of the state or the maintenance of public order (sections 10 and 12*b*). Many persons were held under these provisions in 1977. In 1979, six were in prison under this rubric; another ten were being held under a further section (the 180-day provision — section 215 — of the Criminal Procedure Act of 1955) of the act; and two or three had been detained according to the continous imprisonment authorization (section 55) of the General Law Amendment Act of 1963. In February 1979, the then longest continuously incarcerated detainee was released after seventeen months, the first four of which were spent in solitary confinement. He was Peter Jones, a Black People's Convention organizer who had been arrested with Biko in 1977. Jones was promptly banned.

The extrajudicial aspect of these laws was neatly revealed, in all of its clinical precision, during the inquest into Biko's death. Sidney Kentridge, lawyer for Biko's family, cross-examined Colonel Pieter Goosen, divisional commander of the security police in Port Elizabeth. Kentridge asked Goosen under what authority he had detained Biko in chains. Goosen said that section 6 of the Terrorism Act gave him sufficient authority. The questioning proceeded:

> **Kentridge:** Where do you get your authority from? Show me a piece of paper that gives you the right to keep a man in chains — or are you people above the law?
>
> **Goosen:** We have full authority. It is left to my sound discretion.
>
> **Kentridge:** Under what statutory authority?
>
> **Goosen:** We don't work under statutory authority.
>
> **Kentridge:** You don't work under statutory authority? Thanks very much . . . that's what we have always suspected.[3]

Well before 1979, a pattern had been established. As soon as African or white dissenters became prominent or were thought to be influential, they were questioned and detained or banned. By 1978 serious, nonparliamentary internal opposition had therefore been driven underground, as it had been in the 1960s, and the bulk of the population — both white and black — had effectively been cowed.

3. Quoted in Donald Woods, *Biko* (New York, 1978), 199.

The Parliamentary Opposition

The election of 1977 demonstrated how completely the National party had over the years since 1948 become the leviathan. By successfully banning African movements of protest and preventing their leaders from acting effectively, by using legislation to ensure a minimum of public knowledge and surveillance of the prison system, by mandating a measure of self-censorship by the press, by gaining potentially draconian powers over industry, by extending its ability to declare and sustain emergencies, and by appealing to the voting public as the only possible guardians of its destinies, the National party showed an unquestioned mastery of the existing, permissible politics of South Africa. Having defined the goal of politics as the perpetuation of Afrikaner control and having proceeded to erect a structure of unassailable authority, the National party in 1979 presided over a political system that was effectively beyond the reach of interest groups, opposition groups, public opinion, the press, or other supposed instruments of change. The monolithic National party had become the only guardian of segregation; although it was still a party of and for Afrikaners, it had for the first time attracted substantial English-speaking support. (The old English and Cape Afrikaner standard bearer, the United party, had collapsed of its own inconsequentiality in 1977.)

In parliament the main opposition was the tiny, doughty Progressive Federal party. Representing wealthy white constituencies in the largest urban areas, it espoused political opportunities for Africans, a goal that was anathema to most whites. As a party, its values were those that were increasingly less esteemed in South African official life: equal protection under the laws; freedom of speech, movement, expression, and assembly; and equality of opportunity. In late 1978 the party dropped its insistence upon a qualified franchise and, after some struggle, adopted a detailed program for a future South Africa. The Progressives want to see a South Africa reorganized after a national convention of representatives of all population groups. They envisage a future federal South Africa, with strong, self-governing constituent states. At the national level, the lower house of parliament would be elected by proportional representation, the Progressives rejecting winner-take-all majority rule.

Numerically, as well as by collective achievement, the Progressives could claim not that their increased fraction of the parliamentary seats signified a shift in the sentiments of the electorate, but that they represented a vocal, if small, minority vehemently opposed to the policies of the leviathan and to the consequences for South Africa of the government-enhanced bitterness between white and black. In a parliament that, like most others in Africa, had come to exist primarily in order to provide a faithful claque of sycophants to support the proposals of a ruling oligarchy, they had only one remaining role of consequence. They could not oppose the government, in a meaningful sense, but they could and did embarrass and harry it by asking questions. They could and did compel the government to explain, sometimes to reveal, its intent and now and then called it to financial account. Individually, the members of the opposition could intervene to ameliorate cases of personal hardship. The press could also write about the issues raised in or out of parliament by members of the opposition. In that way the government's domination of information and communication could be minimized, and even the followers of the National party begin to appreciate some of the implications of rule by an absolutist-inclined majority.

The limited relevance of the Progressive Federal party's opposition in 1979 testifies to the National party's successful manipulation of the political system to its own advantage. Change in South Africa thus cannot be expected to come in the normal way by the ballot box, for the Progressives appeal only to a select and demographically distinct fragment of the electorate. It is a fragment that is unlikely to grow, or to be permitted to grow, much larger. In 1979, despite their official status, the Progressives could only carp; in shrill tones question the majority's intent and execution; hone the edges of blunt and damaging legislation; and remain both the conscience of a nation beyond conscience and, with optimism tinged with fantasy, a potential alternative to National party rule should holocaust overtake white domination.

The National Party

Some one-party states in Africa have seen the wisdom of providing electoral alternatives. Party-sanctioned competitors have been allowed to contest seats. Some single-party states even encourage arguments in the single-party caucus, where the leadership can control and channel dissent. New ideas and an awareness of the needs of the masses have thus been returned to some African states; authoritarian though their ruling oligarchies are, the exercise of that authority is at least tempered by a disquiet mediated on the hustings and in the caucus.

The National Party in South Africa has not evolved comparable models, but the conventions of the provincial segments of the party do generate competition and provide a venue for the exchange of information about the whims and qualms of a series of constituencies. The party's isolation from the white electorate is therefore not total. Even so, it is controlled by persons of ministerial rank and those who have unusual prominence in institutions sanctioned by Afrikaner tradition and history. The result is a party that obeys more than it debates and that does favors for special interests and constituents more than it operates as a parliamentary watchdog. Policymaking has increasingly become a cabinet function only, and there is some debate over the extent to which the whole cabinet, rather than powerful members only, plays any meaningful role in this sphere. Especially after 1977's massive electoral mandate, South Africa has been ruled (the word is not too strong) by a prime minister and a small circle of cabinet ministers, only a few of whom have independent political bases. Some owe their positions entirely to the prime minister. Others are rivals even if their rivalry is muted. Most must jockey for position in the next succession crisis, whenever it comes. Few — as white politics in South Africa is now defined — can hope to assert a wholly independent position and survive. Despite the existence of a parliament and several parties, it is reasonable to describe the Republic as an authoritarian state with a police state potential that is already exercised over the vast majority of the inhabitants of the country. For purposes of handy description, at least, South Africa is run by an absolutist oligarchy capable of leading an electorate to which, throughout the 1970s, it gave only safe and unimaginative choices.

Because of the perceived perils of modern life and the steady erosion of democratic values, the white electorate no longer has the kind of independence that threatens or serves as a real check upon the oligarchic dominance of South African politics. Local branches can rarely oppose the party hierarchy effectively; few are sufficiently brave or assertive to try. Their representatives thus gain rewards from the hierarchy, not from their local constituencies. With the death of constituency relevance, so dies the responsiveness of the party (and thus the national leadership) to any kind of constituency-based concerns about the direction of national politics and choices among the nation's available options for the future. South Africa's white leadership is consequently insulated by the successes of the last thirty years; by the rigidity and authoritarian quality of the party, the church, and Afrikaner life generally; by tradition buttressed by a revised legality and an extensive security and intelligence apparatus; by the powerlessness of countervailing corporate and other nonstate institutions; and—possibly most of all—by a clannish solidarity that still reacts to the danger of English as well as African aspirations.

The Ruling Oligarchy

The result is a political system where decisions are made by a small, if shifting, group of men (not women) around the prime minister. Some kinds of internationally focused decisions may be made by a handful, although others that involve alterations in prevailing social codes may be made (or at least scheduled) by a larger group representative of the broad spectrum of Afrikaner life. Admittedly, many of the decisions may reflect what the oligarchy believes to be the feelings of the Afrikaner electorate; they may even be informed about the presumed views of constituents. Further, the policymaking of the oligarchy is often influenced by what its members wish to impute to the Afrikaner electorate. In cold, clinical terms, however, the electorate has become—for political purposes—subservient to the wishes of an oligarchy.

The membership of the ruling cadre is largely drawn from

the ranks of politicians. Historically the leadership of the Broederbond was often included, but the influence of this one-time informal network of power brokers waned under Prime Minister B. Johannes Vorster. Its leadership became comparatively enlightened, or liberal, but it was the strength of the country's purely political oligarchy that tended to diminish the importance of the Broederbond, as also the church, the Afrikaans-medium press, and Afrikaner-dominated commerce. Conceivably the scandal that rocked the National party in 1978 and 1979 may revive the influence of the Broederbond and other parapolitical bodies; yet oligarchic rule has come to dominate South African politics too overwhelmingly to be checked, even in the aftermath of scandal.

Both Vorster and Prime Minister Hendrik Verwoerd were in a position to dominate the coterie of compatriots who composed the oligarchy of their time. Whether or not Prime Minister Pieter W. Botha will be a first among equals or a leader above oligarchy is not yet known. In either case, it is clear that oligarchic rule of South Africa continues and that power is highly concentrated in the hands of men whose vision may remain of the past, not of a challenging future. Nevertheless, although heretofore leading a consciously nonmodernizing oligarchic autocracy, South Africa's rulers may, in response to worsening conditions, have the capacity—precisely because of their independence from the electorate —to become a model modernizing oligarchy.

Remaining an unacknowledged authoritarian state is not terribly difficult where the guardians of white control can point so easily at another alternative that is threatening to most whites. Black dominance—the black peril—fuels authoritarianism, justifies and legitimizes it for whites, and makes the concentration of power in a few hands that much more plausible and self-perpetuating. It was precisely the prevailing climate of fear and subservience that permitted South Africa's Department of Information to spend vast sums of money secretly, and on dubious projects— some of which distorted the direction of South African society— without the country, or even the entire cabinet, being informed. Among various schemes floated by Cornelius Mulder and Eschel Rhoodie, the secretary of information and the plan's "mastermind," were the covert purchase of leading American, British, and French news publications; using front men, the establishment of the *Citizen,* an English-language morning daily to compete with the liberal *Rand Daily Mail;* the secret funding of research institutes, foreign-policy associations, economic seminars, and meetings of various kinds in South Africa and in the United States; the secret financing of programs of the Dutch Reformed Church in South Africa; the covert dispersal of funds to pro-South African front groups in Europe and the United States; gifts of money to European and American politicians; and, allegedly, covert giving to influence American senatorial races. The acknowledged total of all of this largesse was R 73 million, some of which was unaccounted for and some of which was devoted to junkets by Rhoodie and Mulder to funspots in Africa and elsewhere, as well as to the purchase of housing and other material benefits for private consumption. Roelof F. Botha, South Africa's foreign minister, subsequently called the projects of Mulder's Department of Information "naive and half baked." They constituted an "amateurish attempt to serve South Africa's interests [and] in the process caused incalculable hardship to the country."[4]

When the outlines of the department's usurpation of authority became known privately to journalists and to political gossips, it took a full year, charges by the Progressive Federal party in a parliamentary select committee, cautious comments in the English-language press, and jealousies within the cabinet to curtail its activities. Even then it was only because a courageous judge happened upon evidence of the misappropriation of foreign funds and—a rarity in South Africa—chose to speak out that what had long been known to the press and the opposition became public knowledge and politically consequential. Newspapers could not publish without the action of the judge, and only his action breached the cloak of secrecy with which the oligarchy had attempted to cover up extensive ministerial and governmental deceit.

4. R. F. Botha, quoted in *Star Weekly,* February 24, 1979.

The Vorster Era

In South Africa concentration of power came about gradually and naturally in the wake of the hegemony of the National party and the patterns of leadership associated with its heritage. As the Nationalists consolidated their power, so they concentrated the control of that power. Verwoerd brooked little disagreement within the party. Vorster, less well known and less ideological, acceded to his position in 1966 and spent the next four or five years buttressing his prominence with personal as well as positional control. He did so from within the party, as a manipulator as well as an architect, and then from about 1971 began to project himself onto the international stage. By doing so he gained credibility at home and increased stature within the party. Because he was thought indispensable, he was in a position to dominate the party as the party dominated South Africa, and as the leaders of black Africa dominate their own new positions. Like them, Vorster was a man for all seasons. A little less totally but nevertheless in the same ways, he came in the 1970s to personify the state. Behind a dour, delphic countenance and in consultation with political and military cronies, some of whom were interned with him during World War II, he carefully substituted his own for the public will. His was an authoritarianism on behalf of a ruling class and, in particular, on behalf of a majority of the ruling class.

That the prime minister wielded what was essentially personal power occasioned little public comment in South Africa because there was and has been for some time a broad consensus among whites on the only issue of consequence — the maintenance of white privilege and the prevention of black rule. Vorster was seen as a reliable bulwark. Many whites accepted without much thought that a strong leader was necessary to ensure white survival. Yet it was less his person, for Vorster exuded little charisma, than the position that he held and the power that he exercised so assuredly in the face of external harassment and internal danger that made Vorster a true successor to President Paul Kruger, the original shaper of intransigent Afrikaner nationalism. In early 1978 Vorster stood above party and above political rivalry as the unquestioned champion of white survival. Since this public regard was accompanied by overwhelming electoral success, party loyalty, and the fealty of the military and security leadership, Vorster had the local legitimacy and the political freedom to act as boldly as he wished.

During the first half of the 1970s, Vorster established himself as a pragmatist capable of leading with imagination. Despite a reputation as a strong segregationist, he was capable of suspending ideology and of attempting to bring about an entente with a number of black African states, of welcoming black leaders and their wives to Pretoria, and of making the distinction — soon easily accepted — between the need to maintain apartheid at home and the irrelevance of color elsewhere. Vorster was capable of doing what was difficult for Verwoerd and his predecessors — concentrating the minds of his followers on power, not the principle nor the ideology of color for its own sake.

Vorster thus managed profoundly to alter the nature of the debate. He presided over a modification of the strict application of the color bar to all aspects of South African public life. In so doing he succeeded, admittedly at the eleventh hour, in making his own people aware of the necessity for movement. Moreover, there was little opposition to these alterations. Vorster moved cautiously, incrementally, and without any perceptible departure from his usual demeanor. True, too, he downplayed the changes that were introduced and hedged those changes with qualifications capable of modifying their impact on the lives of blacks. Most of all, he offered concessions grudgingly and coupled them with intensified repression. "Troublemakers," liberals, and opponents were harassed, detained, and attacked with as much severity as in the past. Vorster's government cannot be accused of "letting up" — of tolerating dissent. This approach, that of the mailed fist and the velvet glove, permitted Vorster and his government to defuse opposition.

In 1977, with an overwhelming victory at the polls behind him, the potential right-wing dissenters quelled, and outsiders pressing against the South African *laager,* Vorster was poised to bring about change unilaterally. His leadership was unchallenged. Although he feared cleaving Afrikanerdom by moving

ahead too rapidly, the perils and anxieties of white South Africa
cried out for the kind of assertion that only Vorster had the legitimacy to provide. Only he had the authority to bring Afrikaans-
and English-speaking South Africans to realize how precarious
was the future of white privilege and how forthright efforts had to
be to preserve a position for whites in the future. Only Vorster
could make the case that the price of security in the short run
might destroy peace and prosperity for future generations of
whites in South Africa. Only Vorster was in a position to tell his
people that they must modify their dreams of perpetual hegemony. Only Vorster was powerful enough to institute the kind of
reassessments that might conceivably have altered the nature of
the South African confrontation. The terms of the debate had to
be changed, and Vorster was at last in a position to recast them
without much attention to the constraints of white political life.
The opportunity was unique, afforded as it was by the results of
an election and the temporary respite provided by the massive
repression of African dissenters.

Yet Vorster ultimately refused to chart a bold course for
South Africa. Plagued by what was officially called deteriorating
health, he resigned as prime minister in September 1978 without
resolving any of his country's critical problems. (He became president but was also compelled to resign that position, in mid-1979,
after his involvement in the Muldergate scandal became officially
known.)

Separate development remained official dogma despite a
widespread feeling that granting local independence to a handful
of homelands, and the intention to make all Africans, no matter
where they really resided and worked, putative citizens of the
homelands, only obscured the demographic and political realities: blacks would continue to constitute a majority in all the
urban centers of the country, and in the rural, white-farmed
areas as well. No legislative fiction could eliminate their preponderance, their economic relevance to modern South Africa,
their political salience, their capability, regardless of age, of
being mobilized against prevailing norms, their antagonism to
separate development, their distrust of homeland options, the increasing radicalization and nationalism of their politics, the in-

creasing strength of the young in indigenous politics, their new refusal to prefer the option of embourgeoisement to shifts in political fortunes, and their determination to share power instead of merely demanding relaxations in social apartheid. Although many Afrikaner Nationalists, including Vorster and his cabinet ministers, understood how dramatically the politics of post-Portuguese coup and post-Soweto uprising South Africa had shifted from a focus on social rights to the quest for political power, the ruling oligarchy under Vorster rebuffed those within its own ranks who promoted innovative ways of responding to the aspirations of blacks.

Several members of the cabinet attempted at least to begin talking with leading Africans about their future and during 1978 Mulder, minister of plural relations (African affairs), groped for ways of giving urban Africans more responsibility and more residential security within the still unaltered overall framework of separate development and apartheid. Succeeding an obdurate minister, he elevated the debate to a much more practical plane than before. Mulder envisaged a form of autonomy for Soweto as a kind of urban homeland, improvements in living conditions in Soweto and other black cities, and an amelioration of the way in which Africans were routinely treated by the police. Mulder believed in the relevance of embourgeoisement. Although he appreciated that political power was the ultimate question and that the future of South Africa depended upon realistic answers, he persisted throughout his brief tenure as minister in seeking solutions that were cooptive rather than transformational.

Despite the efforts of Mulder, the leaders of the once-powerful Broederbond, and others, the debate remained static under Vorster. Certainly in his last few post-Soweto years, Vorster's leadership was largely hesitant and unimaginative. Although he gave some innovative leeway to Mulder and to Dr. Piet Koornhof, minister of education and sport, he also supported James Kruger's severe and blundering reign as minister of justice and prisons.

When Vorster resigned as prime minister, the unity of Afrikanerdom had not been breached. One of his prime desiderata had thus been achieved, but it was less clear that Vorster had made the future more secure either for whites or for Afrikaners—

surely his more fundamental mandate. Indeed, on the international front his coupling of his resignation with an official *volte-face* over Namibia had revived tension locally and controversy with the West. Whether it was a bargaining tactic (brinksmanship is dear to the hearts of official South Africa), a reflection of new strategic considerations, or merely the price that had to be paid to ensure a smooth political transition within the Afrikaner oligarchy, his about-face represented a refusal to accept the premise that white power in South Africa could no longer be secured by conventional methods of obduracy.

Symbolically, Vorster was returning in resignation almost to the point of his own accession. To his successor he bequeathed not a vision of a future that grew out of his own advances in the early and middle 1970s, but bland assurances about the state of South Africa in the world. On behalf of his cohorts, Vorster was retreating back into a laager that he had so pointedly abandoned years before. By so doing Vorster may have confused responsiveness with weakness and imagination with heresy, but such a confusion also accurately reflects the insidious inner contradiction of the Afrikaner ascendancy. By trying to concentrate power forever in the hands of a narrow élite, and by making that concentration quasi-religious dogma, Afrikaners may have left themselves little room in which to maneuver as the great disparities between white and black privilege ultimately mandate new divisions of resources, changes that, under Vorster, remained officially — but certainly not informally — unthinkable.

The Accession of Botha

P. W. Botha, who succeeded Vorster, inherited the kind of intransigent party posture that doubtless fitted his own temperament. With a reputation as a man who preferred fighting to negotiating, he seemed a natural successor to the Vorster of 1978. Yet he acceded to power over Mulder, who had developed a reputation for pragmatism, largely because of the burgeoning financial scandal that shortly after the election forced Mulder to resign his ministerial and party positions. Botha, too, was not solely the dogmatic, ostrichlike leader of the popular picture.

It is true that many South Africans, especially those of the more liberal wing of the National party and those allied to the Progressives, feared that Botha would not be equal to the challenges facing South Africa in the late 1970s and early 1980s. Those challenges were several. First, black unemployment in 1978 was rising to unprecedented levels; the black dwelling areas were restless; young blacks were still boycotting secondary schools; and violence was—more than ever before—a common accompaniment of daily race relations. One challenge was how best to accommodate black aspirations and black desires for effective political representation to white fears of the loss of power and privilege.

A second challenge was related to the first. Although in 1978 high gold prices had been cushioning the impact of recession on the country, South Africa's economy was weak. Reviving confidence in the future growth of the nation was linked to the first challenge, since Botha would be unable to attract the foreign investment that South Africa desperately needed to grow in real terms without restoring a belief in his country's essential stability.

A third challenge was that of isolation. Vorster refused to battle the West on every front. His willingness in 1977 and early 1978 to negotiate the future of Namibia resulted in the acceptance of a Western formula meant to convey legitimacy to a new government after elections to be supervised by the United Nations. But by coupling his resignation with an about-face on Namibia, Vorster left for Botha the decision whether or not to do battle with the West, and thus potentially to invite broad economic sanctions against South Africa.

Botha, on his record, did not share Vorster's pragmatic belief that cooperation with the West was a useful way of securing the power of Afrikanerdom. He was reputed to see safety for Afrikaners in self-reliant antagonism and appeared, in 1978 and 1979, to oppose all foreign attempts to nudge South Africa into a political posture more acceptable to world opinion. He was suspected of thinking that world opinion was irrelevant.

Botha's critics said that as prime minister he would "hang tough"—that he was not the man for South Africa's season of discontent, or any season. They pointed to his volatility, his excitability in parliament as majority leader, and his reputation as a "cowboy."

Botha had been a member of parliament for thirty years and was sixty-two when he became prime minister. After studying law briefly at the University of the Orange Free State, he became an organizer for the National party, entered parliament (five years before Vorster), and became deputy minister of the interior, minister of Coloured affairs, minister of public works, and, beginning in 1966, minister of defense (a position that he retained after becoming prime minister) and leader of the House of Assembly. Botha was known as a tenacious politician. His contacts overseas were few, however, since he had ventured only rarely outside South Africa before 1978.

Botha is a prime minister sympathetic to some of the Afrikaner political stereotypes. He talks a hard line. Yet because he has long represented a constituency in the Cape Province, where most Coloureds reside, he has never favored extreme discriminatory measures against blacks. He has also spoken out against whites being too insistent on full supremacy over all blacks.

As Botha emerged from the first hundred days of his rule as prime minister, he began to respond to the West over Namibia and to the more liberal element within his own party by replacing Mulder with Koornhof and by refusing at first to give a senior position to Dr. Andries Treurnicht, the party's leading hardliner. Later, in early 1979, he permitted Koornhof, the most articulate and adventurous liberal in the cabinet, to make Africans happy by promising not to destroy the 20,000-strong Crossroads squatter settlement near Cape Town (Koornhof's predecessors had bulldozed two such shantytowns). Koornhof, again with Botha's support, also agreed to maintain Alexandra township near Johannesburg as a residential area for black families rather than convert it into a high-rise hostel area for single migrant workers.

At about the same time as Koornhof, who had renamed the Ministry of Plural Relations the Ministry of Cooperation and Development, was showing more flexibility and courage than his colleagues over African housing arrangements, he unexpectedly began consulting with and taking advice from the African dwellers affected, from liberal and critical academics, and from oppo-

sition white politicians. Further, he appointed a large committee
to recommend changes in the way the state regarded urban-dwell-
ing blacks, thus hinting that the government was prepared to
reevaluate previous policies based on the premise that Africans
were to be regarded as temporary sojourners (out of the homelands) in the urban areas. In announcing the committee, Koornhof also did the unexpected: as members he nominated several
Africans widely respected by militant blacks despite (or because
of, which is the more remarkable) the fact that they had been imprisoned as enemies of the state less than two years ago.

Botha supported Koornhof in these actions against Treurnicht and other members of the National party. When Koornhof
visited the United States in June and said that apartheid was
"dying and dead," Botha defended him against attack from the
right.[5] Later Botha himself, in a hopeful speech to a provincial
congress of his party, told his colleagues that South Africans must
"adjust or die." "We are all South Africans and we must act in
that spirit toward each other," he said. The chief goal for South
Africa should be "to improve the quality of life of all the people
in this country." He rejected both "one man, one vote" and total
separation (oldfashioned apartheid) with white supremacy. He
recognized what South African whites call multinationalism and
foresaw the creation of—unspecified—constitutional structures
that would give these so-called subordinate nations (to employ
Botha's terminology) control over their "own destinies."[6]

The tone of this rhetoric was new. Botha was attempting to
redefine the ideology of the National party and of Afrikanerdom
by giving to pragmatism the status of a refined theoretical set of
formulae. He was insisting that Africans were not subjects to be
controlled, but a part of the solution. Much of the old jargon was
dismissed, which had symbolic value. So did a surprise visit by the
prime minister to Soweto, South Africa's largest black city, in
August 1979. He became the first major National party leader to
set foot in the sprawling, 33-square-mile dormitory area 12 miles

5. *Sunday Times* (Johannesburg), June 24, 1979. See also Robert I. Rotberg, "South
Africa: Can it Go Two Ways at Once?" *Christian Science Monitor,* June 28, 1979.
    6. Quoted in *Star Weekly,* August 18, 1979.; *New York Times,* Sept. 1, 1979.

from Johannesburg. Although his visit was largely ignored by all but a few, and studiously disdained by radical Africans, it indicated a new official white sensitivity to the problems of minority rule. In Soweto Botha promised to transform the area into a city, under black control, but carefully said nothing about the political role of Soweto's 1.3 million inhabitants in the future South Africa.

As South Africa is presently constituted, leadership short of revolution comes from the prime minister and his immediate advisers. Even the scandal that compelled Vorster's and Mulder's resignations could not weaken oligarchic control of the future of Afrikanerdom. Thus if South Africa is to evolve politically, guidance must come from Botha and his coterie. They may respond to international and internationally influenced events, to African-initiated interventions, or to their own sense of the way in which South Africa's future must be reconciled with its past. In any case, they will presumably be directed by an awareness, however belated, of the limitations of any power that is illegitimate and demographically insecure; they will also be motivated throughout by self-interest, not altruism.

The history of Afrikaner politics is marked more by pragmatic responses to the realities of power than by ideological autarky. When it was essential to cooperate with the English, Afrikaners did so. When they were defeated in war, they made the most of the resulting bitterness, bided their time, returned victorious, and determined never again to be denied political primacy. But as the dream of unfettered control has met the dawn of modern politics, so Afrikaners have made accommodations, no matter how grudging and how token. Botha may be a leader capable of saying that Armageddon is preferable to tactical retreat, but if he is, he belies (and perhaps betrays) the lesson of Afrikanerdom. Whether he can respond in a visionary way to the needs of the changing political climate is questionable, but it may be that only a leader of his credentials can afford to think boldly enough to wrestle vigorously with the problems that most Afrikaners now know cannot be dismissed, and will not evaporate of their own accord.

3 | The Response of the Underprivileged

BEFORE THE MODERN ASCENDANCE of Afrikaners, the black majority of South Africa responded to white domination militantly, resourcefully, and pragmatically. In the nineteenth century, at a time when so many other African peoples in Central, East, and West Africa were attempting to forestall the occupation of their countries by Europeans, the more powerful indigenous South Africans also fought the whites — of both Dutch and British extraction — who sought to take their lands of sweet grass and to subjugate them to a thrust of colonialism from the south. In the eastern Cape Colony, in Zululand, and, for a time, in the Transvaal, the superior numbers of the Africans halted the white advance. The Zulu even won a significant victory in 1879. But, like the Ashanti of Ghana, who also defeated the British in a battle, so the Zulu soon lost the war and were incorporated into the folds of white rule. This was not the last manifestation of resistance — the Zulu tax rebellion of 1906 merits that distinction. As in West Africa at about the same time, however, it began the process that was to transform the idiom of indigenous protest from prevention to petition, and from the deployment of the weapons of combat to the adoption of Western-introduced methods of political organization, influence, and bargaining.

When Africans became unwilling subjects of the several white governments of nineteenth-century South Africa, alienation swiftly followed. Competition between white and black for arable land and supplies of water, as well as the mores of the early Cape Colony, led to the extension of segregation into the interior.

61

Most of the peoples affected were as yet otherwise unacculturated to the West and thus politically inarticulate. The gradual emergence of an urbanized, Western-educated middle class of professionals, together with a mission-trained peasantry in the eastern Cape and Natal, provided a focus in the late nineteenth and early twentieth centuries for the expression of newly focused discontent. Nearly always it was reactive in origin, Africans seeking (as they were in West Africa during the same period) to prevent the pathways of advancement and opportunity from being blocked by further impositions of discrimination and intensifications of separation.

To this end, Africans, led by writers, physicians, educators, and other professionals, established political organizations and, from 1912, when the African National Congress (ANC) was formed, to 1948, when the nature of white rule changed, sought to reason with whites in order to redress the grievances of Africans. Reformers who until the 1940s sought participation in politics rather than black rule, the leaders of the ANC were shy of mobilizing the great mass of still rural Africans. They clung to their franchise in the Cape until 1936, when it was taken away, and attempted by their considerable professional achievements, their steadfast moral rectitude, and their moderation to provide both a model for African aspiration and a balm for the fears of whites.

Yet neither the existence and the efforts of the ANC nor the stature of its leaders could prevent the political and economic position of Africans from deteriorating. As educated Africans became more numerous, legislatively mandated taints of discrimination were multiplied. As commercial competition between white and black farmers became more acute, parliament eliminated that competition by confining Africans to tightly drawn reserves and by starving them of developmental capital.

The Emergence of Protest

Both newly ordered restrictions to the franchise and the perception that whites were less and less to be trusted had led as early as the 1880s to the first black political organization, the Union of Africans, in the eastern Cape Colony. In 1894, taking his cue from what was becoming known of the methods that whites in South Africa and Indians in India employed when they wished to concert their forces, Mohandas K. Gandhi established the Natal Indian Congress. At the close of the Anglo-Boer War, Africans in the Cape formed a Native Congress, the Transkei Native Vigilance Association, and the African Political (later People's) Organization. Elsewhere, there was the Natal Native Congress, a Native Vigilance Association of the Orange River Colony, which became a Congress, and both a Transvaal Congress and a Native United Political Association of the Transvaal Colony. The last body vigorously sought the franchise for Africans despite the terms of the Treaty of Vereeniging, which had closed the war and strictly limited black political aspirations.

Both Transvaal Congresses fought the enforcement of pass laws in 1906 and, a year later, Gandhi led his own community in protest against new legal restrictions on Asians, especially the indignity of carrying passes with fingerprints. They picketed registration offices in the Transvaal, and in 1908 Gandhi was jailed, but this first expression of positive nonviolence in modern South Africa availed little. Gandhi would later use similar tactics successfully in India, but the South African racial and colonial context was substantially different, resistant to manipulation, and unresponsive to overseas public opinion. His failure, the victory of the Liberal party in the 1906 election in Britain, and the subsequent British decision to allow Afrikaners to regain many of the prerogatives that they had lost in 1902 placed the fate of all nonwhites in the balance. The deliberations leading up to the South Africa Act of 1909 were a clear signal, perceived by educated Africans and a few liberal whites, that the Union (which came into being in 1910) would unite whites against Africans.

The African National Congress

The African National Congress, formed in 1912 by black lawyers educated in Britain and the United States, by clerics educated in the United States, by a remarkable multilingual editor, by teachers, and by chiefs and descendants of chiefs, was a result of the anxieties of the periods before and after the Anglo-Boer War and of the meaning of Union. It was a response to passes, to taxes, to humiliations, and to a denial of opportunity even to Africans who had broken with and emerged from their traditional ways of life. Yet the ANC could not, in its second year, prevent parliament from passing the Natives Land Act of 1913. Although it built upon the prior setting aside of land exclusively for Africans in the Cape Colony and Natal, as well as the findings of the Native Affairs Commission of 1903-1905 (which espoused territorial partition as the only basis for the development of South African society and politics), the Natives Land Act denoted the determination of whites to confine and curtail African aspirations.

The passage of the Natives Land Act emerged less out of a desire to produce the territorial basis of a just, if segregated, society than in response to the expressed desire of white farmers for continued access to supplies of low-wage labor. A class of South Africans then called "poor whites" was in these years being forced off the land. Combined, the various motives brought about legislation designed to minimize competition by forbidding Africans to purchase land outside of the reserves or to offer themselves as sharecroppers on white-owned land. The reserves were envisaged not as future states but as places wherein the indigenous way of life could be continued. The primary object was to segregate. A secondary object was to limit the number of African families permitted to reside on white-owned farms, especially in the Transvaal.[1]

The act designated 7.3 percent of the land area of South Africa (22.5 million acres) as reserves to be occupied and used by Africans. Most of the land so reserved was at best marginal, and nearly always unsuitable for intensive farming or grazing. It was poorly watered, far from roads and railways, and already crowded and heavily stocked. Moreover, few of the reserves were consolidated. Most were collections of small and large black fragments placed haphazardly — like bewildered chessmen — on the white board of South Africa. Life was soon hard, since the population density in these lands was four times that in the white-

1. Jeffrey Butler, Robert I. Rotberg, and John Adams, *The Black Homelands of South Africa* (Berkeley, 1977), 9-10.

controlled rural areas of the Union. So Africans did what was wanted by whites; they moved off the land, flocking to the white-dominated cities and towns. Their migration never stopped, nor did population increases in the reserves slacken and intense overcrowding and overstocking cease. By the time that the transfer of an additional 15 million acres of land to the reserves was contemplated in 1936, it was already too late to arrest the decline in the productivity of the reserves or to begin to cope even with the natural population increase since 1913. Even if all of the 15 million acres had been transferred (and 20 percent still has not) in accord with the intent of the Native Trust and Land Act of 1936, Africans would still control less than 13 percent of the land of South Africa.

As Africans were segregated, so they were subjected to new forms of discrimination. When the Union-wide compulsory carrying of identification certificates, or passes, was legislated in 1913, and the law applied primarily to blacks, the ANC mobilized a wave of protest in the Orange Free State and later in the Transvaal. In 1913, and then again more successfully and dramatically in 1919, passes were collected and returned in sacks to the government. Protesters marched, sang the 100th Psalm, and courted arrest and lashes. The ANC helped miners strike for higher wages; on the Witwatersrand in 1920, 40,000 African miners downed their shovels. But this heady success in terms of numbers mobilized and crowds aroused did not lead to positive improvements in the conditions of African life. Quite the reverse: whites feared Africans in combination more than ever before, and transformed that anxiety into legislation—especially after an ANC-sponsored court case in 1922 brought about reductions in the levels of the African poll tax.

The Industrial and Commercial Workers' Union

In terms of its impact on African society, and by extension on the shape of the dilemma of South Africa, the ANC would regain similar levels of influence only in the 1950s. In the 1920s it was largely overshadowed in political potential (and in its contacts with the mass of laboring Africans) by the Industrial and Commercial Workers' Union. Formed by Clements Kadalie, a

Malawian, on the Cape Town docks, the ICU, as it was known, grew quickly from its inception in 1919 into an organization of at least 60,000 members (some report 200,000 members in 1926). Bewteen 1923 and 1927 it had the theoretical capacity to transform itself into a force for the reform of race relations in the Union, but the strikes it sponsored in support of minimum wages were undercut by white workers and were ultimately unsuccessful. In addition, the ICU, like the ANC in the late 1920s, was infiltrated and for a time dominated by individuals friendly to the Soviet Union. This infiltration led to internecine squabbling, the collapse from within of the ICU, and the severe weakening of the ANC. In 1935, shortly before the government managed to remove Africans from the voting rolls in the Cape Province, the convening of an All-African Convention heralded the resurgence of African protest and the renewal of bonds with Asian and Coloured politicians, who attended the convention. But neither the convention nor African protest more generally halted the juggernaut of segregation.

The Response to Apartheid

The politics of African protest remained for the most part a tool of the reforming élite until the electoral victory of the National party in 1948. Until then a residual faith in the good intentions of whites sustained Africans. But in 1948 the way in which their stake in even a discriminatory society was about to be destroyed became clear, and altered the direction and the methods of protest. Within the ANC, still led by older men of determinedly bourgeois outlook, the triumph of the Afrikaners in 1948 emphasized the need for radically new, urgent responses. Already, in 1943, the ANC had demanded the abolition of discriminatory legislation, land redistribution, universal adult suffrage, and the right to organize collectively in the industrial sector. In the same year, a cadre of young lawyers and other professionals, including Nelson Mandela, Walter Sisulu, Oliver Tambo, and Anton Lembede, had established a Youth League within the African National Congress and had begun the kind of systematic strategic and tactical planning that had never been attempted by their elders.

In 1949, in response to the Afrikaner victory and the reactions of the leaders of the Youth League, the ANC adopted a "Program of Action" that demanded political independence and committed its organization to boycotts, strikes, and civil disobedience in order to achieve its new aims. In 1952, together with the South African Indian Congress, the ANC, which had a membership at the time of about 100,000, implemented the first phase of its Program of Action by calling for the defiance of six "unjust" laws: the Group Areas, Separate Representation of Voters, Suppression of Communism, and Bantu Authorities Acts, compulsory cattle-culling regulations, and requirements that Africans carry passes. Their methods were to be civil disobedience, the courting of arrest, and the crowding of jails with opponents of these laws. Similar tactics had stirred British consciences in India and on the Gold Coast and had been used by Asians in the Union. In South Africa, however, the government responded by imposing harsher penalties and jailing 8,500 Africans, Asians, and Coloureds, and a few whites. There were riots in Port Elizabeth, Johannesburg, and elsewhere, in which forty people were killed. The result was additional repressive legislation and an acknowledgement that the ANC's Program of Action would not, on its own, prove capable of disrupting the grand design of apartheid.

Throughout the remainder of the 1950s, the ANC, in cooperation with Asian and Coloured political bodies, and with some support from communists, attempted to sustain and mobilize active mass participation and protest through exhortation as well as through determined opposition to the growing legal apparatus of apartheid. The deliberations of nearly 3,000 black, brown, and white delegates at a Congress of the People in 1955, and the Freedom Charter that they ratified, helped to legitimize the maintenance of concerted, cooperative forms of protest.

But the boycotts promoted by the ANC in accord with the Program of Action and the aims of the Freedom Charter succeeded more in swelling jail populations and in increasing the number of new laws than in impeding the implementation of the apparatus of apartheid or contributing to a sense of African power. A national strike against and the campaign of passive resistance to the removal of Africans from the long-established inner-city borough of Sophiatown in 1955 was easily thwarted by the government. A boycott of schools to gain repeal of the Bantu Education Act of 1953, which had transferred control of African education from the provinces and the missions to the national government, took 6,000 students out of school in 1955, but only for a few weeks. In 1955 and again in 1956, when 20,000 women defied arrest in Pretoria, opposition to the extension of the pass laws to black women was expressed dramatically—but without effect.

General strikes to withhold African labor were sponsored by the ANC in 1957 and 1958, but these expressions of solidarity were ill disciplined, and they were observed with enthusiasm only in widely separated parts of the country. In fact, whether because of insufficient organizational ability, rifts within the leadership of the ANC (now dominated by the founders of the Youth League), or the antagonism of the police, which used newly obtained powers to detain, arrest, and otherwise intimidate and coerce African protesters, broad-gauged, generalized movements of protest were acknowledged by the late 1950s to have little utilitarian value. More immediately promising were narrowly focused economic boycotts, where Africans could use their collective power as consumers to overturn nonpolitical decisions.

In 1956 bus services were boycotted in Evaton, a black township 28 miles from Johannesburg, until fares were reduced, but this demonstration of African economic solidarity had been sponsored not by the ANC but by local groups. During the first four months of the next year the Congress did involve itself significantly in a bus boycott in Alexandra, Johannesburg, with more than 50,000 Africans walking long distances to and from work. (Buses were also boycotted in Lady Selborne, Pretoria.) Eventually the penny fare increase that had precipitated the boycott was repealed, whites having been compelled to consult with the leaders of the boycott. In 1959 a boycott by Africans of the purchase of potatoes was also successful in that it contributed to temporary modifications in the system under which Africans served prison sentences virtually as unpaid laborers on white-owned farms.

Africans were far worse off politically in 1959 than they had been in 1949. As a riposte to the defiance campaigns promoted by the ANC, parliament had enacted even harsher laws, and the National party had won two elections more decisively than in 1948. Thousands of Africans had been jailed or otherwise deprived of their civil liberties throughout the decade; 156 leaders had been charged under the Treason Act of 1956 for their participation in the Congress of the People; although only 28 were eventually brought to trial, all were banned until 1961, when all were acquitted.

The Pan-Africanist Congress

Throughout this period there had naturally been disagreements within the ANC over tactics and ideology. Chief Albert Luthuli, its charismatic president beginning in 1952; Mandela, deputy president from 1952 to 1953, when he was banned; and Tambo, secretary-general from 1954 to 1958, then deputy president, all favored continued cooperation with the Asian and Coloured congresses and with communist sympathizers, many of whom were white. They opposed the employment of violent methods and continued to espouse nonracial democracy as the goal toward which the ANC should direct its efforts and energies. However, younger, more militant, somewhat more intellectual members of the ANC, notably Robert Sobukwe, a language teacher at the University of Witwatersrand, had begun to question the determination and ability of the leadership. They believed that its involvement with non-Africans had weakened, distracted, and—conceivably—even sabotaged the effectiveness of the ANC. Certainly, said Sobukwe, it had caused "interference from . . . so-called left-wing or right-wing groups of the minorities who arrogantly appropriate to themselves the right to plan and think for Africans."[2] He and his supporters wanted to use any and all means to wrest power from whites—the ruling "pigmen-

---

2. Robert Sobukwe, address at the inaugural convention of the Pan-Africanist Congress, April 4, 1959; quoted in Thomas Karis and Gwendolen Carter (eds.), *From Protest To Challenge* (Stanford, 1977), III, 515.

tocracy" — in order to establish a government of, by, and for Africans, with minority rights assured for individuals, not groups designated by color. The result of this fundamental disagreement about how best to emancipate Africans was the formation in 1959 of the Pan-Africanist Congress (PAC) by breakaway followers of Sobukwe, who became its president. Potlako Leballo, an ANC organizer from Orlando, became its secretary-general.

Rivalry between the old and new congresses occasioned competition. The PAC was determined to show that its complaints about the ANC's failure of will had been justified. The ANC was equally determined to limit the appeal of the PAC, which claimed nearly 25,000 founding members. The ANC therefore began to promote another campaign against the pass laws, planning a day of national defiance on March 31, 1960. The PAC countered by scheduling a similar protest ten days earlier. Its call was largely ignored, however, except in Cape Town and in the southern Transvaal, especially at Vereeniging. There, from 3,000 to 20,000 people (witnesses differ) presented themselves at the local police station without their passes, thus inviting arrest. The police panicked, shooting and killing 68 and wounding 186. This was the Sharpeville massacre, reports and photographs of which were flashed around the world. Within South Africa, African mobs rampaged in and around Soweto and Langa, near Cape Town. In Johannesburg, Port Elizabeth, and especially Cape Town, a week of mourning was accompanied by work stoppages sponsored by the PAC and the ANC.

This local version of the European general strike paralyzed Cape Town after March 28. Africans demanded the abolition of passes, an increase in wages to $98 a month, and immunity for the strikers. The government declared a state of emergency and began arresting and beating Africans. On March 30, Philip Kgosana, a twenty-three-year-old local PAC leader, led 15,000 Africans from Langa toward parliament, where he intended to demand an interview with the minister of justice. Diverted by promises that the minister would see him and that police brutality would cease, he dispersed his marchers, 30,000 of whom had gathered, only to be denied an interview later that day and to be arrested along with his principal cohorts. Nearly 12,000 others, including Sobukwe, Leballo, and many of those freed during the long sittings of the treason trial, were also arrested. The Cape Town locations were surrounded until the strike was broken, and, a few days later, the PAC and the ANC were both banned in accord with the provisions of the hastily enacted Unlawful Organisations Act.

After Sharpeville

After Sharpeville, African opposition to apartheid became increasingly desperate. In 1961, once the earlier state of emergency had expired, the leaders of the ANC who had not been banned or whose banning orders had expired, including Mandela, organized a large conference in March; there the National Action Committee was formed with Mandela as its secretary. It demanded the calling of a national convention of black and white leaders to chart the future of the country. Yet a national strike, called by the committee for the end of May—the eve of the inauguration of the Republic of South Africa—collapsed when the police arrested up to 10,000 Africans, including the suspected leaders of the committee. Mandela went into hiding.

From late 1961, opposition to apartheid became violent and clandestine. The white-led National Liberation Committee, which advocated urban sabotage, began setting off small bombs in post boxes and against telephone and electricity installations in August and October 1961, before a scheduled election. Later in the year Mandela's Umkonto we Sizwe (Spear of the Nation), the new militant wing of the ANC, demonstrated its commitment to violence by attacking electricity substations, Bantu Administration buildings, and post offices in Port Elizabeth, Johannesburg, and Durban. Poqo (Only Ourselves), the underground continuation of the PAC, was less well controlled than Umkonto. It attacked police stations, railway lines, and power plants in the eastern Cape and the Transkei in 1962 and 1963. During the same years, it murdered chiefs and headmen in the Transkei, fomented a riot in Paarl, killed informers in Cape Town, and sponsored disturbances in Langa.

Mandela's arrest in 1962, the arrest of several hundred members of Poqo, and the discovery of Umkonto's headquarters

at Rivonia near Johannesburg, all in mid-1963, effectively ended
the immediate threat that Africans could mobilize massive support and ultimately overthrow the state by sabotage and terrorism. Although the tiny white-led African Resistance Movement
(successor to the National Liberation Committee) bombed the
Johannesburg railway station late in 1963, the security forces
were in effective control of the country by mid-1964. Detentions
and exile had been the fate of the blacks, Coloureds, Asians, and
whites involved. Mandela, Sisulu, Sobukwe, and others were
jailed under harsh conditions on Robben Island or in Johannesburg. Others, like Tambo and Leballo, were compelled to reorganize the ANC and the PAC from offices in London, Dar es
Salaam, Algiers, Cairo, and elsewhere. With backing from the
Organization of African Unity for the ANC, from the Soviet
Union for the ANC or segments of the ANC, and from Algeria,
China, and Egypt for the PAC, the ANC and the PAC underwent
the painful transformation from political movements with widespread indigenous support into exile pressure groups dependent
upon the receptivity of their host countries and the largesse of a
number of manipulative patrons. Over the years the ANC, linked
at least loosely to the Soviets, managed to maintain its standing.
By the mid-1970s, however, support for the PAC had largely
withered away. Squabbles among the exiled leaders, the decision
of once-prominent members to join the governing ranks of Transkei, and the death of Sobukwe in 1978 lessened the viability of the
PAC as a movement of liberation.

Long before the end of the 1960s, too, the forceful discour-
agement of the expression of African dissent inside the country by
conventional political means (boycotts, protests, petitions, and so
on), and the elimination of violent manifestations of discontent,
had ushered in a transitional era between two periods of political
confrontation between blacks and whites. The transitional era
was marked by the systematic harassment of white and any remaining black dissidents and by the enlargement of the security
forces, a resultant surface calm, the gradual emergence of a generation of new urban and rural spokesmen, and the limited
adaptation of the state's policy of separate development to black
ends.

Black Consciousness

The vacuum created by the effective elimination of black politics on the national level was gradually filled by voices from the homelands and the upsurge of an emphasis upon black consciousness. Although historically related to the stress placed by the PAC upon being Africanist, the elaboration of a black-consciousness position owed much to the black-power movement in the Americas, the writings of Frantz Fanon, Malcolm X, and others, and a new generation's perception of the strategic and thus the ideological mistakes of its predecessors. Conceivably, in surroundings that denied nonwhites a role in society, the notion of separation, and thus of a determination to rely on one's own, could not have been as foreign in the late 1960s and early 1970s as it once was. The dream of an integrated society was fading. The burden of the message of the new black consciousness was self-reliance. "The emancipation of the black people of this country," resolved the first of the new organizations, "depends entirely on the role black people themselves are prepared to play."[3]

This was the byword of the South African Students' Organization (SASO) in 1970, a year after its formal inauguration and eighteen months after Stephen Biko and thirty other black students had decided to break with the white-led but strongly anti-government National Union of South African Students (NUSAS). Biko was then a student at the nonwhite medical school of Natal University. Born in Kingwilliamstown, where his father was a clerk employed by the government, he had attended St. Francis College, a liberal Roman Catholic secondary boarding school at Mariannhill, in Natal. Although he had been a delegate to NUSAS congresses from his medical school, Biko became the architect of black consciousness and, in 1969, the initial president of SASO. At first Africans were suspicious of an exclusively black, and therefore separatist, body, but by 1971 SASO was well established at all the segregated nonwhite universities, at the Transvaal College of Education, in two seminaries in the eastern Cape,

3. Quoted in Gail Gerhart, *Black Power in South Africa* (Berkeley, 1978), 262.

and on the Witwatersrand through a branch catering to students, working on higher degrees by correspondence.

Biko was a remarkable publicist, educator, and organizer. Dropping his medical studies, he was the energetic center of SASO and the consummate theoretician of its evolving ideology of black consciousness. He saw a trap for Africans in their involvement with whites, especially white liberals. He railed against any acceptance of black powerlessness, sometimes called accommodation. Both were psychologically crippling for a people in need of revolution, not the yoke of oppression. He fought the growing recognition of the political relevance of the leaders of homelands, since it undercut the awareness of the need for independence in the face of oppression. It followed that Biko favored confrontation, even if blacks were insufficiently educated and prepared (here he differed with Fanon), for, above all, Biko was alarmed that the absence of agitation would perpetuate itself and strengthen the forces of white domination.

Biko's revolutionary stance, rather than the "realism" of older politicians, some of whom had been members of the ANC Youth League and now ran urban and rural self-help associations, professional bodies, and similar groups, infused the Black People's Convention (BPC) when it was established in 1972 as an overtly political outgrowth of SASO. It extended into the urban high schools of Soweto, where the South African Students' Movement (SASM) was later established, and throughout the rural areas of the country as the National Youth Movement. Black consciousness spread to the university campuses and, after a prominent student critic of the government was expelled from the University of the North in mid-1972, also led to a wave of student strikes and what amounted to a student rebellion. There were disorders on the campuses again in 1974, after the BPC and SASO sponsored rallies in Durban and Pietermaritzburg and at the University of the North in favor of Frelimo, the Marxist soon-to-be ruling party in Mozambique. But the major contribution of SASO and the BPC to African political life and thought was the lifting of the self-esteem of a people, especially younger generations, who had come to accept their status of subjugation.

Biko and his colleagues mitigated the psychological impact

of the stultifying years after 1964. They cleared the way for the new outburst of militance that has characterized the period since 1976. With their organizations, they also provided a counterpoint, of far greater importance than the relatively small number of their adherents, both to the new strategies of the white government and to the rapid development in the early 1970s of the politics of the inner periphery that were being pursued through the homelands. After 1973, however, hardly any of the founders of SASO or the BPC could participate actively in political life. In that year the government began banning Biko and the others, leaving few who could speak openly for either organization after 1974. Nine SASO leaders were also arrested under the Terrorism Act and jailed in 1976 for five to ten years for their part in the rallies of 1974. In 1977 Biko died in police custody, presumably from a battering inflicted by his captors (pathologists reported five brain lesions) and from the after-effects of being shackled naked in a cell and then being driven, still naked, 750 miles to a prison hospital in the back of a landrover. "We end," said his family's counsel at the inquest into the circumstances of his death, "with Steve Biko dying a miserable and lonely death on a mat on a stone floor" in a prison cell.[4] With him died a unique brand of leadership. But black consciousness, and its contribution to the African way of addressing their problems, had become common property, and remained alive.

Separate Development

Biko and others of his nationalist persuasion and urban orientation were alarmed in the early 1970s by the rise to prominence of the leaders of the homelands. Although the components of South Africa had been segregated before 1910 and the Union itself had created reserves in 1913, only in the Transkei and the Ciskei before 1953 had Africans participated directly in the process of local government. Local councils were created in 1894 in the Transkei; by 1931 the councils, which had been established in all of the districts of the reserve, were federated to form the United Transkeian Territories General Council, or Bunga. Three

4. Sidney Kentridge, quoted in Donald Woods, *Biko* (New York, 1978), 255.

years later a Ciskei General Council was established. Both were intended to devolve at least some authority to Africans but, like the African Representative Councils in Northern Rhodesia (later Zambia) and Nyasaland (now Malawi), the South African councils were advisory, their debates and resolutions being forwarded to the minister of native affairs, and rarely reaching parliament. Even the Union-wide Natives Representative Council, which was created in 1936 partially to replace the loss by Africans of their common-roll franchise in the Cape Province, functioned little more than as a "talking-shop"; its evident powerlessness obscured its value as a common, national forum for a people otherwise voiceless and voteless.

Before 1948 successive South African governments had assumed that the African majority would remain predominantly but not exclusively rural, with specific ethnic as well as common national loyalties. Afterwards, for political as much as ideological purposes, the National party quickly sought to divide Africans according to a false, but strategically astute, model of the past. In 1951 parliament passed the Bantu Authorities Act. It established a hierarchy of Bantu authorities — tribal, regional, and territorial — with limited legislative, executive, and judicial powers, each guided and controlled by whites. Local chiefs (already on the government payroll) and white officials would appoint the members of the tribal councils. Regional authorities covered two or more tribal authorities and were permitted to run schools, construct and maintain public works and hospitals, involve themselves in the practice of agriculture, levy taxes, impose fines, and make bylaws. These regional authorities were, in turn, made subordinate to territorial authorities (as defined by the Promotion of Bantu Self-Government Act of 1959), with powers over essentially the same range of subjects. By exercising their political aspirations within these three categories of local government, Africans were expected by the national government (which had also abolished the Natives Representative Council) henceforth to be unconcerned about national issues. Indeed, the government was introducing political segregation to accompany its policy of territorial segregation, both urban and rural.

The Bantu Authorities Act worried Africans. Chiefs were

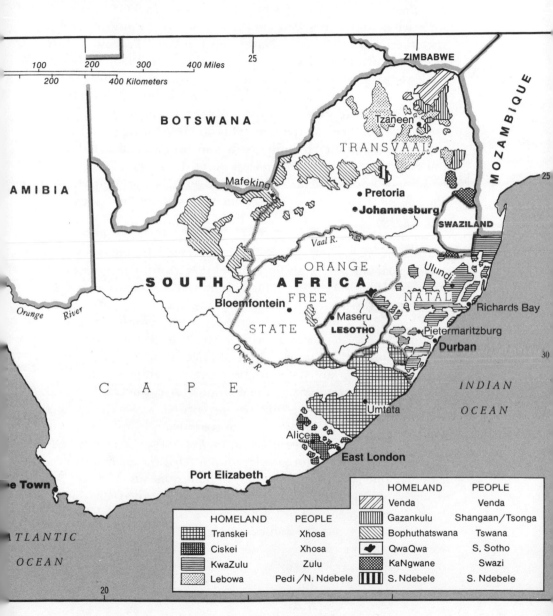

HOMELAND	PEOPLE
Venda	Venda
Gazankulu	Shangaan/Tsonga
Bophuthatswana	Tswana
QwaQwa	S. Sotho
KaNgwane	Swazi
S. Ndebele	S. Ndebele

HOMELAND	PEOPLE
Transkei	Xhosa
Ciskei	Xhosa
KwaZulu	Zulu
Lebowa	Pedi /N. Ndebele

The Black Homelands of South Africa

suspicious of the law; educated, politicized Africans were un-
equivocally hostile. It was retrogressive legislation, and at first
few chiefs and traditional councillors could be persuaded to accept the rearrangements envisaged by the act. In 1953, however,
three tribal authorities were established in the Transvaal, and a
few others followed suit in Natal and the Cape Province. Only
when the Bunga voted to accept the scheme in 1955, however,
could the government boast of significant indigenous support for
the law.[5] Two years later the Transkeian Territorial Authority,
composed of chiefs and indirectly elected councillors, replaced
the Bunga and became the first subordinate African government
within the Republic. It built roads and bridges and acted as a
pressure group for African interests in the Transkei. Thus it realized minor improvements, but it could exercise no unique control; popularly this first experiment with separate development
was regarded with great suspicion.

Prime Minister Hendrik Verwoerd gave ideological rigor to
the hitherto vague and unspecific yearnings of Afrikaners for separate development. He also presumed that growing international
hostility to South Africa could be minimized if Africans were seen
to receive political rights at least in their own areas. Moreover,
only by giving separatism an expandable framework could Verwoerd and his successors have claimed that South Africa was
composed of many nations, white, brown, and black, and that
the government wanted to promote the "separate freedom" of
blacks. Only by emphasizing the division of Africans into cultural
groups could they assert that the undivided white nation was
larger than any one of the African nations and thus was not a
ruling minority. The preamble to the Promotion of Bantu Self-
Government Act therefore declared that Africans formed diverse
national units, that Africans were not homogeneous, and that Africans should gradually acquire home rule in their "national"
units. Even so, neither the act nor the parliamentary debates ac-
companying its passage indicated timetables or foreshadowed
complete independence. It took the international furor occasioned by the Sharpeville massacre, as well as the prospect of con-

5. Butler, Rotberg, and Adams, *Black Homelands,* 29.

tinued internal violence, to propel Verwoerd in 1961 publicly to commit South Africa to the advancement of self-governing homelands and to their independence.

Homeland Leadership

Paramount Chief Kaiser Matanzima and his supporters in the territorial authority of the Transkei judged that more could be achieved for themselves, and for other Africans, by supporting separate development under the new dispensation than by opposing it. Since Africans could no longer hope to regain representation in the national arena, Matanzima reasoned, a large measure of local control could prove an acceptable, if avowedly temporary, substitute. He and his colleagues were prepared to turn Verwoerd's cynical public relations exercise to their own advantage. Yet there was widespread opposition within the Transkei as well as the Republic. Poqo even attempted to assassinate Matanzima. Nevertheless, in 1963, the Transkei became a self-governing territory with Matanzima as chief minister and a legislative assembly dominated by appointed chiefs. The powers of the new local government were circumscribed, autonomy being limited to local education, local security, agriculture, and a host of minor issues. And for many years it was but a token exemplar of devolution within the tightly controlled authoritarian society of South Africa.

By the late 1960s the central government had demonstrated a willingness and capacity to preserve order at any cost. It had maintained its determination to pursue its professed goals of political and social segregation. Multiracial politics, always limited in scope and effectiveness, were eliminated by the Prohibition of Political Interference Act of 1966. Organized expressions of African dissent had been driven underground. It thus became apparent to many that African political advances would be more likely to occur in the foreseeable future within the context of separate development. Matanzima, widely called a collaborator, was also demonstrating that the logic of apartheid could at times be exploited to African advantage. By 1970, furthermore, Prime Minister B. Johannes Vorster's government had decided that the movement of homelands along the road to independence could

help South Africa sell its program of apartheid to a skeptical
world. The Bantu Homelands Constitution Act of 1971 declared
"the firm and irrevocable intention of the government to lead
each nation to self-government and independence."[6]

Throughout the 1950s and 1960s most of the ethnic congeries into which the black population of South Africa had been
arbitrarily divided had been sorted into tribal and regional authorities. Several had established territorial authorities as well.
The last to succumb was the largest in terms of population. A
Zulu Territorial Authority came into being only in 1970, with
Chief Gatsha Buthelezi, a young, university-educated former
member of the ANC, as its chief executive. "Homeland leaders,"
he said in 1971, "have accepted separate development . . . because it is the only way in which Blacks in South Africa can ex-
press themselves politically." He went on: "I am not prepared to
say that separate development is the only hope, but it may be a
contribution to the unravelling of the problem, insofar as, if we
attain full independence, our hand will be strengthened. Gone
will be the days then, one hopes, when people will think of us
simply as 'kaffirs.' " Whether or not Buthelezi was representative
of the other homeland leaders in his decision to make of separate
development an instrument for the enhancement of an African
political role, his soon became the banner behind which the others began to marshal their efforts. Buthelezi publicly declared
his determination to see that the government delivered "the goods
on the basis of its own scheme."[7]

Well before the grant of local independence to the Republic
of Transkei in 1976, Bophuthatswana in 1977, and Venda in
1979 (in 1978 the Ciskei established an international commission
to advise on the merits and demerits of independence), the thrust-
ing of a measure of local autonomy upon the homelands had
given them a political salience unintended by the architects of
separate development. By 1972, because the homeland leaders
alone among Africans had, as a result of their official positions,
the prerogatives of free speech, the right to travel within and out-

6. Quoted in ibid., 36, where other sources will also be found. Much of this chapter is
derived from the analysis contained in *Black Homelands*.

7. Ibid., 33, 35.

side the Republic, and—for practical purposes—immunity from banning and arrest, they, like Biko, served to fill the yawning void that existed after the banning of the ANC and the PAC, the dissolution of the Liberal party, and the incarceration and muzzling of any and all successors to Sobukwe and Mandela. With Buthelezi in the vanguard, they took advantage of their institutional bases and privileges. They articulated the grievances of all Africans, not only their ethnic kin. They criticized the policies of the central government. They praised Mandela and Sobukwe. Cautiously, with Buthelezi jabbing at the underbelly of official resistance, they quickly carved out what, for the time, was a surprisingly broad zone of political relevance. So long as the government needed their services to give flesh to the bones of separate development, they could expoit the system to the advantage of Africans.

Protected by the edifice of separate development, the homeland leaders—as representatives of Africans—could not be ignored. They were quoted in the English and Afrikaans press. Buthelezi even wrote a weekly column, which was published in most of South Africa's English-language morning newspapers, throughout 1974 and 1975. The homeland leaders criticized and embarrassed the government; they addressed white, black, and multiracial groups, taking their message even into such strongholds as the Afrikaans-language universities. Overseas, they decried the policies of the National party. Public assertiveness in this way kept African protest alive and encouraged a shift in the relations between white and black from the solely hierarchical to the hesitantly equal—at least in political terms. It contributed immeasurably to a revival of self-esteem among blacks, especially when the dominant white oligarchy was seen, beginning in 1974, to be bargaining (however tentatively) with Buthelezi, Matanzima, and others both individually and collectively. For whites to have recognized a black sphere of responsibility, and to negotiate over its enlargement, were important steps in the evolution of any potential black/white compromise.

Buthelezi and Biko presented different strategic alternatives. Buthelezi consistently espoused multiracialism and nonviolence. "The whole system under which we are ruled as Blacks is structured on violence," he said in 1975. "It is a form of violence to forbid my children to go to a school of their choice because of their colour. It is a form of violence that I cannot enter the Post Office [through] a door reserved for Whites . . . The influx control regulations and pass laws are a form of violence . . . The whole colour bar system is based on violence and violence is used every day to enforce it." But "our people can never meet violence with violence."[8] From 1971 Buthelezi, like Mandela in 1961, has demanded the calling of a national convention in order to seek a *modus vivendi*. He has explored the notion of federalism as a solution to the South African problem; according to his scheme, separate, autonomous black- and white-run states would be linked federally in a manner that would ensure their cooperation on matters of joint concern. Common machinery would be established and, in time, "mutual confidence could grow to a point where agreement could be reached at the centre as well."[9]

This was a federalism, however, that would not fracture black unity. Buthelezi also believed that the homelands should work in concert, even against the white government. Before Transkei's independence he had hoped to link KwaZulu with Transkei, thus forming a bloc containing 37 percent of the total African population of South Africa. He early espoused black unity. "We would be fools," he said, not to follow the white example and join forces. At a summit meeting of all black homeland leaders in 1973, Buthelezi made his point more strongly. Before a crowd cheering in the street below, he appeared on a hotel balcony in full traditional regalia. Giving a clenched-fist, black-power salute, he told the crowd that "we are doing the same thing as the banned African liberation movements, but we are using different methods. Through this unity, as sure as the moon is in the heavens, we shall liberate ourselves. With power and with God on our side we shall overcome."[10]

Fourteen months later, in 1975, at the height of his influence, Buthelezi stormed out of a meeting with Vorster. He handed the press a copy of a memorandum that he had read to

8. Ibid., 81.
9. Ibid., 85.
10. Ibid., 87.

the prime minister. "We have been prepared to endure abuse," he had told Vorster, "in the hope that the government's policy may be a road to real fulfillment for Blacks. If this road . . . is leading only to a cul-de-sac, then our only alternative is to seek fulfillment not in unreal 'separate freedoms' but in . . . the only seat of power which is Parliament." He continued, "I feel that it is my moral duty . . . to point out, the only logical alternatives we have, if we do not want our people to resort to civil disobedience and disruption of service in this land. Not that I intend leading my people in this direction at the moment [a phrase the prime minister was quick to condemn], but . . . I should point out that if no meaningful change is forthcoming for them . . . this will come as a logical alternative . . . I cannot be expected to successfully ward off the venting of pent-up frustrations . . . if the government continually fails to offer [my people] anything meaningful." The time to "deliver the goods" had come. Otherwise disaster could not be avoided. The next day Buthelezi said that blacks must discuss "other means of taking the initiative and impressing their demands upon the Republic."[11]

These threats may have fallen on deaf ears, but within a few months the government had announced a series of limited reforms beneficial to black urban dwellers. Consultation and negotiation, when accompanied by criticism and fearlessness, had been seen to bring about results consonant with the inclusionist liberalism of the ANC. But however positive the possible consequences for all black South Africans of Buthelezi's homeland-based attack on the system, the real concessions obtained were few, and he and his cohorts were still in other ways promoting the aims of apartheid. Certainly criticism within a framework of collaboration was dangerous, and many urban Africans were prepared, at most, to acknowledge the utility of the homelands only as transitional objects. That is, Buthelezi and others could chip away at the underpinnings of apartheid only until such time as national, transethnic protest again proved possible.

There was and remains another fear. The government of Prime Minister Pieter W. Botha asserts that Africans are foreign-

11. Ibid., 103.

ers, residing in white-dominated South Africa only so long as their labor is required. If most or all of the homelands become independent (a goal that Buthelezi and Dr. Hudson Ntsanwisi, chief minister of Gazankulu, have disavowed), then it will become much more difficult for Africans to assert their rights as citizens of the greater South Africa. In such a circumstance it will become easier for whites to exclude Africans from the resource base of the country and to convert the arbitrary and unequal distribution of land and population into a permanent, debilitating partition. The disabilities of the homelands might also then become obscure, despite their variety and their existence as bars to meaningful, internationally recognized, independence.

The homelands, whether denominated independent or merely self-governing, remain wholly dependent upon South Africa's parliament for over 80 percent of their recurrent budgets. Thus, without the acquisition of a fairer portion of the resources of the Republic or without outside assistance, the homelands will find it impossible to achieve self-sustaining growth and a rising level of social services for their citizens within at least the next generation. Doing so without the consolidation of their existing, scattered pieces of territory is impossible (KwaZulu, for instance, consists of 48 major and 157 minor segments separated by stretches of white-controlled land). Even the inclusion of contiguous areas, now farmed by whites, within the various homelands would not redress the long-standing disparities between black and white land, since 87 percent of the population is still allotted 13 percent of the total land mass. That 13 percent is almost entirely impoverished, overcrowded, and unhealthy. Per capita incomes are low by world and especially by South African standards. In terms of natural resources and infrastructure, they are poorly endowed. The soils of the homelands are not conducive to the easy development of cash crops. Except for Lebowa and Bophuthatswana, their mineral potentials are limited. Finally, the dominance of the Republic prevents all of the homelands from overcoming their limitations or influencing developmental choices except at the margin, since the homelands are dependent upon the Republic for public services, trade barriers, fiscal services, and — most of all — an outlet for surplus labor. As economic entities, the homelands as presently constituted, arranged, and ruled are not viable. Whatever their nominal constitutional status, they remain clients of a jealous sovereign. So long as their existence is designed to serve the domestic needs and the international dreams of South Africa, they will remain powerless, their leaders cynical, and their urban critics unpersuaded that their existence has any positive attributes.

Since 1976 the homelands have played a reduced role within the politics of black self-assertion. The coup in Portugal and the consequent independence of Angola and Mozambique under Marxist black governments diminished the relevance of the homeland strategy as a useful alternative for a South Africa no longer surrounded by white allies. Since 1975, by which time both former Portuguese colonies had achieved their majority, the ANC and the PAC have been able at least to hope to pursue a strategy of liberation from friendly territory adjacent to South Africa — a possibility that had never existed before. In that year, too, Matanzima broke with Buthelezi and announced his determination to seek independence for the Transkei in 1976. Whatever the conceivable advantages in theory, by so doing he was seen to be playing precisely into the hands of Vorster's government, and buttressing the apartheid of the 1970s. But it was the spontaneous, unprecedented urban disturbances that began in June 1976 in Soweto and that later spread throughout the country that returned black politics to the center and greatly vitiated the perceived need for a rurally rooted, nonviolent, integrationist program like that of Buthelezi. Many urban dwellers who cheered him in 1974 and 1975 turned against him when the rioting of 1976 had reclaimed the initiative for those who believed in confrontation, not artful manipulation.

The Soweto Uprising

The death and destruction that engulfed the 28 townships (33 square miles) of Soweto in 1976 and spread rapidly to the African ghettos of Pretoria, Port Elizabeth, East London, Cape Town, Witbank, Ladysmith, Carletonville, and Klerksdorp (160 communities in all) and to the segregated university campuses, began on June 16, 1976, when the police fired into a large crowd (estimated at 20,000) of schoolchildren who were marching through Orlando in order to protest black educational and political disadvantages. The proximate cause of African ire (students had already begun to boycott classes and attack teachers) was the government's rigid insistence that elementary schools should begin to teach most of their subjects in Afrikaans rather than English. But Africans had many other grievances, too, their consciousness having been raised by the activities of SASO, SASM, the BPC, Buthelezi, and new groups like the Soweto Students' Representative Council (an outgrowth of SASM with a strong appreciation for the ideological stand taken by Biko). Moreover, Frelimo, the party of black Marxists, had become the government in nearby Mozambique and guerrillas in both Rhodesia and Namibia had mounted credible offenses that were giving hope to those who believed in the efficacy of externally supported liberation.

Whatever the precise contribution of each of these factors to the motivations of those who took to the streets of Soweto, marched on Johannesburg and Cape Town, kept Africans away from work, attacked their elders for collaborating with whites, tried to destroy the beer halls and *shebeens* (illegal bars) of the ghettos, forced the resignation of the Soweto Urban Bantu Council (the local advisory council), promoted school boycotts that kept nearly all of the schoolchildren of Soweto (and many in the Cape and Pretoria) away from their studies in 1976 and much of 1977, and undermined the economic vitality of the country, there is no doubt that most of their leaders were young, desperate, and prepared brashly to show older generations how to give their lives for a cause. On the eve of the riots Leonard Mosala, a member of the Soweto Urban Bantu Council, had warned of impending trouble. The students, he said, "won't take anything we say because they think we have neglected them. We have failed to help them in their struggle for change in the schools. They are now angry and prepared to fight and we are afraid the situation will become chaotic at any time."[12]

The toll of the combat that convulsed Soweto from June 16

12. Quoted in *World,* June 15, 1976.

through August and then erupted sporadically in Soweto and elsewhere throughout late 1976, 1977, and part of 1978 included 140 killed during the first week and at least 661 dead (all black except for about fifty Coloureds and a few whites) in the first eleven months. Most of those who died were young, usually under twenty-five, sometimes as young as twelve or thirteen. Of the 661, between 350 and 400 died in Soweto; between 42 and 72 in the rest of the Transvaal; between 23 and 33 in Port Elizabeth; and 153 in the western Cape. During the months between June and October 1977, another 29 people died in Port Elizabeth and Uitenhage. Given undercounting and confusion, 700 is a credible round figure (more than seven times the Sharpeville toll) by which to appreciate the extent of the convulsion in 1976 and 1977. This is not to imply that all 700 died of police wounds. A state pathologist said in 1977 that only two-thirds of the Soweto deaths were the results of gunfire. The police said that of 97 killed in the Cape during a part of 1976, they shot only 92. Official postmortems indicated that in Soweto, more than half of the dead had been shot from behind, a quarter from the front, and a quarter from the side.[13] In addition to the deaths, over 4,000 people were wounded and 1,000 arrested during the first seven months. Hundreds of schoolchildren, university students, adherents of SASO and SASM, and union organizers were detained, as were 18 black journalists. In early 1977 the minister of justice reported that he had detained and was holding 236 boys and 23 girls under eighteen years of age.

    Later in the year, when the violence in the streets had all but ended, the minister rounded up large numbers of adults as well. Biko had died in detention, and the true facts of his death were only becoming known when, on October 19, 1977, a month before the national election, the government banned SASO, SASM, the BPC, the Black Parents Association (a group formed after the Soweto riots), the Black Women's Federation, the Union of Black Journalists, the Christian Institute, the *World* (the country's major black daily, with a peak circulation of 178,000), and a host of

13. The fullest account of those terrible days is John Kane-Berman, *Soweto: Black Revolt, White Reaction* (Johannesburg, 1978), 26-33.

other organizations. Percy Qoboza, the editor of the *World;* Dr.
Nthato Motlana, a physician and a leader of the Soweto Committee of Ten (a new nationalist organization); Curtis Nkondo, chairman of the Teachers' Action Committee; Donald Woods, the
white editor of the East London *Daily Dispatch* and a close friend
of Biko; a number of churchmen; and virtually anyone else who
had recently spoken outside of parliament in opposition to the
government was either detained without trial or, like Woods,
banned.

Revolution?

Six months later Qoboza, Motlana, and other moderate
leaders were released to resume their occupations and their roles
as nuclei for above-ground movements of outspoken, rational
protest. Woods had escaped to Lesotho, Britain, and the United
States, where he became an antagonist of the regime both on the
lecture circuit and as an overseas syndicated newspaper colum-
nist. Many of the young who had led the actual episodes of rage
were either jailed, on trial, dead, or in exile. Biko's legacy was the
widespread acceptance of his message. Organizationally, his
groups, never large, had been destroyed by the actions of the government against individuals. Yet the townships were full of young
people who instinctively sought the goals of black consciousness.
They had been politicized by the events of 1976 and 1977. They
remained capable of being mobilized, and the actions of the government had done no more than to dampen the desires of the
young adults for revolution. How and when and to what their
emotions and intentions would be harnessed was the question of
1979.

There were at least two answers. From outside the country,
the ANC (more than the PAC) had lately shown an ability to infiltrate armed cadres into South Africa. Clashes between guerrillas and police came increasingly to the attention of the press.
Caches of arms were discovered. Trials were held of men smug-
gled with their weapons from Mozambique and Swaziland. Possibly those captured represented only a few compared with the
many uncaught, but they may also have been a majority of the
attempted intruders. As of late 1979 there was little evidence

that the ANC had either the means or the men to plant agents deep into the fertile countryside of South Africa; that they had an underground organization sufficient to support the agents and provide them with secure local facilities and escape routes to sanctuaries in Mozambique; or that Mozambique was prepared to risk sponsoring an attack on South Africa from its territory (certainly Lesotho, Swaziland, and Botswana were not). Nor was it clear, for all of these reasons, that an externally aroused, ANC-backed revolution was about to occur.

The events of Soweto and its aftermath had eclipsed Buthelezi in the eyes of urban Africans. At Sobukwe's funeral in Graaff Reinet he was jeered and harassed by young blacks. Men like Qoboza and Motlana had turned against him. Throughout 1978, however, he was active in transforming his Zulu-based Inkatha yeNkululeko yeSizwe (National Cultural Liberation Movement) into a political body of about 250,000 dues-paying members, both urban and rural. After winning KwaZulu's elections resoundingly early in the year, he strengthened the organization of Inkatha in urban areas with large concentrations of Zulu. Then he forged the South African Black Alliance (SABA) by bringing together Inkatha, the Labour party (the leading political organization of the Coloureds),[14] the Reform party (an opposition Asian group), and a political party representing the tiny homeland of QwaQwa. SABA was the largest nonwhite but multiracial political force in the country's history.

Given Buthelezi's political skills and his massive rural and urban support, at least among Zulu, it remained possible that Buthelezi could take his message of negotiation out of the homelands and into the national arena. If he could either successfully negotiate improved working conditions for blacks in industry (one of Inkatha's main aims) or persuade Botha's government to begin the delicate process of political change through bargaining (the crux of the South African question), his legitimacy as a polit-

---

14. In 1979 the Reverend Alan Hendrickse was elected to lead the Labour party. He proclaimed it a militant organization and promised that it would cooperate with the ANC, but not with a strategy of violence, and that it would oppose the government's constitutional proposals, favor a national decision-making convention, and demand a unitary society based on one man, one vote.

ical figure would be restored. An attempt was made in February 1979, for example, to strengthen Buthelezi's position with urban blacks. On his instructions, Inkatha urged blacks not to "sell their birthright" by taking out Transkeian or Bophuthatswanan citizenship, Africans having been given until 1981 to do so. Inkatha issued about 100,000 pamphlets calling on blacks in the "name of a greater South African patriotism" to retain their South African citizenship.

Later Buthelezi began feuding with Motlana and the Committee of Ten and forged an alliance with its archenemy, the leader of the Soweto Community Council. In October 1979 he startled the committee by promising to win the 1980 Soweto elections. This flaunting of his rural power and urban pretensions, he felt, was tactically more useful than seizing the opportunities of apartheid. Even more brazen was his clandestine meeting in London in November with the leaders of the banned ANC. Afterward he claimed that the ANC and Inkatha recognized each others' legitimacy. If the ANC supports Buthelezi and Inkatha, which would be politically salient, it will pose serious problems for both the black-consciousness movement and South Africa.

Whatever the effects of this development, neither Buthelezi, nor Inkatha and SABA, can be ignored, since no others can criticize, make demands, or compel the government to "deliver the goods." Buthelezi remains a potential bridge between the politics of repression and the politics of reconstruction and renaissance.

Men like Motlana, the young on trial, and older heroes in prison or in exile would be able to lead or assist that reconstruction. They have been better bridges to the urban discontented, and their legitimacy was hardly dissipated by detention and official enmity. Yet, because the size of their following remains unknown, and because the power of the Azanian People's Party (AZAPO)—resurrected in 1979 under Nkondo—is uncertain, Buthelezi can muster his strength more easily than they. In the early 1980s, unless new violence engulfs the country, Motlana and Buthelezi will, following their different strategies, continue to enunciate the discontent and aspiration of their fellow Africans.

4 | Economic Strengths and Vulnerabilities

SINCE ITS FIFTEEN-YEAR BOOM ended in 1976 with the importation of the world's recession, South Africa has struggled to achieve more than negligible real economic growth. In 1978 the Republic's gross domestic product, thanks to soaring metals prices and a return of internal consumer demand, grew by about 2.5 percent. But that amount failed to enable the country to keep pace with population growth: average real income fell by 4.4 percent; white real income alone fell by 4.5 percent. When it began, 1979 had been predicted as a much better year, with a doubling in real growth over 1978. Tight monetary and fiscal policies and increased export earnings together had put South Africa in a position of much greater strength than that which prevailed in the mid-1970s. But the addition of at least 30 and possibly 40 percent to the cost of petroleum and taxes to fund the construction of an oil-from-coal plant had a dramatic deflationary impact in the first half of 1979. It was estimated that petroleum-caused price rises would deprive consumers of at least $1.2 billion during the year. An upsurge in imports of machinery for the expanded liquid-fuel plant, continued combat-readiness on the borders, and the onset of double-digit inflation would take their toll. No longer was it possible confidently to forecast that South Africa, despite its many political problems, was about to resume growing, and average real incomes were again expected to fall.

Only unprecedented prices for gold, strong markets for several of South Africa's base minerals, and record coal and steel ex-

ports enabled South Africa in both 1978 and much of 1979 to pay
for the escalating costs of imported oil and still maintain a positive current account. The price of gold rose to over $200 a troy
ounce in late 1978 and was $400 or more a troy ounce for much of
1979. Platinum prices were well over $450 a troy ounce; other
primary products, but not all, were in great demand throughout
the period. The sale of 6 million Krugerrand gold coins (30 percent of all South African gold sold abroad) in the United States
and Western Europe in 1978, for a total value of $1.2 billion, also
helped measurably to convert the 1976 current-account deficit of
$1.9 billion into a surplus of $1.7 billion in 1978. In 1979, even as
oil prices increased, so the price of gold, tied as it was to a weak
dollar, remained high. The 1979 current-account surplus was expected to reach $3.6 billion.

Local and foreign investment fell dramatically after 1975,
especially after the Soweto riots of 1976. Capital outflows, both
long and short term, continued at record rates throughout 1978,
when more than $1 billion left the country legally. Without rising
gold sales this amount would have been costly to the economy and
have had a decisive recessionary impact. The government's decision in 1979 to create a realistic "financial rand" was designed to
make investment opportunities more attractive for overseas corporations by encouraging the easy repatriation of newly introduced assets at par. It helped limit the impact of capital flight
and stimulated the employment of excess liquidity. No matter
what happened, the foreign exchange position, which was $2.6
billion ($2.1 million was in gold) in early 1979, was expected to
remain healthy into the early 1980s.

By early 1979 confidence in the South African economy had
largely returned. No longer depressed by the world recession and
the aftermath of the Soweto riots and buoyed by the price of gold,
prospects for local prosperity, and therefore for funds with which
to be creative economically and socially on the domestic front,
seemed excellent. Yet the elimination of assured oil supplies and
escalated prices for replacement oil vitiated much of the expected
enthusiasm. South African financial managers also knew that renewed rioting, other indications of internal instability, or the on-
set of foreign-sponsored boycotts could plunge what had become

a recovering but fragile economy back into serious recession. The most bullish of official South Africans recognized the tenuous nature of the economic balance in early 1979. "I can fortunately say," he told a conference of businessmen, "that most recently the outlook for South Africa has been turning to the good. I admit that it would be premature to say that on the socio-economic side we are out of the woods, but I think that there is reason for business people both here and abroad to be less apprehensive about South Africa's outlook."[1]

Employment

Of South Africa's economically active population of nearly 8 million (according to the 1970 census), more than 5.6 million were African, 1.5 million white, and 0.9 million Coloured and Asian. Of all black workers, about 0.5 million were foreigners from neighboring countries. The agricultural sector, including subsistence farming, employed nearly 30 percent of the total in 1970, but that proportion is known to have fallen in recent years. Services accounted for 20 percent of the total in 1970; the percentage is doubtless higher now. Manufacturing absorbed 13 percent; commerce, 11 percent; and mining, only 8.5 percent of all employment. In 1978 unemployment was running at about 25 percent of the African population (white, Coloured, and Asian unemployment was less than 1 percent). Although official figures estimated only 800,000 unemployed Africans in early 1979, a generally accepted and reliable figure (used by the major banks) was at least 1.3 million of those actually seeking employment (that is, not counting subsistence agriculturalists). The 1976-78 recession increased the pool of underemployed, unemployed, and unemployables; so did a rapidly growing labor force due to African population increases estimated at about 3 percent per year. Thus only a return to the growth rates of the pre-1976 period will permit South Africa to avoid exacerbating the problems of structural unemployment, pressure on urban services among those categorized as unproductive, and the obvious social and political

1. Christopher Heunis, minister of economic affairs, quoted in *Star*, January 31, 1979.

consequences of increasing lack of opportunity for blacks. As a prominent member of the opposition told parliament, "If whites want to sleep at night they must ensure that blacks have jobs during the day."[2]

Only industry, mining, and some forms of service are likely to expand, and provide more jobs, in the best of times. Whether or not the 1980s will be economically prosperous for those sectors depends more on political than on economically determined variables.

Foreign Trade

Although South Africa produces about 80 percent by value of what it consumes, it is still dependent, in terms of foreign exchange, for earnings with which to afford vital imports, such as the 60 percent composition by value of imported components incorporated into its own manufactured goods. Of South Africa's total export earnings in 1978 of R 11.3 billion, gold contributed 35 percent based on sales worth R 3.9 billion, or 54 percent of the mining export total of R 7.2 billion. The other prime net sources of foreign exchange were uranium, with a sales value of R 500 million; diamonds, R 446 million; coal, R 325 million; ferroalloys, R 306 million; steel, R 300 million; and wool, R 181 million. From 1970 to 1978, the growth in the value of exports doubled; in constant 1970 prices, however, growth has been about 1 percent.

Until 1978 Britain remained the largest importer of goods from South Africa, the United States exceeding British levels for the first time in that year. In 1978 Britain took more than 16 percent of all nonbullion exports, especially wool, fresh and canned fruit, asbestos, manganese, and platinum, for a total of R 1.22 billion. The United States imports a range of minerals (discussed later in this chapter), canned and fresh fruit, sugar, and wool, a total of R 1.37 billion in 1978.

Britain, Germany, the United States, and Japan together supplied South Africa with 51 percent of its imports in 1978. This amount represented about 2 percent of Britain's total overseas sales, but only 0.7 percent of American exports. Nevertheless, a

2. Harry Schwartz, quoted in ibid., March 3, 1979.

1975 estimate suggested that 66,000 jobs in the United States were directly dependent upon exports to South Africa. Most were in the aircraft industry (South Africa has purchased its transcontinental air fleet and most short-haul aircraft from the United States), locomotive, electrical, automobile, and computer industries.

Britain and South Africa are historically important trading partners. In 1977 Britain exported about $1.3 billion worth of goods to South Africa; in 1978 its total gross income from trade with South Africa was about $4.2 billion. In the same year, it was estimated that about 70,000 British jobs depended directly upon exports to South Africa. As a percentage of South Africa's total trade, however, the British connection was a massive 22 percent in 1978.

South Africa replaced Nigeria as West Germany's main trading partner in Africa in 1978, when total trade between the two amounted to R 2.5 billion, an increase of 7.5 percent over 1977. Exports from South Africa were R 1.1 billion, a decrease of 3 percent over 1977; imports went up 18.6 percent. Nevertheless, trade with South Africa only amounted to 1 percent of West Germany's total foreign trade. South Africa is West Germany's seventeenth-largest market.

Although trade with the developed world is much more important to South Africa than trade with the nations of black Africa, the latter trade is much more extensive than is usually appreciated. In 1977 the South African Foreign Trade Organization claimed that the value of trade with the rest of Africa exceeded $1 billion in exports and $0.5 billion in imports. However, the official figures for 1976 were $521 million and $356 million, respectively.[3] Rhodesian trade, about half of all totals, was included in the estimates and the official figures.

As late as 1978 South Africa said that it was trading with 49 African states. Thirteen of the states have long admitted that they had such ties; most if not all of the others refuse to acknowl-

3. International Monetary Fund figures, cited in Andrew B. Sisson, "Africa's Economic Relations with South Africa," *Fletcher Forum*, III (1979), 95; *New York Times*, April 8, 1979. South Africa discontinued the publication of country-by-country trade statistics for Africa in 1964.

edge such links and/or obscure them by trading (expensively) through intermediaries. The first category includes South Africa's neighbors and obvious trading partners: Botswana, Lesotho, Swaziland, and Zimbabwe. Mozambique, from which South Africa imports labor and through which pass much of South Africa's exports to Europe and Asia, is also an important purchaser of South African goods and services. From Mozambique, South Africa imports labor, food, and 90 percent of the power output of the Cabora Bassa hydroelectric facility. Zambia relies upon South Africa for a range of consumer goods, maize, and mining machinery and other industrial equipment. Zambian and Zairese copper is exported in part through South Africa. Their imports of manufactured goods and agricultural produce come directly from South Africa or through its ports. Malawi imports consumer goods and agricultural produce and exports tea. Mauritius, Gabon (which exports timber to South Africa), and the Ivory Coast (which supplies coffee) are other acknowledged traders.

The second category, of clandestine traders with South Africa, is thought to include Ghana, which imported South African mining machinery and consumer goods until its foreign exchange position deteriorated dramatically, Togo, Benin, the Central African Republic (previously Central African Empire), Guinée, Burundi, Rwanda, the Comoro Islands, Kenya, and Nigeria. South Africa claimed to be obtaining crude oil from Nigeria in 1979. It allegedly exported food there, too, but by means of third-party transfers. For instance, a South African trading company reported in 1977 that it sent "quite a few foodstuffs by ship . . . they stop at Cotonou [in Benin] or Lome [in Togo] and the stuff is discharged and then brought on fishing boats or by roads into Nigeria."[4] In addition, the Seychelles and the Republic of Cape Verde both permit South African Airways to land; they derive important foreign exchange in the form of landing fees.

Within southern Africa, Botswana, Swaziland, Lesotho, and Zimbabwe obtain supplies of refined petroleum from South Africa. The Republic is also a major service center for those economies, and for Zambia, Zaire, and Mozambique. Its maintenance

4. Quoted in *Wall Street Journal,* December 9, 1977; also quoted in Sisson, "Economic Relations," 94.

facilities, for example, service airplanes from as far away as Gabon. The equipment of war reaches Zimbabwe through South Africa. During the second half of 1977, as much as 38 percent of Malawi's total imports came from South Africa, although its shipments there were only 7 percent of all exports. As receivers of their labor and as a consequent remitter home of foreign exchange, South Africa is also important. In 1978, more than 200,000 contract workers came to South Africa from neighboring nations.

Manufacturing

From 1946 to 1976, the contribution of manufacturing to the nation's gross domestic product rose from 17 percent to 25 percent, making manufacturing the largest single ingredient in South Africa's transformation from a supplier of raw materials to the developed world into a regional-level industrial power. By 1977 manufacturing dwarfed the contribution of wholesale and retail trade (13.1 percent), mining and quarrying (12.7 percent), transport and communications (11.1 percent), finance and business services (10.3 percent), general government (9.8 percent), agriculture, forestry, and fishing (7.9 percent), and several minor categories to total domestic gross product. In 1978 total sales in manufacturing were R 24.5 billion. Without its large and growing industrial sector, South Africa in the 1980s would be more vulnerable to consumer boycotts, less able to move in many areas toward manufacturing self-sufficiency, and less robust as an economy with a rapidly growing population.

In terms of gross value of output and the percentage of the total gross value of output for all manufacturing industries, food processing is South Africa's largest. It also employs the greatest number of workers. Excluding the manufacture of food, however, the four largest manufacturing categories in South Africa by value are iron and steel, metal fabrication, chemicals, and automobile and truck manufacture. The textile and clothing industries, which employ large numbers of workers, are almost as large, but the wood, furniture, paper, printing, leather, and rubber industries are all considerably smaller both in value and as sources of employment.

Continued growth in the industrial sector is limited by the insular and isolated nature of contemporary South Africa. In present circumstances South African industries cater almost exclusively to the small local market. The core of that market is a relatively affluent white and Asian population of 5 million, added to which are the large but underendowed Coloured and African populations, amounting to another 22 million. When these last two groups are allowed to participate fully in the prosperity of South Africa, the local market will expand toward its local potential. In recent years the growth in black consumer spending has been the single most prominent feature of the South African economy, real white incomes having remained stagnant. If and when South African goods are traded openly in black Africa — the rest of its natural market — then, too, South African industrial expansion will be able to produce effectively for a broader, economically more rewarding market.

These limitations in the size of the market for South African goods, the relatively large number of firms competing within that market, the underutilization of the available labor pool (making for artificial promotional barriers and overpayment of white labor), and traditions and regulations that make multiple-shift and continuous operations rare, combine to increase capital costs and to make most manufacturers uncompetitive with imported finished products. The automobile industry, for example, has installed a manufacturing capacity more than two and a half times what is needed for local market demand.

High tariff barriers and other forms of protection for local industry have thus been necessary. The government has also encouraged industrial consolidation, output-sharing, and price-fixing as a means of limiting competition and maximizing the capability of those manufacturing industries that have an important strategic potential. It has established its own domestic production facilities both through the Industrial Development Corporation (as in the recent decision to make diesel engines locally) and by the state domination or control of various aspects of industry through large state-owned corporations with special pricing and accounting methods.

South Africa's most important single industry now is the

making of iron, steel, and ferroalloys. With sales in 1978 of R 2.4 billion, the bulk of which was in primary steel products, it amounted to about 10 percent of total domestic manufacturing output. It is small by world standards, accounting for 7.9 million tons (compared with 124 million tons in the United States) or about 1 percent of total world steel production in 1978, but in the rankings of that year it was seventh in the world, immediately after Japan, China, and Brazil, and before Australia, South Korea, and Taiwan. Since 1975, in an industry dominated by the state-owned Iron and Steel Corporation (ISCOR), South Africa has also become largely self-sufficient, turning a sizable import deficit into a surplus that was exported with increasing success through 1978. The sale of 2 million tons of steel products abroad in 1978 contributed nearly R 300 million to South African foreign exchange earnings. Since Iran was a major importer of South African steel, however, and since the European Economic Community, another significant importer, has an internal surplus and has erected new barriers, South Africa may not be able to sustain its exports in 1979 and afterwards with the same success.

As is not generally the case in other parts of the world, the chemical industry in South Africa is old, having been established before 1900 as a necessary adjunct to mining. It is dominated by AECI (African Explosives and Chemicals Industry), the world's largest producer of industrial explosives. South Africa also makes fertilizers, pesticides, plastics, synthetic fibers, synthetic rubber, and basic chemicals. Self-sufficiency has not been achieved, but the government is using a variety of subsidies and forms of import restrictions to hasten the day when South Africa can be self-reliant in most of these areas.

The South African motor vehicle industry was responsible in 1978 for sales of R 1.7 billion. As an industry, it is characterized by a high degree of competition; only a few of the many firms (twenty firms existed in 1975, mergers and takeovers having reduced the total number through 1979) hold market shares that are economical without the advantage of substantial governmental protection. Volkswagen and Datsun sell the most cars and trucks. Ford and General Motors, the American-owned companies that have had South African plants since the 1920s, have but 4 percent and 3 percent stakes in the local market, respectively. Lately the government has been attempting to reduce the number of firms by requiring each vehicle sold in South Africa to include specified amounts of locally manufactured content by weight. Since 1978 this figure has been 66 percent, resulting (since automobile components vary considerably in weight-to-value ratios) in a local content by value of 40 percent.

Few of the firms in the automobile industry have been very profitable since 1970, and profits overall between 1971 and 1975 averaged about 5 percent of earnings before taxes as a percentage of total assets. Moreover, profits from 1976 through 1978 were largely negative. Most of the firms eagerly await the opening up of South Africa's internal market among blacks. Ownership of motor vehicles by blacks increased from 32,000 in 1961 to 207,000 in 1975; in the year 2000 blacks are expected to own more than 1.5 million cars and trucks. Many firms thus endure small losses now in order to maintain a presence in what promises to be Africa's largest market at the end of the century.

Mining

Gold has been the mainstay of the South African economy since the 1890s. More than half of the world's known reserves are South African. In 1978 the Republic's 36 active mines produced nearly 700 tons (23 million troy ounces) of the metal, roughly half of the total mined throughout the globe. Because of a weak American dollar and other demand forces, the world price of gold rose dramatically during 1978, averaging $194 a troy ounce over the year. In late 1979, the price was over $400 an ounce. Gold earnings thus amounted during 1978 to $4.1 billion for South Africa, a record $1 billion more than 1977. This windfall ensured a $1.7 billion surplus on current account in 1978 (1976 and 1977 were deficit years). Without favorable prices for gold, South Africa would have plunged deeply into recession.[5]

Of South Africa's total export earnings in 1978, mining contributed R 7.2 billion, or about 64 percent. Within that percent-

5. Production percentages and figures, reserve totals, and total sales for minerals discussed individually on the following pages are based upon data contained in Economist

age, gold (and the sale of Krugerrands) accounted for 35 percent of the total and 54 percent of the mining subtotal. Likewise, the contribution of mining to the gross domestic product in 1978 was about 18.1 percent; gold accounted for two thirds of that total. Diamonds were responsible for a further 1 percent of the gross domestic product and for 7 percent of total overseas earnings from mineral exports. All of South Africa's other mineral resources, important as they are to foreign industrial end users, contribute only about 5 percent to export earnings and less than 1 percent to total gross domestic product. South Africa may therefore be far less dependent for its own growth upon the mining and consequent availability of base minerals than highly industrialized countries without other sources of these minerals or ready substitutes. The expectation that South Africa would necessarily continue, even in times of confrontation, to make these minerals available to a hungry market is thus unmerited. So long as sales of gold and diamonds continued, South Africa could — under certain circumstances — stop selling base minerals vital to the industries of the West without putting its own economy in serious jeopardy.

South Africa gains considerable strength in any future contest of wills by virtue of its enviable supply position. It is the world's first, second, or third most important provider of nine significant minerals, and the dominant supplier of platinum, gold, vanadium, andalusites, and antimony. It ranks second in the world among exporters of manganese and chrome. South Africa has about 81 percent of the world's known reserves of chrome, 75 percent of manganese, 71 percent of platinum, 49 percent of vanadium, and 17 percent of fluorspar. It is obvious that South Africa has been blessed by the richest mineral resources in the non-Soviet world; on the globe its abundance can only be matched by the Soviet Union.

In 1977 Japan imported 90 percent of its mineral require-

Intelligence Unit, *Quarterly Economic Review of Southern Africa,* 1978 and 1979, and *Annual Supplement* for 1978; Standard Bank Investment Corporation, *Review,* monthly issues for 1979; Barclays Bank, *Business Brief,* monthly issues for 1978 and 1979; *Financial Mail,* supplement, July 28, 1978; information supplied by Philip Christenson; figures from Nico Czypionka of Standard Bank, April and September 1979: the daily press.

ments, the countries of the European Economic Community imported 75 percent, and the United States as much as 15 percent. Despite the relative self-sufficiency of the United States, in 1977 that country imported 86 percent of its asbestos, 91 percent of its chrome, 88 percent of its platinum, 56 percent of its antimony, and 99 percent of its manganese. South Africa provided the United States directly with 43 percent of its antimony, 30 percent of its chrome, 25 percent of its diamonds, 21 percent of its chromite and 35 percent of its ferrochrome, 36 percent of all of its ferromanganese, 48 percent of its platinum, and 57 percent of its vanadium. (Additionally, many American imports of these metals from other nations with no indigenous resources originate ultimately in South Africa, for example platinum refined in Britain and ferroalloys in France.) In value the mineral exports from South Africa amounted in 1978 to $1.5 billion. Europe as a whole draws upon South Africa for 52 percent of its manganese, 31 percent of its chrome and chrome alloys, and 24 percent of its platinum. Britain depends upon South Africa for large proportions of its minerals: chrome, 45 percent; manganese, 35 percent; platinum, 55 percent; antimony, 80 percent; and vanadium, 15 percent. West Germany imports 60 percent of its chrome and 48 other raw materials (especially manganese, asbestos, and wolframite) from South Africa.

In other words, given present industrial patterns in the developed countries of the northern hemisphere, South Africa possesses an importance as a raw material supplier crucial at least in the short run to the peak performance of several major economies. Defense-related and ferrous metals industries are the most vulnerable. Even so, South Africa acting on its own cannot be said to possess a power of dislocation similar to that of the Organization of Petroleum Exporting Countries (OPEC). At a price, most metals can be replaced by substitutes, if sufficient quantities of the substitutes exist. Alternatively, in time, processes of manufacturing can be altered to compensate for the unavailability of otherwise essential commodities, but, again, only at high cost. It is not yet evident, moreover, that under most foreseeable circumstances South Africa would want to run the considerable political risks of a conscious countervailing strategy of resource denial.

South African cabinet members have occasionally uttered such threats, but more for domestic consumption than for serious consideration overseas.

Used with precision, the employment of economic might could give a beleaguered South Africa weapons with which to combat sanctions against itself. Dangers would remain, however. An inability to forecast the exact consequences of a policy of resource denial, the potential economic and political side effects of such a policy, and the likelihood of an international backlash would compel South Africa to hesitate. Ultimately, South Africa derives leverage more in theory than in practice from its wealth underground.

South Africa's strengths and weaknesses become more evident when its resources are examined mineral by mineral.

Antimony

Antimony, a soft metal, is primarily employed in alloys with lead for automobile and storage batteries and in the detonators of explosives. Antimony oxide is a flame retardant used for upholstery and clothing.

In 1977 South Africa overtook Bolivia as the world's prime producer of antimony, supplying 22 percent of the total. In South Africa antimony is found in small deposits scattered across the Transvaal. Consequently, it is expensive to mine.

Consolidated Murchison is South Africa's only producer of antimony sulphide concentrates (the usual form). It is jointly owned by the Anglo-Transvaal Mining Corporation and Johannesburg Consolidated Investments. Antimony Products, a partnership between Consolidated Murchison and Chemetron, an American firm, produces antimony oxide. South Africa's production of antimony concentrates in 1978 totaled 12,000 metric tons, worth R 11 million. The price of antimony in 1979 was $2 per pound.

The United States depends on imports for 95 percent of its primary antimony, but for only 56 percent of its total needs because of a high rate of secondary recovery. Of the 95 percent, South Africa in 1974 supplied a third. Much of the rest came from Bolivia, China, and Mexico. The capacity to supply all

American needs exists in those countries, assisted by more efficient methods of secondary recovery.

Asbestos

Canada and the Soviet Union are the world's two largest producers of asbestos, mining nearly 75 percent of the total. Although South Africa is the world's third-largest supplier of asbestos, it contributes only 9 percent of the total. In 1976 that amounted to 370,000 metric tons, which earned R 133.4 million in 1977 and R 113 million in 1978.

Although two of the three basic types of asbestos, crocidolite (blue) and amosite (brown), are unique to South Africa, all three forms are for most uses interchangeable. All can be used in the fabrication of specialized cement because of the reinforcing qualities of asbestos and because asbestos resists alkaline cement solutions. Chrysotile is employed for brake linings and accounts for only 28 percent of total South African production. Amosite, 25 percent, is fabricated into lightweight, fire-resistant insulation boards. Forty-seven percent of South African production was of crocidolite, which is widely preferred for the manufacture of cement asbestos products.

The General Mining Corporation is the main producer in South Africa, selling asbestos in the form of cement products (recently, especially, piping for irrigation and sewage disposal) to the United States, Australia, Japan, Europe, and the Middle East. Although the United States obtains 86 percent of all of its asbestos requirements outside its own borders, and depends on South Africa for amosite, most of its asbestos still comes from Canada.

Chromium

Chromium is essential to the production of high-quality stainless steel, superalloys for jet engines and other space-age applications, and high-technology weapons systems. Food-processing machinery is made with stainless steel and chrome-plated steel. The petrochemical and chemical industries use stainless steel in processes that require corrosion-resistant vessels and piping. Chromite (the raw material), usually in combination with magnesia, is employed in the manufacture of heat-resisting (refractory) bricks used for the construction and maintenance of industrial furnaces, mainly in the steel industry. Some chromite is used in moulding sands for foundry applications. Chromite is also the source of many valuable chromium-bearing chemical compounds. Lead chromate is the main constituent of high-quality chrome yellow, red, and green paints. Chrome stabilizes green and brown pigments in paints and inks, and the green ink used, for example, on the special paper that becomes American dollars. Chrome tanning compounds, in the form of crystalline chrome alum, are basic to the leather industry, which employs about 275,000 persons in the United States; vegetable-based compounds are an alternative, but a less attractive one economically. Another 25,000 people are employed in chrome-pigment factories in the United States.

Of the identifiable world resources of chromite, 97 percent is located in South Africa and Zimbabwe. South Africa alone has 81 percent of the total reserves of the world, although the Zimbabwean ore is higher in chromium content. In 1978 South Africa was the world's second-largest supplier of chromite, contributing 2.5 million tons, or 28 percent of the total. Of that amount, about a third was in the form of chrome alloys. In 1978, for example, South Africa, the world's leading producer, exported about 525,000 tons of ferrochrome. Two-fifths went to the United States, about 160,000 tons to Europe, and about 130,000 tons to Japan. In late 1978 charge-grade ferrochrome exports were fetching about $400 a ton on the world market. In 1978 South Africa exported R 89 million worth of chromite and ferrochrome.

Three South African companies, General Mining, Rand Mines, and Samancor (South African Manganese, Limited, and African Metals Corporation, Limited), dominate chromite extraction in South Africa. Union Carbide has one mine, in Lebowa, and a 49 percent interest in a ferrochrome smelter on the edge of Lebowa (General Mining holds the other 51 percent). Union Carbide manages the smelter, which cost $48 million to construct in the early 1970s and has a capacity of 125,000 metric tons a year.

Before Union Carbide perfected its Argon Oxygen Decarburization process, South Africa's low-grade, friable, chromite ores were less useful than those of Rhodesia for the manufacture of ferrochrome used in the production of stainless steel. By the mid-1970s, however, the Union Carbide process permitted the widespread utilization of the more abundant, less expensive high-carbon ferrochrome (charge chrome) of South Africa. South Africa also supplies virtually all of the chrome ore used by the United States chemical industry.

The United States mines no chromite. It is dependent upon imports for 91 percent of its supply, the remainder being derived from stockpiles and recycling. Before the repeal of the Byrd Amendment (which permitted the United States to import chromium from Rhodesia despite United Nations trade sanctions against the breakaway colony) in 1977, the United States obtained 7 percent of its chromium needs from Rhodesia and 30 percent from South Africa. Thus about 40 percent of its chromium requirements are now customarily satisfied by imports from South Africa. The Soviet Union, Turkey, and the Philippines together provide the remaining 50 percent (some of the Soviet chrome was alleged to have been originally Rhodesian in 1979). However, since at present extraction rates the known deposits of chromite in the Soviet Union, Turkey, and the Philippines will be exhausted in nine, nine, and five years, respectively, and since the refractory-grade chromite of the Philippines is more valuable for refractories than for metallurgical or chemical applications, the American reliance upon South Africa's chromium is even greater than those percentages would imply, and it will grow. The importance of chromium to American industry, and of employees in chrome-related industries as a fraction of overall American employment, is also more extensive than is generally realized.[6] In the simplest terms, chrome is much more important

6. An experimental process, announced in 1979, may someday permit manufacturers of stainless steel and other alloys greatly to reduce their dependence upon chromium. Rather than mixing 2 to 3 percent chromium with 97 to 98 percent steel to give the steel a corrosion-resistant finish, for example, highly energized chromium ions would be driven under pressure onto the outside of a steel product. The product would be coated, but precisely, and only a fraction of the chromium usually required for stainless steel (or another alloy) would thus be necessary. *New York Times*, March 7, 1979. Extraction and exhaustion rates are from U.S., Bureau of Mines, *Mineral Commodity Summaries* (1978).

to the United States, and to the other developed nations of the noncommunist northern hemisphere, than it ever will be as an earner of foreign currency for South Africa. Chrome, along with platinum, manganese, vanadium, and, possibly, uranium, provides South Africa with a unique source of economic leverage.

In 1978 Japan purchased 50 percent of its chromite and 90 percent of its ferrochrome from South Africa.

Copper

Although South Africa exported R 210 million worth of copper concentrates, anodes, and castings in 1978, and copper thus contributed measurably to the foreign earnings of the Republic, in world terms South Africa is not an important producer. It was the world's tenth-largest producer in 1976, supplying only 2 percent of the total trade in copper. Its reserves are large, but it still ranks thirteenth (with 2 percent of all known reserves) on the list of the world's countries with copper deposits. In Africa, South Africa ranks far behind Zambia and Zaire, but ahead of Zimbabwe and Namibia in terms both of production and proven reserves. South Africa also has a limited capacity to refine copper, and thus it cannot add appreciable value to copper as a raw material.

Copper earns money for South Africa (R 147 million in 1978) but provides no leverage of a kind potentially available from scarcer metals. One American corporation, Newmont Mining, has a stake in the richest South African copper deposit, holding 57.5 percent of the O'Okiep mine in Namaqualand (northern Cape Province).

Diamonds

Diamonds, especially those larger in size than 1 carat, have industrial uses that are more important to the economies of developed countries than is often realized. Diamonds as jewels remain a significant form of consumption, but for strategic purposes diamonds are irreplaceable in petroleum drilling bits and the cutting edges of machine tools. South Africa is the world's premier producer of industrial diamonds, as well as a major gemstone producer. It also supplies the raw materials for synthetic diamonds. About a fourth of all diamonds imported into the United States come from South Africa.

In 1978 South Africa's diamond exports were worth R 446 million. It was the world's third-largest producer, with 12 percent (7 million carats) of the world total. It ranked second on the list of countries with sizable known reserves, having 7 percent of the world's total. However, the De Beers Corporation, which mines all diamonds in South Africa, has since expanded production from its Namibian alluvial working and is opening up a rich, new, open-cast mine in Botswana. Both developments will diminish the relative share of South Africa's diamonds as a proportion of world supply, and contribute to a lessening of any countervailing influence that South Africa may be able to derive from its favorable position as a diamond exporter. Even so, De Beers, through its Central Selling Organization, effectively manages the supply of diamonds in the noncommunist world. That dominance of diamond sales will continue, and will ultimately give South Africa some as yet undetermined and unspecified economic and political influence.

Fluorspar

A nonmetallic base mineral that, in South Africa, averages about 25 percent calcium fluoride, fluorspar is vital to the production of steel and aluminum, where it is used as a flux. It is also utilized for petroleum refining and uranium enrichment, although the amounts required are small. Fluorspar is essential to the manufacture of fluorocarbon propellants, but after 1979, when the United States banned most such propellants, this use was sharply reduced.

With the expansion of existing mines and the opening of a new one (by Chemspar, Limited, a wholly owned subsidiary of Phelps-Dodge, in 1977), South African production rose by 75 percent over 1975 figures. In 1978 Chemspar mined 70,000 tons of acid-grade fluorspar and sold a total of 75,400 tons, up appreciably from 1977, when total fluorspar production earned R 16 million. South Africa produces metallurgical-, ceramic-, and acid-grade fluorspar and briquetted flotation concentrates, its total production in 1978 being 424,000 tons, worth R 23.3 million.

In 1977 South Africa became the world's third-largest supplier of fluorspar (after Mexico and the Soviet Union). France, Spain, West Germany, Thailand, and China also mine fluorspar, but their reserves are being depleted rapidly. In 1977 total world production was 5.1 million tons.

South Africa has the largest proven reserves of fluorspar in the world, about 17 percent of the total. As other countries exhaust their supplies, South Africa, by the mid-1980s, is expected to become the world's most important exporter. Only then will South Africa derive political benefit from fluorspar. The United States may still be protected by virtue of long-term contracts with Mexican mines.

Iron Ore

Iron ore, of which South Africa holds but 3 percent of the known world reserves, is important to South Africa internationally only as a substantial earner of foreign exchange. In 1978, iron ore exports declined to R 165 million from R 206 million in 1977, but remained well above R 80 million in 1976 and R 42 million in 1975. Sales to local steel producers were worth an additional R 54.6 million in 1978. ISCOR produced 7.9 million tons of steel in 1978.

In terms of sales, but not leverage, iron ore brought in more total foreign exchange than manganese, chromite, and other more strategic minerals. Copper was in a similar position in 1977.

Manganese

Ninety percent of the world's available manganese is consumed in the manufacture of steel. It is a critical hardening element; without manganese, steel stays brittle. Precision instruments are also formed of manganese. Given present methods of steel-making, which differ only in the percentage of manganese required to produce each ton of steel, there are no known substitutes.

The Soviet Union mines more manganese than South Africa, the world's second-ranked producer with about 24 percent of the total, but Soviet steel mills are unusually heavy consumers of the metal. As a consequence, little Soviet manganese is exported to the West. Brazil, Gabon, Australia, and India also mine manganese, but South Africa is by far the largest supplier to the non-Soviet industrial nations, being responsible for 40 percent of their imports. The United States has no indigenous access to manganese, and is thought to depend on South Africa for about 55 percent of its total requirements. Since South Africa holds 75 percent of world proven and probable reserves, American dependence upon South African manganese is certain to grow as long as steel production methods remain the same. In the United States about 26 percent of all manufacturing is steel-related; thus South African manganese may be even more important to the United States than is generally appreciated. The holding of stockpiled manganese would certainly cushion the shock of any abrupt loss of access to supplies from South Africa. But in the longer run, American reliance on imports of manganese could only be reduced significantly through the exploitation of the manganese that now sits on ocean beds in the form of nodules.

Samancor is government-owned and the main producer of manganese ore and ferromanganese. In the recent past it has mined about 6 million metric tons a year. The other South African manganese producer is Associated Manganese, which is owned by the Anglo-Transvaal Mining Corporation and African Mining and Trust. It sells about 1.8 million tons of manganese ore a year. In 1977 total exports fetched R 120 million, down from R 131 million in 1976. In 1978 total export sales fell to R 88 million.

Platinum Metals

South Africa and its homelands are the world's leading producers of platinum, palladium, rhodium, and rare related metals, supplying 47 percent of the world total and 87 percent of the non-Soviet bloc total. Of platinum alone, in 1976 South Africa mined 68 percent of the total; of palladium, 30 percent. Canada and the Soviet Union are the other large producers of both metals, but there they are mined as byproducts of nickel. South Africa is the world's sole primary producer of both metals. About 71 percent of the proven reserves of the world are within its borders and the borders of its subordinate homelands.

The six metals of the platinum group can usually be employed interchangeably by the chemical, petroleum, and electronics industries of the northern hemisphere. Outside the group, however, substitutes are either unavailable or inferior in performance. Platinum is unusually ductile and malleable, does not oxidize in air, and has the quality of changing the nature of the substances with which it comes into contact without altering its own properties. It does not flake, and can be used to make optical glass. It resists friction, and is used in screens through which synthetic fibers are drawn. Because of its high melting point, it is employed to line furnaces and aircraft engines. As a catalyst, it upgrades the octanes of gasoline. But it is as the main constituent in antipollution devices—the catalytic converters of American-made automobiles—that platinum becomes essential to ordinary consumers. Without platinum (unless rhenium can be substituted) these automobiles would have to be designed differently, at great expense. Platinum is also used extensively for fashioning jewelry in Japan, but not in the United States.

Palladium is used especially for the coating of telephone contact points because of its resistance to friction. Rhodium has nearly all of the characteristics of platinum and palladium, but is much rarer and costs far more. Rhenium, which is not found in South Africa, has a very high melting point (nearly twice that of platinum) and is used in electrical contacts and high-temperature thermocouples.

The United States depends upon foreign sources of platinum, palladium, rhodium, and rhenium for about 80 percent of its needs. South Africa alone supplies about 33 percent directly. Another 23 percent comes from a refinery in Britain with strong South African connections. In the event of a South African decision to withhold supplies, American and European industry would be limited in their options, especially since the alternative Canadian and Soviet supplies, being byproducts of nickel extraction, cannot rapidly expand.

In 1978 South Africa and the Soviet Union each produced about 3 million of the 6.4 million troy ounces of platinum-group metals mined in the world. In that year the price of platinum rose from $200 to $350 a troy ounce due to new demand forces (catalytic converters) and the withdrawal of Soviet supplies from the world market as a result of a mine disaster. In 1979 the price of platinum soared above $400 an ounce. Palladium had reached $90 an ounce; the price of rhodium was $650 an ounce.

Of South Africa's total production, at least two-thirds is mined in Bophuthatswana, a homeland to which South Africa gave a local version of independence in 1977. Rustenburg Mines, the largest platinum producer in the world, operates two mines in Bophuthatswana and one in the Transvaal. The Union Corporation operates Impala Platinum Mines, another major Bophuthatswanan producer. Both companies and two smaller ones also won 700,000 of South Africa's total 1.8 million ounces a year of palladium from the subsoil of Bophuthatswana. Thus that homeland, and not South Africa, is the true center of the world production of both metals, a reality that, under some circumstances, could limit the strategic value of platinum to South Africa. Bophuthatswana also produces chromite, copper, asbestos, and manganese.

Titanium

QIT-Fer et Titane, a two-thirds-owned subsidiary of the Kennecott Corporation, began exporting titanium slag and low-manganese pig iron in 1978 from a smelter located at Richards Bay and owned by Richards Bay Minerals. (That company, in turn, is owned 32 percent by QIT, 30 percent by the Union Corporation of South Africa, 20 percent by the South African Industrial Development Corporation, 11 percent by one South African insurance company, and 7 percent by another.) The titanium slag, used as titanium dioxide in white paint pigments, is produced by smelting ilmenite, which in turn is mined or dredged from the sands south of Richards Bay. In 1979 Richards Bay expects to reach full production with 400,000 metric tons of slag and 217,000 metric tons of iron. From the same mining venture it also expects to export 115,000 tons of zircon sand (used by the ceramic, foundry, and refractories industries) and 56,000 metric tons of rutile (used in paint pigments and by fabricators of welding rods). Despite these figures, South Africa will for some time rank behind Australia, Canada, the United States, and Norway in the sale of all three of these metals.

Vanadium

South Africa is the world's largest producer of this metal, with an annual output of about 54 million pounds, or 40 percent of the world total and about 52 percent of total Western capacity. South Africa's reserves of nearly 8 million metric tons of vanadium pentoxide are also the world's largest and about half of proven global supplies. The Soviet Union is self-sufficient in vanadium and exports to Eastern Europe. In the West, the other main producers are the United States (35 million pounds) and Finland (11.5 million pounds). Namibia, which is a declining factor in the world supply situation, and Chile also mine vanadium.

Vanadium is an important alloying element in the manufacture of specialty steels, 90 percent of all vanadium being consumed in this way. The remainder is employed in the fabrication of titanium-based alloys and the production of catalysts for use by chemical industries. Traditionally, steel mills used vanadium to produce conventional full-alloy steels and, along with tungsten and molybdenum, in tool steel to form complex carbides that impart hardness, strength, and wear characteristics. Since the 1960s, vanadium (in the form of solid vanadium nitride) has been a crucial component of high-strength, low-alloy steels used for the construction of buildings, bridges, pressure storage tanks, and, notably, oil and gas pipelines. Increasingly vanadium is also used for automobile steel in order to meet new United States weight-economy and damage vulnerability standards. Columbium, molybdenum, titanium, tungsten, and tantalum can sometimes, depending upon specific end uses, be substituted for vanadium, but columbium (a byproduct of tin mining in Nigeria, Brazil, and Canada) and tantalum are usually in short supply.

Three companies produce vanadium in South Africa from titaniferous magnetite containing 1 to 2 percent vanadium pentoxide. Highveld Steel and Vanadium, a division of the Anglo-American Corporation, South Africa's largest conglomerate, annually produces about 39 million pounds; Ucar Minerals, a Union Carbide subsidiary, 12.5 million pounds; and Transvaal Alloys, a South African firm, 4.5 million pounds. In 1978 the total South African production was valued at about R 50 million.

In the United States, vanadium oxide is produced by a number of companies as a byproduct of uranium mined on the Colorado plateau. It is also derived from vanadium-bearing ferrophosphorous slags, along with phosphorous production, in Idaho; from spent catalysts; and from the vanadium-rich ash that results from the combustion of high-sulphur petroleum. The main source of American-produced vanadium as a single entity, however, is a Union Carbide vanadiferous clay-extraction process in Arkansas. The major American sources of supply have comparatively short lifespans.

In Finland, vanadium oxide is extracted as a single product as well as a coproduct with titania from a titaniferous magnetite near the Arctic Circle. Australia, Canada, India, China, and Eastern Europe have titaniferous magnetites that could yield large quantities of vanadium if they ever become economically viable sources of iron. Vanadium is also recoverable from the desulferization of Venezuelan oil and Canadian tar sands. In the short term, certainly, the importance of South African vanadium to American steel producers will grow from its present 56 percent of total imports as the ability of indigenous sources to supply American needs (now 63 percent satisfied) declines.

Other Minerals

Uranium is discussed separately, in the next chapter. Coal and petroleum are discussed together later in this chapter. South Africa also produces and has sizable reserves of a variety of minerals which have not yet been mentioned because they are economically and politically marginal to an appreciation of South Africa's future. Nevertheless, South Africa has the world's largest reserves of andalusite (aluminum silicate); vast supplies (the second most abundant reserves in the non-Soviet world) of vermiculite, a class of micaceous hydrated silicates used as heat insulation; kyanite, lead, zinc, nickel, phosphates, silver, and traces of tin. It is the world's largest producer of andalusite, with 30 percent of the total; but in terms of tin, silver, zinc, and lead, its share of the world market is 1 percent or less in each case. However, these last shares may increase after 1980 with the opening of the Black Mountain mine in the northern part of the Cape Province. Black Mountain, 51 percent of which is owned by Gold Fields of South Africa and 49 percent by Phelps-Dodge, is expected to produce 132,000 tons of lead concentrates, 35,000 tons of zinc concentrates, 22,000 tons of copper concentrates, and 249,120 pounds of silver annually.

Employment in the Mining Sector

Mining in South Africa employs 16 percent of all and 24 percent of total black industrial and commercial labor. Mining is significant because of its strategic role, because it earns sizable amounts of foreign exchange, and because it is a major provider of jobs for blacks. In late 1978 mining and quarrying ventures in South Africa (including Bophuthatswana and Transkei) employed 662,000 workers, 90 percent of whom were blacks. At the beginning of the 1970s, when total mining employment was larger, a mere 20 percent of all black miners were South Africans, the remainder being migrants on short-term contracts from neighboring Mozambique, Namibia, Botswana, and Lesotho, and from Malawi and Angola. But by 1978, 60 percent of all blacks employed by the mines were South Africans (including those resident in Transkei and Bophuthatswana). About 61 percent of the total were involved in the extraction of gold, down 5 percent since 1972. In September 1978, of that 61 percent, South Africa supplied 235,000 men; Lesotho, 92,000; Mozambique, 41,000; Malawi, 21,000; Botswana, 20,000; Rhodesia, 13,000; Swaziland, 9,000; Namibia, 1,800; and Angola, a mere 126. Coal mining is the second largest employer of black labor, followed by the iron-ore, chrome, and manganese industries. The last four employed 126,000 blacks in 1977 despite increasing mechanization. About 17 percent of all nongold employment (45,000 workers) is centered on the platinum, chrome, copper, manganese, and asbestos mines of Bophuthatswana.

Given a 526 percent increase in the average monthly per capita cash earnings of black miners from 1972 to mid-1978 (from R 23 to R 121)—when the pay of white miners rose only 219 percent (from an average of R 402 to R 881 per month)—the ratio of white to black earnings dropped from 17:1 to 6.2:1. The percentage of blacks housed in married quarters rose in the same period from less than 1 percent to about 3 percent. The five-year period was also characterized by a total inflation of more than 60 percent. Furthermore, although average black earnings rose faster in the mining than in the manufacturing sector of the South African economy, average cash earnings of blacks in mining remained considerably below those in manufacturing.

In mining the wage gap measured not in ratio terms but as an earnings differential between whites and blacks has widened significantly. In 1977 it was 77 percent higher than 1972 (R 669 compared with R 379), with little prospect, given current remuneration patterns in the mining sector, of narrowing differentials significantly until 1985. By this measure blacks are far less well off today compared with whites than they were in 1972, a paradox that will continue unless and until black job advancement and the acquisition of skills by blacks (limited now by the terms of the Mines and Works Act and by the restrictive practices of white trade unions) makes increased black productivity possible. For example, the act prevents blacks from obtaining a blasting certificate and thus from receiving pay for what in fact they do routinely, if under the nominal supervision of whites. They perform all the manual tasks connected with the smelting and refining of gold into ingots but are paid a fraction of the wages received by the whites who by law must oversee the process.

In early 1979 the 17,000-member white Mineworkers' Union slowed the production of most South African mines for nearly a week when it decided to protest the advancement of three Coloureds to skilled positions on the O'Okiep copper mine, but the strike was ultimately called off without a union victory. In the course of the strike, however, the leader of the white miners made absolutely clear his opposition, and that of his men, to the elimination of legal and customary barriers to black advancement. Arrie Paulus, the general secretary of the union, said that South Africa would forever belong to whites. Blacks must seek their rights in their homelands. "You must know a black," he said, "to realize that he needs somebody to be his boss. That's the way it is now, and that is the way it will always be."[7]

7. Arrie Paulus, quoted in *New York Times,* March 10, 1979.

Fuel and Power

In terms of its total energy requirements, South Africa is self-sufficient to a degree most other nations can but envy. Only 25 to 30 percent of energy demand needs to be satisfied by imports (the United States is 40 percent dependent); South Africa's ample reserves of coal relieve the country of what would otherwise be an intolerable, even crippling, reliance upon externally derived sources of power. However, in the crucial transportation sector, South Africa is wholly dependent (for up to 95 percent of its needs) on petroleum obtained elsewhere. How South Africa maximizes its self-sufficiency and minimizes its dependence will to some extent determine the Republic's vulnerability in the 1980s to overseas economic and political influence.

Coal

South Africa has an estimated 32 billion metric tons of coal in reserve, about 2 percent of the world's total. At present rates of local consumption and export, it has sufficient coal to last 250 years, and probable reserves sufficient for hundreds of years longer. Moreover, most of its supplies are found in thick, easily worked seams near the surface, and a good proportion is mined in close proximity to major industrial centers. Yet most of South Africa's coal is of the soft, bituminous variety with a low calorific value and a high ash content (mostly above 25 percent). Its quality, overall, is well below that of American and British soft coals. South Africa also mines little anthracite and less coking coal (in 1979 only about 8 percent of its coal could be converted into coke). Despite these limitations, South Africa has a distinct advantage: it produces its coal inexpensively and transports it at subsidized rates. For those reasons, and as a result of its failure to find petroleum, coal is burned to generate nearly 90 percent of the country's electricity (half of all South African coal is used in this way), is the basis of a new industry that by the mid-1980s may greatly reduce South African dependence upon imported petroleum, could again provide the locomotive power for South Africa's railways, and in recent years has also become an important source of foreign exchange.

In 1977 coal became South Africa's most prized export commodity after gold and diamonds. In 1967 only 45 million metric tons were mined. In 1973 South Africa was exporting only 1 million metric tons (at R 6 per ton); in 1977 more than 90 million metric tons were produced and 10 million metric tons exported at R 19 per ton; in 1978, 15.3 million metric tons were exported at R 20.9 per ton, or R 325 million. The vast growth of coal exports was due to inflated oil prices, aggressive sales activity, massive new local investment, and the construction of specialized coal export facilities at the new Richards Bay harbor. By 1978 South Africa was supplying about 25 percent of the world market for internationally traded coal and 23 percent (second only to Poland) of the requirements of the European Economic Community countries in competition with the United States and Australia. France imported nearly 7 million metric tons and West Germany more than 1 million metric tons. Thanks to long-term contracts with Israel (1 million tons a year from 1980) and Japan, South Africa expected to be selling at least 25 million metric tons overseas by 1985.

Petroleum

Of all strategic minerals, oil is the one of which there are no known reserves in South Africa. The government and foreign multinational corporations have tried at least since 1965 to discover supplies on and offshore. Southern Oil Exploration Corporation (SOEKER), the state-owned oil research corporation, has spent nearly R 130 million without discovering economically exploitable reserves.[8] Total, the French petroleum company; Caltex, an amalgam of Standard Oil of California and Texaco; and Exxon have searched with no better luck.

Until the Shah of Iran was tumbled from his throne, South Africa obtained 90 percent of its petroleum needs (about 400,000 barrels per day in 1978) from oilfields there, with the rest coming from Iraq, Saudi Arabia, Venezuela, and other less important

---

8. SOEKOR has depended heavily on SEDCO of Dallas to supply the technology required for drilling offshore (especially in the vicinity of Mossel Bay), where prospects seem best.

sources. Since the Shah's overthrow, South Africa has been buying petroleum wherever it can find it, paying a premium over posted OPEC prices per barrel, and probably paying inflated concessionary and high tanker transport fees (sometimes in gold) as well. As a cabinet minister said in early 1979, "We do not have a country from whom we can purchase oil. We buy our oil in strange places and under strange circumstances, and we pay a lot for this oil."[9] An analysis of tanker movements suggested that large amounts of crude oil were reaching South Africa from the United Arab Emirates. Press reports indicated that South Africa was buying oil from Nigeria, Mexico, and Indonesia, but it was probably doing so through brokers, and without any assurance of uninterrupted supply. Moreover, the South African refineries were facing technical problems resulting from the purchase of a mixture of crude oils with varying characteristics.

An obvious response was mandatory conservation. Of the 400,000 barrels imported daily in 1978, about 173,000 were consumed by trucks, cars, aircraft, and diesel-burning locomotives. Rhodesia and other countries (and international shipping) took 80,000 barrels per day; 70,000 were added to the stockpile; 36,000 were used by agriculture; 26,000, by industry; 7,000, for power generation; and 5,000, by the mines. Of the 173,000 barrels a day used for transport, 47 percent was sold as gasoline, 28 percent as diesel fuel, 20 percent as industrial fuel oil, and 5 percent as kerosene. The government's response to Iran's refusal to continue selling oil (and to the Arab oil boycott, which had been in effect since 1973) was to try to reduce imports by 20 percent without intensifying inflation. At first it lowered the highway speed limit from 55 to 50 miles per hour, maintained Sunday shutdowns of service stations, and raised the price of gasoline and other fuels by 35 percent to 40 cents a liter or $1.75 a United States gallon (in 1973 it was 10 cents a liter, and in 1978, 30 cents a liter.). The government also purchased smaller vehicles for cabinet ministers and other officials, considered consumer ra-

9. Louis le Grange, minister of tourism, quoted in *Star,* February 24, 1979. There are somewhat lower oil import figures in *Financial Mail,* June 29, 1979. "Energy Supplement," 19. Brunei also supplies oil to South Africa.

tioning, tried to alter the mix of products produced by the country's four refineries, thought about replacing diesel with coal-burning locomotives, and planned to expand the production of liquid fuels from coal. By June 1979, it was apparent that those restrictions and innovations would be insufficient to cushion the country's shortfall and compensate for the growing scarcity and cost of crude oil. South Africa therefore raised gasoline prices a further 40 percent, to the equivalent of $2.43 a U.S. gallon; sharply lowered town speed limits to 43 miles per hour (this was later modified), and closed service stations on Saturdays.

Petroleum Substitutes

In 1955 South Africa constructed a small plant (SASOL I) to burn coal, steam, and oxygen under pressure and thus transform the coal into a gas and then into liquid fuels. It was located near Sasolburg in the northern Orange Free State, 40 miles southeast of Johannesburg, near coalfields and the Vaal River (the source of the large amounts of water needed for coal gasification). By 1976 coal amounting to nearly 3 million tons a year was producing about 4,500 barrels a day (50 million gallons a year) of low-octane gasoline and diesel fuel. This amounted to about 5 to 7 percent of South Africa's total petroleum requirements.

By 1977 the state-owned South African Coal, Oil and Gas Corporation (SASOL) had begun building a second plant, known as SASOL II, at Secunda in the Transvaal, 80 miles east of Johannesburg. In 1979, as a response to the loss of Iranian supplies, SASOL announced a further extension. The total cost of SASOL II and III would approach $7 billion; they were expected to be completed in 1982 and would absorb the greatly expanded output of a nearby coal mine. When the plants are finished, South Africa will have the ability—according to its plans—to produce 500 million gallons a year, or about 47 percent of its liquid-fuel requirements.[10] In addition to gasoline, diesel fuel, aviation spirits, liquefied gas, and kerosene, SASOL II and III will provide

10. The figure of 47 percent may prove a gross overestimate. For a thoughtful discussion of this question, see Stephen Ritterbush, "South Africa's Energy Needs and National Security," unpub. (Cambridge, Mass., 1979), 19. See also David M. Liff, "The Oil Industry in South Africa" (Washington, D.C., 1979), 19.

ammonia and sulphur. They will consume about 27 million tons a year of coal, employ about 7,500 persons, and — during the construction phase — provide jobs for 20,000 laborers. The general contractor is the Fluor Corporation of Los Angeles. Major American, German, French, and local firms are also involved as equipment suppliers and subcontractors. To some extent the success of the project also depends upon Lesotho, since additional supplies of water from the headwaters of the Vaal River, which lie in that country, are crucial to the SASOL expansion. Without that water, production will be limited and risky.

Economic Pressure

Until 1982, when SASOL II and III are due to become operational, South Africa will remain vulnerable to petroleum boycotts. For that reason it will use economic and legal means to demand conservation and limit growth. It will also continue to stockpile petroleum underground in keeping with a storage project begun in 1958. In 1979 it was variously estimated that South Africa had reserves in disused coal mines equivalent to between eighteen months' and three years' supply (at current rates of consumption). Holding such reserves would limit the catastrophic impact of any international boycott of South Africa's petroleum.

Of South Africa's refineries, the state's National Petroleum Refiners of South Africa (Natref) controls (in partnership with the National Iranian Oil Company, with 17 percent, and Total, with 30 percent) the largest single share. Mobil, Caltex, and Shell-BP are the other refiners. Two of the refineries are located near Durban and obtain their supplies of crude oil primarily from a single offshore mooring facility. The Caltex refinery, recently expanded, is in Cape Town. The fourth, operated by Total for Natref, is near Johannesburg.

Because supplies of petroleum for Botswana, Lesotho, and Swaziland normally come from South African refineries, South Africa could hold those countries at ransom if its own supplies are limited. Under the Petroleum Supply and National Supplies Procurement Acts of 1977, the minister of economic affairs can also hold the companies hostage by requiring them to sell oil to the government (and the military) for stockpiling or other purposes despite commercial or any other preferences. (They also must always maintain specified minimum stocks of various refined products.) An amendment to the first act in 1979 made it an offense to divulge information about South Africa's petroleum crisis and how it copes with it, or otherwise to endanger supplies.

Agriculture

In recent years the agricultural, forestry, and fishing sector (both its white- and black-dominated parts) of the South African economy has contributed less than 8 percent to total gross domestic product (GDP). In 1976 the figure was 7.8 percent; in 1977, 7.9 percent. This proportion fell from about 30 percent in 1950 despite healthy 4 percent increases in output during the same period. From 1970 to 1978 South Africa increased the gross value of its agricultural production from R 1.5 to R 2.6 million. At the same time, total employment in agriculture fell from 1.6 to 1.4 million workers, of whom only 14,000 were white and 233,500 Coloured and Asian. Taken together, these figures provide further confirmation of South Africa's dramatic shift from a country dependent in the 1950s upon the production of raw materials to a country dominated in the 1970s, in terms of GDP, by manufacturing.

With the exception of meat, rice, coffee, tea, and specialty commodities, South Africa produces enough to feed itself, and usually has a surplus sufficient to export 20 to 25 percent of total output (predominantly maize, raw sugar, and fruit in canned and fresh form). Maize is by far South Africa's major crop. In 1973-74, 11 million metric tons were harvested; ln 1976-77 the total was 9.7 million metric tons. The total for 1978-79 was only 6.5 million metric tons, reflecting conditions of severe drought early in the growing season. About a fifth of the total was exported. About 1.6 million metric tons of wheat, 9 percent of which was exported, was harvested in 1978-79. The production of oats (50,000 metric tons), rye (6,000 metric tons), and sorghum (400,000 metric tons) was also depressed because of the drought. Only barley (134,000 metric tons) grew well. Cotton production in 1978-79 reached a record 52,000 metric tons, of which 4,500 metric tons were exported.

Although sugar production grew steadily throughout the 1970s to more than 2.3 million metric tons in 1976-77, the 1978-79 crop totaled 2.1 million metric tons, about half being sold locally. Another 775,000 metric tons was exported, the United States taking as much as 10 percent of the total and Canada (which subsequently withdrew long-standing imperial tariff preferences), 33 percent. The surplus (more than 200,000 metric tons) was in part shipped overseas as molasses and animal feed, especially to West Germany and Spain. The export earnings for South African sugar in 1979 were not expected to reach the R 187 million of 1978.

South Africa exports fresh and canned fruit to Europe, to the rest of Africa, and even to the United States. In 1978, 421,000 metric tons of citrus fruit alone earned R 181 million from exports. Apples, table grapes, and other noncitrus fruit earned more than R 200 million in the same year.

South Africa is also a significant producer of peanuts, oilseeds, sunflower seeds, and tobacco for local and export consumption. It has traditionally exported rock lobster from South African and fishmeal from Namibian waters, but by 1979 overfishing and altered ocean currents (without an internationally recognized authority South Africa could not protect Namibian waters with a 200-mile economic zone) in the South Atlantic had destroyed the run of pilchards. Prospects for an immediate revival of the industry were poor.

Sunflower seeds, grown for their oil, have long been grown in and exported from South Africa. But the potential economic significance of sunflowers to South Africa was unappreciated until 1979. At midyear, in an unexpectedly manic moment, the country's minister of agriculture decided that the farmers of South Africa could help supply liquid fuel for tractors and other diesel-consuming vehicles. He said that the technology for replacing diesel with sunflower oil was proven. All the farmers of South Africa had to do was to harvest masses of sunflowers — to turn the arable fields of South Africa over to growing vegetable oil rather than wheat or maize. In 1979, too, there were many proposals to devote surplus sugar cane or grain to the production of ethanol, which in Brazil had satisfactorily powered automobiles. However, for ethanol a shortage of available crops and land was clearly apparent.

South Africa is the world's fourth largest exporter of wool. Mohair and greasy-wool production decreased slightly, from 227 to 218 million pounds in 1978-79, but export earnings (90 percent of total output) increased by 6 percent to R 181 million. The wool was derived from about 35 million sheep; beef consumption, from 18 million cattle; and pork and bacon, from about 1 million pigs.

Only 3.7 million acres (including 1.2 million in African areas) of South Africa supports timber. About 71 percent of the total is in the hands of 2,400 private growers. They sell sawn timber and pulp worth about R 500 million a year; of this, the pulping industry absorbs about 39 percent of the total by value, timber for construction purposes, about 31 percent, and mining (mostly for props), 26 percent. Pine and other softwoods are used for structural purposes locally and form the bulk of South Africa's modest timber exports (in 1977, R 22.5 million; in 1978 about R 30 million), mostly of eucalyptus chips for pulping. Japan is the most important market. Other African countries and Britain follow.

The mines use hardwoods, primarily species of eucalyptus, but will use less in the 1980s as the gold mines (which take 90 percent of all timber required by the mines) gradually switch to hydraulic props or concrete packs. Paper and paper products are made largely from hardwoods (again primarily varieties of eucalyptus) that are unsuitable for underground use, and, to a lesser degree, from softwoods. But as late as 1978 the market for pulping-quality wood was poor and that for construction and mining timber somewhat better (all three being related directly to the state of the local economy). Only export demand was strong.

Employment in agriculture supports an estimated 40 percent of the black work force of South Africa, and about 28 percent of the total economically active population. There are about 90,000 white-owned farms, comprising about 222 million acres. Only a portion of those farms are judged efficient, in local terms. Twenty percent of the white farms supply 80 percent of total production. Moreover, by 1979 the total debt burden carried by the white farmers of South Africa had increased to R 2.6 billion (the equivalent of about two years' oil supplies or 44 new gold mines), up at least 50 percent in the three years prior to 1979.[11] Fixed capital formation in the agricultural sector reached R 578 million in 1978, up by 7 percent over the previous year.

Cultivated land in South Africa was estimated in 1965 to cover 24.7 million acres in the white areas and only 4.9 million in the homelands; pasture covered 173.0 million acres in the white areas and 29.7 million in the black areas. In 1978 about 3 million Africans farmed in the white areas for whites.

About a quarter of the total production of the white farms, and a negligible percentage of the production of black farms in the homelands, is dependent upon export markets. Fruit crops, produced in the western Cape Province, and sugar, produced in Natal, are the most vulnerable. Britain alone took 20 percent of South Africa's exports of fruit in 1978. Zaire buys maize to feed Shaba Province. Zambia has also become a large importer of South African maize. Aside from South Africa's immediate neighbors, they are the only countries obviously dependent upon South African agriculture. In turn, South Africa relies upon Botswana to make up what would otherwise be a meat-consumption deficit.

In terms of export earnings, agriculture contributed R 1 billion in 1978. This was 13 percent of total earnings from exports. However, with the price of gold and other minerals expected to remain high into the early 1980s, the importance of agriculture to foreign earnings will diminish.

Foreign Investment and Lending

South Africans concede the importance of foreign investment and foreign lending to the continued strength of their economy. In the 1960s and early 1970s the flow of foreign capital and loans to South Africa played a major role in transforming an

---

11. *Star*, February 17, 1979.

economy heavily dependent upon the export of primary products into a user and industrial processor of many of those raw materials. The availability of foreign capital permitted South Africa to grow economically more rapidly than its population increased, to modernize its infrastructure as well as its manufacturing capability, and to enhance its military and security capabilities. At the end of the 1970s, after several years of minimal real economic growth, South Africans were acutely aware that their real outputs per capita would almost certainly stagnate if new injections of foreign capital remained scarce and if lenders continued chary of requests for multiyear borrowings. After the Soweto uprising in 1976, external investment and lending declined sharply in volume. Even aggressive multinationals came to regard South Africa as unstable and, as its economy fell into recession, as an economic as well as an obvious political risk. In 1979 that assessment remained widespread, if not universal. It was supported by the large net outflow of capital (much of which consisted of ordinary and accelerated repayments) from the Republic in 1977 and an even larger outflow (over $1 billion) in the first nine months of 1978.

Direct and indirect foreign investment in the 1970s, concentrated largely in manufacturing, finance, mining, and tourism, was attracted to South Africa until 1976 by unusually high returns. In 1974 American corporations were reported to be earning an average of as much as 19 percent per year on investments in South Africa. British-owned companies counted upon average earnings of about 20 percent. In that year about 14 percent (17 percent in the developing world) was a general average for other external investment opportunities. Since 1976, however, returns have averaged much less, with most American and British concerns reporting yearly earnings of about 5 to 6 percent. Likewise, at the end of the 1970s South African borrowing costs were higher than those of many industrial economies, and sometimes well above the standard London Interbank Offered Rate. Supplies of short-term loans (under one year) had remained steady, but longer-term funds were much more difficult to obtain in 1978 and 1979 than they had been in the halcyon years of the previous decade.

British and German Investment

About half of all direct foreign investment in South Africa, and a large share of indirect investment, as calculated by book value, is British. In 1978, 500 British companies held assets worth $8.4 billion. Significantly, too, the British investment in South Africa in 1977 represented the nonnegligible figure of about 10 percent of total British-controlled overseas direct investment. The income from that tenth of total British investment outside of the United Kingdom plays a much larger role in the British economy and its foreign exchange earnings than do the smaller stakes in South Africa of West Germany, the United States, France, Japan, Israel, or other direct and indirect investors.

Although new British investment in South Africa declined considerably after 1976, and although disinvestment became important, most subsidiaries of British corporations were thought to be expanding because of the reinvestment of locally generated profits and, to some extent, because of Eurodollar borrowings. In 1978 eight British firms disinvested, selling assets worth about $200 million. The largest was Tate and Lyle, the giant sugar producer; it sold its final 52 percent share in African Products, a sugar refiner, to a South African competitor for R 15 million after negotiating a complicated remittance arrangement with the South African reserve bank. Racal, the General Electric Company (not affiliated with the United States corporation), and the Guardian Royal Exchange also diminished their holdings in 1978. In 1979 another four British firms reduced their investments in South Africa, with British disinvestment in 1978 and 1979 exceeding R 200 million.

At the end of 1978, as a result of a sudden surge of investment capital, the book value of West German holdings in South Africa reached $2.3 billion. West Germany thus became the second-largest foreign investor in the country. About 350 West German firms operate in South Africa through either direct representation or joint-venture agreements. Investment is concentrated in those areas where the Germans have traditional interest and expertise: in the chemical, engineering, and automotive industries. As a proportion of total overseas investment, however,

West Germany's direct activity in South Africa was only 2 percent.

American Investment

The book value of direct American investment in South
Africa in 1978 was $1.9 billion, about 17 percent of all foreign in-
vestment there. This amount represented no more than 1 percent
of direct American overseas investment, and only about 40 percent of American direct investment in all of Africa. In 1975, 45
percent of American investment was in South African manufacturing, 20 percent in petroleum refining and distribution, and 10
percent in mining. Additionally, in 1978 it was estimated that indirect American investment, mostly in the stock of South African-
controlled gold and base-metal mining companies, totalled about
$2.3 billion (about 25 percent of all shareholding in this sector,
but without comparable impact on management). The British
indirect share is as large in mining, and exists as well in the industrial sector.

About 300 American firms are active in South Africa. They
employ only about 77,000 workers, 65,000 of whom are black. In
addition to the 300 concerns, another group, estimated to include as many as 600 firms, buys and sells in South Africa
through agencies. Recently there have also been a dozen American companies, mostly involved in engineering design and management, which play a major role in the South African economy,
are profitable, employ thousands, and yet hold no significant assets there.

Total numbers of foreign firms doing business in, and holding assets in, South Africa are approximations, for there is no
centrally maintained register. Even the comprehensive 1977 survey by the United States Senate's Subcommittee on African Affairs was unable to develop complete lists of American economic
involvement in Africa. Of the 300 American firms, it could only
locate 260 to which to send questionnaires. After analyzing the
returns, and drawing upon other available documentation, it
could also develop only a series of alternate lists of the dozen or so
corporations that bulk by far the largest (accounting for about 75
percent of total investment, sales, or employment) among all

American firms in South Africa. In 1977, in order of size of assets, the biggest American companies were: General Motors, Mobil, Exxon, Caltex, Ford, ITT, General Electric, Firestone, Goodyear, Minnesota Mining and Manufacturing (3M), IBM, and Caterpillar. According to sales and assets combined, Mobil and Caltex were the largest in 1976. The largest employers in 1979, according to a survey by the United States Consulate General in Johannesburg, were Ford, General Motors, Coca-Cola, ITT, Goodyear, Mobil, Firestone, General Tire, General Electric, Caltex, Union Carbide, IBM, Newmont Mining's O'Okiep Copper Company, Lion Match (owned by Allegheny Ludlum), 3M, NCR, Carnation, Masonite, International Harvester, and Otis Elevator. Joy Manufacturing, Cyanamid, Gillette, and John Deere also appeared on the United States Department of Commerce list of leading companies.[12]

American-owned firms have been active in South Africa since the 1880s, when General Electric and Singer began operating there. Petroleum companies followed, Mobil before the turn of the century, Esso and Caltex before World War I, and Valvoline (Ashland Oil) in 1928. By that date Goodyear had begun to make tires, Ford and General Motors automobiles, and International Harvester farm machinery. Yet by 1977 some of the larger American firms controlled only limited percentages of the total South African domestic market; smaller firms, however, in some cases dominated significant sectors of specialized domestic markets. According to the Senate report, for example, an Exxon subsidiary distributed 45 percent and Tokheim another 45 percent of all petroleum pumps; Kellogg had a 41 percent share of the breakfast-cereal market; Norton manufactured 45 percent of all abrasives, 65 percent of all hand tools, and 90 percent of all buffs. Geosource sold 85 percent of all liquid flow meters. Celanese controlled about 50 percent of the market for specialty polymers. Borg Warner's axles and automotive components were 55

12. U.S., Congress, Senate, Committee on Foreign Relations, *U.S. Corporate Interests in Africa* (Washington, D.C., 1978). Most of the data on American corporate activity in South Africa are taken from this account, updated by the United States Consulate General's survey, reported in *Financial Mail,* August 3, 1979. See also E. J. Kahn, "Annals of International Trade," *New Yorker,* May 14, 1979.

percent of the total sold. Colgate Palmolive had a 27 percent share of the soap and detergent market. Otis Elevator manufactured and serviced 40 percent of the country's lifts. American-owned firms were responsible for 40 percent of petroleum sales. American computer firms, especially IBM and Control Data, were thought to share about 70 percent of the market, but by 1979 British and Japanese firms had begun decreasing the traditional American dominance, especially in areas important to the maintenance of South African military strength and overall security. Even so, the average for South African sales as a percentage of total overseas sales of American companies was 0.5 percent.

Other Investment

After the British, German, and American shares, French and Japanese investment is significant both in terms of value of assets and in terms of the penetration of sectors important to South Africa. About 5 percent of total foreign investment is French; slightly less, Japanese. French ownership and investment is concentrated in the construction and petroleum sectors. Because the Japanese government officially prohibits investment in South Africa, a large proportion of the Japanese stake has been achieved by investment in European or American firms with subsidiaries in South Africa. (Japanese products in South Africa are often assembled by South African-owned firms.)

Loans to South Africa

In recent years up to 30 percent of all South African investment capital has been borrowed overseas, predominantly by the state and state-owned corporations. In the early 1970s bank lending to South Africa grew enormously, tripling in volume between 1974 and 1976 and doubling as a proportion of total foreign investment during the same years. The debt burden of South Africa, which had stood at about $200 million in 1969, reached $7.6 billion by the end of 1976. Of that total, nearly a third, or $2.2 billion, was owed to United States banks. Of the $3.5 billion that was borrowed by South Africa during those three years, about $3 billion was obtained for projects in the public sector. South African parastatals (government-controlled corporations) have traditionally been dependent upon external borrowing for the construction of massive infrastructural projects; this was especially true between 1974 and 1976. By 1979, however, when borrowing had become more difficult, internal financing began to play a proportionally larger role in the expansion of major state-controlled enterprises. According to the World Bank, the South African government managed to borrow only $24 million of long-term money in 1977 and $206 million in the first half of 1978.

Before 1977 the major American lenders to South Africa (of a total of 47) were the Chase Manhattan Bank, Citibank, Irving Trust Company, the Bank of America, Manufacturers Hanover Trust, the Central National Bank of Cleveland, Morgan Guaranty Trust, First Wisconsin National Bank, the Pittsburgh National Bank, the Chemical Bank, and the First National Bank of Boston. Since the uprising in Soweto, however, the downturn in the South African economy, and domestic pressure on the banks from church groups, universities, and labor unions, have encouraged bank managements to rethink their lending strategies regarding South Africa. Several, including Wells Fargo and First Pennsylvania, have stopped lending to South Africa. The First National Bank of Boston decided to limit its loan exposure in South Africa to $20 to 30 million, the level in 1978. Chase Manhattan publicly declared in 1978 that it would make no loans that furthered the "apartheid policies of the South African government or reinforce[d] discriminatory business practices." In late 1977 Citibank (less than 0.5 percent of its worldwide assets and profits is in South Africa) reversed a long-standing policy and announced that it would no longer make loans to the South African government or its parastatal bodies, nor would it make balance-of-payments loans. Citicorp told its shareholders that the bank would limit "its credit, selectively, to constructive private sector activities that create[d] jobs and . . . benefit[ed] all South Africans." In 1979 Merrill Lynch said that it would never underwrite securities sold by the South African government, nor would

its banking subsidiaries lend to that government (they had
stopped in 1976).[13]

Official agencies of the United States government played a
significant role before 1977 in the expansion of the South African
economy. The Export-Import Bank, which insured, guaranteed,
and discounted credits that finance United States exports, supported more than $200 million of credit ($142 million for insurance) for South Africa between 1972 and 1976. The Commodity
Credit Corporation financed the sale of $46 million worth of
United States commodities (mostly rice) to South Africa in the
same period. But in late 1978, the United States Congress, having
earlier in the year attempted to prohibit further lending by the
bank to South Africa until that country achieved majority rule,
decided to limit lending by the bank only to the support of sales to
American corporations or others that had implemented the Sullivan principles (discussed later) and recognized black trade
unions' rights. In 1979 it was expected that this addition to the
Export-Import Bank Authorization Bill would substantially curtail official American support for lending to South African firms.

With increasing American private and public reluctance to
lend or lend as heavily as before to South Africa, the relative importance for South Africa of borrowing in Europe, especially
from British, Swiss, and West German sources, has become apparent. British, Swiss, and West German banks have not been
fastidious about lending to the public sector. French finance has
also remained available. The extent of this availability was hard
to discern, however. South African officials remained guardedly
confident in 1979, when the need to finance crucial infrastructural needs had again become significant.

Disinvestment and Pressures for Change

In addition to disinvestment by corporations like Tate and
Lyle, the issuance of restrictive policy statements by American
banks, and congressionally imposed limitations, rising concern in
the United States and Western Europe about the appropriateness

13. *South African Update,* April 11, 1979; *Citicorp Stockholder's Information Pam-
phlet,* March 10, 1978, 20; Chase Manhattan Bank, "Chase's Policy on South Africa,"
April 18, 1978.

of continued economic relations with South Africa has led, since about 1976, to a thoroughgoing reevaluation of the operating practices of foreign companies doing business there. In Europe and the United States, student, trade-union, and church-related bodies have questioned the morality of investing in and lending to South Africa; these groups, and stockholders, have advocated withdrawal from or disassociation with South Africa on strategic, tactical, and moral grounds. They have tried to boycott banks and businesses refusing to heed their suggestions; they have urged depositors in banks to withdraw and holders of stock in corporations continuing to invest in South Africa to sell. Reasoning, persistence, harassment, and occasional strikes and sit-ins (mostly at American universities) have had an effect exemplified by the heightened sensitivity to the South African problem, and what to do about it, on the part of corporate and bank executives and directors, university presidents and trustees, and the public generally, especially in the United States. The bank declarations already cited, the sales of stock in American corporations doing business in South Africa by colleges and universities, and the withdrawals of deposits by pension funds and church groups from banks that have lent to South Africa are indicators of the success of this effort. So is the broadly based acknowledgment by many American and some European-owned multinational corporations of what has been defined as their social obligations as investors in and lenders to South Africa.

In 1977 the Reverend Leon H. Sullivan, pastor of the Zion Baptist Church of Philadelphia, the founder of a job-training program, and a member of the board of General Motors, persuaded twelve American businesses to sign a set of principles that he had designed to promote fair employment practices in South Africa. By early 1979, 116 American corporations (including two major banks) had endorsed his principles. Originally rather generally and gently worded, the principles by 1979 had been greatly amplified, taking on a tougher tone. A mechanism for monitoring corporate adherence to the principles had also been devised and tested. The principles (see table 1) pledge American companies to desegregate all facilities, ensure fair employment practices (including the right to form and join trade unions), pro-

Table 1   The Sullivan Code: Six principles for corporations operating in South Africa

---

Principle 1: Nonsegregation of the races in all eating, comfort, and work facilities.

Each signator of the Statement of Principles will proceed immediately to:
- Eliminate all vestiges of racial discrimination.
- Remove all race designation signs.
- Desegregate all eating, comfort, and work facilities.

Principle II: Equal and fair employment practices for all employees.

Each signator of the Statement of Principles will proceed immediately to:
- Implement equal and fair terms and conditions of employment.
- Provide nondiscriminatory eligibility for benefit plans.
- Establish an appropriate comprehensive procedure for handling and re-solving individual employee complaints.
- Support the elimination of all industrial racial discriminatory laws which impede the implementation of equal and fair terms and conditions of em-ployment, such as abolition of job reservations, job fragmentation, and ap-prenticeship restrictions for blacks and other nonwhites.
- Support the elimination of discrimination against the rights of Blacks to form or belong to government-registered unions, and acknowledge gener-ally the right of black workers to form their own union or be represented by trade unions where unions already exist.

Principle III: Equal pay for all employees doing equal or comparable work for the same period of time.

Each signator of the Statement of Principles will proceed immediately to:
- Design and implement a wage and salary administration plan which is ap-plied equally to all employees regardless of race who are performing equal or comparable work.
- Ensure an equitable system of job classifications, including a review of the distinction between hourly and salaried classifications. Determine whether upgrading of personnel and/or jobs in the lower echelons is needed, and if so, implement programs to accomplish this objective expeditiously.
- Assign equitable wage and salary ranges, the minimum of these to be well above the appropriate local minimum economic living level.

Principle IV: Initiation of and development of training programs that will pre-pare, in substantial numbers, blacks and other nonwhites for supervisory, ad-ministrative, clerical, and technical jobs.

Each signator of the Statement of Principles will proceed immediately to:
- Determine employee training needs and capabilities, and identify employ-ees with potential for further advancement.

Table 1 — *continued*

- Take advantage of existing outside training resources and activities, such as exchange programs, technical colleges, vocational schools, continuation classes, supervisory courses, and similar institutions or programs.
- Support the development of outside training facilities individually or collectively, including technical centers, professional training exposure, correspondence and extension courses, as appropriate, for extensive training outreach.
- Initiate and expand inside training programs and facilities.

Principle V: Increasing the number of blacks and other nonwhites in management and supervisory positions.

Each signator of the Statement of Principles will proceed immediately to:
- Identify, actively recruit, train, and develop a sufficient and significant number of blacks and other nonwhites to assure that as quickly as possible there will be appropriate representation of blacks and other nonwhites in the management group of each company.
- Establish management development programs for blacks and other nonwhites, as appropriate, and improve existing programs and facilities for developing management skills of blacks and other nonwhites.
- Identify and channel high management potential blacks and other nonwhite employees into management development programs.

Principle VI: Improving the quality of employees' lives outside the work environment in such areas as housing, transportation, schooling, recreation, and health facilities.

Each signator of the Statement of Principles will proceed immediately to:
- Evaluate existing and/or develop programs, as appropriate, to address the specific needs of black and other nonwhite employees in the areas of housing, health care, transportation, and recreation.
- Evaluate methods for utilizing existing, expanded, or newly established in-house medical facilities or other medical programs to improve medical care for all nonwhites and their dependents.
- Participate in the development of programs that address the educational needs of employees, their dependents, and the local community. Both individual and collective programs should be considered, including such activities as literacy education, business training, direct assistance to local schools, contributions, and scholarships.
- With all the foregoing in mind, it is the objective of the companies to involve and assist in the education and training of large and telling numbers of blacks and other nonwhites as quickly as possible.

The ultimate impact of this effort is intended to be of massive proportion, reaching millions.

(*cont.*)

Table 1 — *continued*

Periodic Reporting
The signator companies of the Statement of Principles will proceed immediately to:

- Utilize a standard format to report their progress to Dr. Sullivan through the independent administrative unit he is establishing on a six-month basis, which will include a clear definition of each item to be reported.
- Ensure periodic reports on the progress that has been accomplished on the implementation of these principles.

---

vide color-blind wage scales, train substantial numbers of blacks for increased responsibilities, promote without regard to color (especially into management and supervisory positions), and improve the lives of employees outside the work place (in such areas as housing, schooling, and the provision of medical care).

By mid-1979 the results were mixed. It was clear that American-owned concerns had begun, in some cases strenuously, to adhere to at least most of the principles. A few had given assistance to unions, many had desegregated at least part of their working areas, most had contributed financially to the upgrading of employee life outside the work arena, many had started training schemes, and a few had managed to breach racial barriers and evade legal restrictions to promote Africans upwards in the corporate hierarchies. None had appointed Africans to the local boards of their subsidiaries; many were proceeding with an emphasis on gradualism. A few were well behind in pay levels. There was more effort than ever before, but the Sullivan monitoring group could not report that the pace was everywhere sufficiently rapid. Moreover, a United States embassy survey of a small sample of firms in 1978 showed that none had black senior managers and that fewer than 1 percent of total middle managers were black.[14] A few European-owned and many locally owned corporations had done as much as or even more than American firms. To some extent this reflected the management imperatives

14. Arthur D. Little, *First Report on the Signatory Companies to the Sullivan Principles* (Cambridge, Mass., 1978); *Boston Globe*, April 19, 1979; *Post* (Johannesburg), April 18, 20, 25, 27; ibid., May 4.

of individual companies. It also followed in part from adherence by European-owned concerns to the corporate responsibility principles enunciated in 1977 by the foreign ministers of the European Economic Community. Those principles were more forthright than Sullivan's, particularly in their support for black-run trade unions and advancement opportunity. A monitoring effort indicated that German firms were lagging behind on pay and maintained segregated facilities. British companies were reluctant to support unions.[15]

Chief Gatsha Buthelezi's Inkatha movement in 1978 had explicitly added the potential pressure of its large following to the impetus for corporate responsibility. His attention was directed initially at foreign, especially British, firms, but there was the implicit threat that Inkatha would act against other companies that were slow in improving the conditions of African employment. Buthelezi was especially anxious to persuade corporations to recognize and support black trade unions.

The principles enunciated by Sullivan, Buthelezi, and the foreign ministers of Europe hardly satisfy those who would employ sanctions either to wound South Africa commercially or to induce South Africa to scrap apartheid. Those who want to end lending and mandate private disinvestment believe that the very existence of foreign corporations in South Africa props up a cruel, unfair system. Withdrawals and the threat of withdrawal would make white-ruled South Africa change its policies, and reform. For these and other complex reasons, at least ten American universities had divested themselves of some or all of their South African-related holdings by May 1979. Tiny Hampshire College, with a miniscule endowment, sold everything not once, but twice (its investment firm misunderstood the first instructions). The University of Wisconsin liquidated nearly $11 million worth of stocks. Columbia University sold shares in three banks worth $2.7 million (about 1 percent of all Columbia's investments exclusive of real estate, and 15 percent of its stock in financial institutions). The university sold those stocks, and not those of the forty-one other companies that do business with South Africa and were

15. *Post,* January 24, 26; ibid., February 7-8, 9, 11, 14, 16, 28.

part-owned by Columbia, because the three banks were lending
to the South African government. The three were the Detroit
Bank Corporation, Manufacturers National Bank of Detroit, and
Rainier Bancorporation of Seattle. Yale sold $1.6 million worth
of stock in the J. P. Morgan Company because its Morgan
Guaranty Trust refused to promise to cease lending to the government of South Africa. Boston University decided to sell stock in
any company that was not "constructively seeking" an increase in
black opportunities and wages and supporting an end to apartheid. Brandeis University sold a nonvoting Ford Motor Company
bond because that manufacturer supplied vehicles to the South
African police and army.

Other North American groups and institutions followed this
lead. The California Nurses' Association withdrew $10 million in-
vested in the Wells Fargo Bank of California. The Canadian
Union of Public Employees took 1 million Canadian dollars (C$)
from the Imperial Bank of Commerce. The University of Guelph,
in Ontario, took its C$70,000 from the same bank. Dawson Col-
lege, in Quebec, withdrew C$25 million from the Bank of Mon-
treal.

Obviously, even the strongest supporters of such action can
provide little direct evidence that the government of South Africa
has been or will be responsive to disinvestment. They can point
much more securely to South African economic and fiscal responses to the shortage of new capital during the late 1970s, but
without proof or much confidence to positive, politically related
reactions to the threat of foreign economic pressure. In 1979, in
order to stimulate an influx of new capital, the government
greatly relaxed the monetary conditions under which new foreign
capital and profits could be repatriated. But this also constituted
a fiscal response and an acknowledgment that the health of South
Africa's domestic economy was improving. The government
made no moves dramatically to alter the political configuration
of South Africa in order to stimulate investor interest.

Nor did South Africa relax any of its many restrictions on
disinvestment. Foreign corporations are practically and legally
constrained from removing themselves from South Africa by
strict case-by-case interpretations of foreign exchange regula-

tions, which make even the sale or disposal of externally owned companies unrewarding. Physical asset stripping is barred by law. The National Supplies Procurement Act of 1977 permits the minister of economic affairs to order foreign (and domestic) companies to produce any goods or perform any services as directed by the government. Under the act the minister may also prohibit companies from revealing the content or the existence of such orders. In effect, foreign-owned companies can be commandeered or, in time of emergency as declared by the state president, nationalized. Thus the South African government has protected itself against disinvestment by individual companies or by the companies of virtually all individual countries together. Britain is an exception; were all British firms to act together, the result might prove salutary. It is also true that some American and European firms supply and dominate strategically important sectors of the market; these firms are therefore important, but their activities are in nearly all cases not irreplaceable. Locally owned or, more usually, foreign-based firms can — if pressed — substitute for the skills and products of the outsiders.

The South African economy is not invulnerable from outside assault. It would feel the effects even of a short-term deprivation of externally supplied petroleum. It would be affected by the withholding of new investment and a narrowing of borrowing facilities. As in the nuclear area (discussed in chapter 5), South African growth could be impeded by specific trade or supply boycotts. Each of these and additional focused attacks on the economic well-being of the Republic would have an undeniable impact; the cost of carrying on as before would be increased for South Africa as a whole and for its people. The sum of several or all of these modes of attack would, if introduced simultaneously, be much more threatening to the economy of South Africa than the separate, uncoordinated employment of the same kinds of means. There would be a synergistic effect. Even so, it is not obvious that the political impact would be equal at any stage to the economic impact. It has never been demonstrated that hurting South Africa economically would result, directly or in ways susceptible to unambiguous measurement, in an appropriate political response. The government of South Africa is not impervious to economic influence, but, as has already been discussed at length, its bottom line is the maintenance of power, not the maintenance of affluence without power or the spread of prosperity in the absence of power.

Economic means (both punitive and incentive) are therefore unlikely to provide the sole or even the primary motivating force capable of bringing about significant alterations in the political organizing principles of South Africa. As an economy, South Africa has too many advantages: energy needs that are only 25 to 35 percent externally supplied; a transportation economy about 47 percent of which is expected to be supplied from internal resources in 1982 (meanwhile, stockpiled petroleum could be drawn from storage if South Africa ceases to be able to purchase crude oil and refined products on the world market); and its fortuitous but real preeminence as a supplier of a variety of raw materials on which the economies of the developed world rely for the production of steel and the fashioning of the implements of high technology. Most of all, South Africa has an economy that is subject to state control and direction and a government that has never responded overtly or been compelled to respond to pressures from local commerce and capitalism. Thus the impact of external manipulations of the economic variables of South African life is much more likely to be felt if and when political change is underway. Then, and mostly then, the threat of one or more forms of economic deprivation and/or pressure could accelerate the rate of change. It could also help to shape the nature of that change.

5 | Uranium and the Nuclear Industry

WRITTEN IN COLLABORATION WITH NORMA KRIGER

IN ADDITION TO ITS HISTORIC ROLE as a major producer of gold, diamonds, coal, and base metals, South Africa has a growing role as one of the non-Soviet world's largest and most rapidly expanding producers of uranium oxide (U_3O_8). With French assistance, South Africa has also embarked upon an ambitious program of constructing nuclear energy plants. When completed and operational, these facilities will lessen South African dependence upon fossil-fuel-based power supplies. But, given abundant supplies of relatively inexpensive coal, the precise place of and need for reactor-generated energy in South Africa's future is imperfectly understood. Moreover, South Africa may already or may shortly have the capability to produce fissionable material from its enrichment facility. South Africa probably has the capacity to construct nuclear explosives.

Supplies and Exports

Even after Namibia becomes independent, South Africa will remain a significant source of the Western world's low-cost uranium. As table 2 indicates, its known proven reserves of uranium oxide, extracted at a cost of up to $30 per pound, were the third largest, after those of the United States and Sweden.[1] Since

1. U.S., Congress, House, Committee on Government Operations, *Facts on Nuclear Proliferation: A Handbook* (Washington, D.C., 1975), 69. In May 1978, *Africa Research Bulletin*, XV (May 31, 1978), reported that the South African Atomic Energy Board believed that its reserves amounted to 306,000 tons, with 42,000 tons of additional likely reserves, at an extraction cost of $36 per pound. The Swedish reserves are very low grade.

141

Table 2   Proven uranium reserves in the Western world

Country	Tons of uranium oxide	% Western world
United States	454,000	26.7
Sweden	300,000	17.6
South Africa and Namibia	276,000	16.2
Australia	243,000	14.2
Canada	166,000	9.7
France	55,000	3.2
Niger	50,000	2.9
Gabon	20,000	1.2
Others	142,000	8.3
Total	1,706,000	100.0

Source: "Pressure on African Countries to Produce More Uranium," *New African Development*, XI (1977), 252.

the table was compiled, too, estimates of South African reserves have increased. At higher prices South Africa may have even larger reserves equal to at least 20 percent of total non-Soviet supplies.

These figures may not hold into the 1980s, for new technology is being perfected that may enable the profitable mining of more expensive ores. Furthermore, given all the intensive exploration of the late 1970s, the aggregate total of proven world reserves may be expected to be revised upwards on a regular and continuing basis. In 1978, for example, what could be the world's most extensive deposits of uranium were delineated in the Northern Territory of Australia and in Saskatchewan. Uranium may be in surplus throughout the 1980s.

Although the presence of uranium in the gold-bearing ores of the Witwatersrand reef was known from the early 1920s, it was not until 1941 that its existence and properties became fully appreciated. The separation of uranium from gold-bearing conglomerates began in 1952 as a result of American and British initiatives and investments during World War II and the decision by their Combined Development Agency to promise to purchase the uranium production of South Africa at a cost sufficient to

cover operating deficits. This externally derived encouragement
made possible the initial development of the low-grade ores of
South Africa. It financed the first central calcining plant, which
transformed slurries of liquid uranium into a dry powdered oxide
capable of being shipped overseas.[2] From 1953 to the mid-1960s,
South Africa was a major supplier of uranium oxide to the United
States.

Production

In 1967 parliament amended the 1948 Atomic Energy Act.
It gave responsibility for the processing and marketing of South
African (not Namibian) uranium to a new Nuclear Fuels Corporation (NUFCOR). Controlled by eight mining finance houses—
including the Anglo-American Corporation, which has 50 percent; the Union Corporation, which has 30 percent; General
Mining; Gold Fields of South Africa; Johannesburg Consolidated
Investments; and others—it assumed responsibility for the calcining plant and for the provision of technical, administrative,
and financial services for the mining sector of the uranium industry. (Uranium from the remote Palabora copper mine and from
Rössing in Namibia is, however, marketed by Rio Tinto Zinc of
Britain). NUFCOR finances all new exploration activity.

South Africa began production at the West Rand Consolidated Mine in 1952 with an output of 40 metric tons. Within
three years nineteen mines were active, as were twelve extraction
plants. The total tonnage was 3,000. In 1959, twenty-six mines
and seventeen extraction plants produced a total of 6,000 tons,
but by 1965 (after the Combined Development Agency reduced
its guaranteed purchases), only 2,650 tons of uranium oxide were
available from seven mines and seven extraction plants. Since
then South Africa has increased its production beyond 1965 levels, without as yet attaining the high mark of 1959. Table 3 pre-
sents detailed production figures (in kilograms).

2. Barbara Rogers, "Namibia's Uranium: Implications for the South African Occupation Regime," unpub. (June 1975), 36; R. E. Worrall, "Pattern of Uranium Production
in South Africa," *Mining Survey,* LXXXI (1976), 16-22; James H. Jolly and Charles W.
Sweethood, "Republic of South Africa," *Minerals Yearbook,* III (1974), 812.

Table 3 South African uranium output since the start of operations

Year	Metric tons treated (thousands)	Uranium oxide produced (kilograms)	Revenue from sales (rands)
1952	116	40,177	356,016
1953	2,566	514,923	8,474,340
1954	7,408	1,466,118	54,587,196
1956	16,903	3.962, 590	73,030,582
1957	20,288	5,174,475	94,969,460
1958	22,042	5,668,718	104,592,762
1959	22,370	5,846,229	107,262,476
1960	22,481	5,813,906	108,411,204[a]
1961	15,536	4,960,750	79,371,625[a]
1960	22,481	5,813,906	108,411,204
1961	15,536	4,960,750	79,371,625[a]
1962	12,805	4,557,874	74,390,652[a]
1963	11,414	4,111,677	66,953,956[a]
1964	10,483	4,032,638	58,068,474[a]
1965	7,403	2,669,230	—
1966	8,620	2,981,138	—
1967	9,525	2,915,366	—
1968	12,389	3,522,488	—
1969	12,937	3,609,579	—
1970	13,976	3,738,819	—
1971	14,253	3,800,007	—
1972	14,609	3,629,265	—
1973	12,828	3,093,982	—
1974	14,654	3,074,418	—
1975	14,873	2,809,490	—
1976	17,267	3,111,366	—
Totals	331,430	88,101,248	—

Source: Chamber of Mines of South Africa, *87th Annual Report* (1976). Statistics includes nonmembers of the chamber; the information was provided by the producers.

a. Value of exports of prescribed materials. "Revenue from sales" not available.

In the late 1960s and throughout the 1970s, the production of uranium in South Africa was affected by low world prices for the metal as well as by the world price of gold. All uranium in South Africa except that from Palabora (0.3 percent of the total) is mined in conjunction with gold (new discoveries in the Karroo and a new, exclusively uranium mine in the Orange Free State will change the percentage). After the price of gold rose substantially from 1974 and permitted poorer gold aggregates to be mined, new sources of uranium were also brought to the surface. However, the average grade of uranium in the ore fell, and total production grew slowly.[3]

In 1978 nine gold mines produced uranium. The most important was Vaalreefs, owned by Anglo-American and producing 1,013 tons per year. Total output from all the seventeen mines reached 4,500 tons. By 1980, given the likelihood of reopening old mines, starting new ventures, and the reprocessing of the gold tailings piled high along the eastern and western reaches of the Witwatersrand, South Africa's total output of uranium oxide is expected to surpass 1959 levels and reach a predicted 6,000-ton total.

South Africa apparently has perfected an unusually efficient leaching process for the extraction of uranium from dilute ammonium slurries. In 1978 NUFCOR exported 96 to 98 percent pure uranium oxide. Additionally, a countercurrent ion exchange technique is apparently being used at Palabora and Rössing and is especially suitable for uranium from heavy metal concentrates. The gold mining houses foresaw doubling of the world price of uranium in the mid-1980s, sufficient justification for their own renewed interest and heavy capital investment in the uranium extraction industry. However, in late 1979 expectations for the uranium market appeared very discouraging.

South Africans anticipate that the reopening of old mines, the expansion of existing operations, and intensive exploration and development will be supported by foreign investment and by loans negotiated for this purpose by NUFCOR. In the mid-1970s, annual lending from abroad in this sector ranged from $60 mil-

3. Worrall, "Pattern of Uranium Production," 16-19.

lion to $150 million. In addition, such loans were a useful method of importing foreign exchange.[4] There was direct lending, as well, with the French Atomic Energy Commission providing the funds — approximately $100 million — for reopening the Rand-fontein mine in return for a ten-year contract guaranteeing 900 tons of uranium oxide annually.[5]

Trade

Authoritative reports predict that South Africa will soon replace Canada as the second-largest uranium producer, after the United States, in the Western world.[6] With an anticipated output of 13,000 tons in the early 1980s, South Africa may hold as much as 25 percent of the world's exportable stocks of uranium. Although the United States produced 9,800 tons of U_3O_8 in 1976, it generally exports only about 3 percent of its total production. Canada has estimated that 21 percent of its total proven reserves will be needed for its domestic industry. Exporters are thus permitted to draw on the excess only insofar as the needs of installed or planned reactors are covered for thirty years. Canada also subjects its exports to stringent safety and monitoring standards. Overall, these twin guidelines may minimize Canada's importance in export markets over the next decade.[7] Australia, with at least 20 percent of the West's reserves of low-cost uranium, may rival and surpass South Africa in export markets, but its new mines will become operational only in the 1980s. Moreover, Australia has traditionally imposed safeguards more rigid than those demanded by the International Atomic Energy Agency. South Africa asks that its customers abide by the guidelines of the agency, and claims to be especially wary of unorthodox customers.

4. Sinclair Smith, assistant general manager, NUFCOR, interview with Norma Kriger, January 1978.

5. *Financial Mail,* July 8, 1977; *Economist,* July 9, 1977. NUFCOR denies that it has ever agreed to such an arrangement. Financing of that kind would be taxed as mine revenue at 70 percent and would therefore be acceptable only to mines that wanted to set large losses against such gains. Interview with Smith, January 1978.

6. Worrall, "Pattern of Uranium Production," 18.

7. "Reserves: Canada Ups Estimates," *Nuclear News,* XX,11 (September 1977), 48; Henry D. Jacoby, "Uranium Dependence and the Proliferation Problem," *Technology Review* (June 1977), 20.

As a producer dependent upon exports, South Africa was a member until recently of an international producer cartel that set prices, maintained them at an artificially high level, and divided up much of the stable world market. This was distinctly to the advantage of South Africa's NUFCOR and Rio Tinto Zinc. Between 1972 and 1977, the cartel intended to give Canadian firms 37 percent, NUFCOR and Rio Tinto 24 percent each, Australia 8 percent, and France 4.5 percent of the market.[8] But, with unexpectedly high prices for uranium, the cartel became irrelevant after 1973. Without a cartel, and in the face of competition from Australia, an independent Namibia, Canada, and newcomers, South Africa in the future may be able to compete on a price basis only if industrial stability and its present wage structure continue.

Since NUFCOR does not reveal the identity of its trading partners nor, since 1965, disclose the sales value or volume of its exports, it is impossible to be precise about the identity of South Africa's uranium customers, their contracts, and the amounts that they purchase. However, Japanese utilities have apparently agreed to buy 12,000 tons of uranium oxide between 1984 and 1993 (Japan has no uranium of its own).[9] Taiwan has purchased uranium from South Africa; Israel allegedly uses South African uranium in a reactor supplied by France; and until 1979 Iran depended upon South Africa's promised output for its two not-yet-completed reactors.[10] West Germany depends for 50 percent of its needs on South Africa.[11] The United States now imports no uranium from South Africa for domestic use.

8. Barbara Rogers and Zdenek Cervenka, *The Nuclear Axis: Secret Collaboration between West Germany and South Africa* (New York, 1978), 151. But see *Nuclear News,* XX,12 (October 1977), 57; *Nuclear Engineering International,* XXII,264 (November 1977), 7; *New York Times,* November 19, 1977.

9. Rogers and Cervenka, *Nuclear Axis,* 124, have different figures. According to them, Japan has contracted to import 76,600 short tons of yellowcake (uranium oxide) from South Africa from 1975 to 1985 (not 1984 to 1993); they cite *Star,* June 25, 1974, and a Japanese international trade and industry publication.

10. "Nonproliferation Issues," *Senate Hearings* before the Subcommittee on Arms Control, International Organizations, and Security Agreements (1976), 367; Rogers, "Namibia's Uranium," 43, 45.

11. Interview with Smith, January 1978.

NUFCOR exports earned $170 million in 1977 and $575 million in 1978, and were expected to earn only $500 million in 1979.[12] The prospective figures are even higher, however, since 80 percent of South African uranium is sold under long-term contracts, the value of which was about $1.5 billion in 1978.

Nuclear Weapons, Power, and Processing

South Africa benefited for two decades from American co-operation in the area of nuclear-derived energy. In 1965 Allis Chalmers, an American firm, completed the installation of a $4.5 million research reactor at Pelindaba. It was used in engineering tests, isotope production, and fuel-element development. From 1969 until 1977 the reactor operated close to its design level of 20 megawatts, burning about 29 pounds of highly enriched uranium per year. But, beginning in mid-1975, the United States' refusal to continue to supply highly enriched uranium until South Africa signed the Nuclear Non-Proliferation Treaty (under which nations not in possession of nuclear weapons renounce the right to acquire them) and acceded to United States nuclear policy generally has prevented the reactor from operating with new fuel elements. It has thus been functioning at no more than about 40 or 50 percent of capacity, and in 1979 was thought to be performing only at 15 percent of capacity. From 1965 to 1975 the United States supplied 229 pounds of 90 to 93 percent enriched uranium elements (fabricated by United Nuclear, an American firm, in 1975, and in Britain from 1965 to 1974) and trained South Africa's nuclear scientists and engineers at the Oak Ridge and Argonne research laboratories of the Atomic Energy Commission (now facilities of the Department of Energy).[13] But the highly enriched uranium was supplied in small quantities and in the form of prefabricated fuel rods. Moreover, the use of the rods was subject to careful on-site inspection and, until 1977, all

12. *Economist,* February 25, 1978; *Star Weekly,* March 31, 1979; *Rand Daily Mail,* August 1, 1979.

13. See Colin Legum (ed.), *Africa Contemporary Record, 1976* (New York, 1977), B-829.

of the rods were returned to the United States for checking and resupply.

American assistance was given under a bilateral cooperation agreement, dated 1957, and a trilateral agreement with the International Atomic Energy Agency. The first agreement runs until 2007, having been extended in 1967 and 1974. It provides for the long-term supply of enriched fuel and the reprocessing of spent rods in the United States. The trilateral agreement, dating from 1965, as amended in 1967, provides for the operation of the reactor under agency safeguards until 2007. Both agreements compel South Africa to use all of its highly enriched uranium (from the United States) for civilian purposes, and to return equipment and materiel in case of default. As of 1977 inspectors of the International Atomic Energy Agency and the Americans who had received the spent fuel rods were satisfied that no diversion of the very small amounts of plutonium produced by the reactor in the rods had occurred.[14] What has been at issue since 1977, however, is the degree to which South Africa will cooperate with American and international demands for inspection of its enlarged enrichment plant. That plant is a much more likely site of diversion.

As of late 1979, the United States was still withholding the export of 57.3 pounds of highly enriched uranium in the form of fabricated fuel elements.[15] Pending the settlement of South Africa's disputes in the nuclear field with the United States, this boycott will continue. So will South Africa's research reactor continue to run at very low levels of efficiency, at least until such time as sufficient fuel is obtained from its enrichment facility. South Africa in 1982 will also want the United States (unless the French agree to do so) to fulfill its contract for the supply of low-

14. However, a confidential International Atomic Energy Agency *Special Safeguards Implementation Report* (1977) implies that the agency feared that South Africa had altered or could easily alter its records so as to circumvent inspection. Even more ominous, newspaper and government accounts suggest that South Africa has a small, secret plutonium plant capable of reprocessing spent fuel from the research reactor and later from Koeberg. See Rogers and Cervenka, *Nuclear Axis*, 198, 206.

15. *Nuclear Engineering International*, XX, 262 (September 1977), 48; *Africa Research Bulletin*, March 31, 1977.

enriched uranium to the two Koeberg nuclear power plants.
Whether it does so will depend, again, upon South Africa's accession to the Nuclear Non-Proliferation Treaty and to other safeguards. (France, so far cooperating with the United States, has
also refused to supply South Africa with fuel for the reactors.)

Nuclear Plants

South Africa began building full-scale nuclear plants in
1976, signing a contract in that year for two 922-megawatt light-
water reactors to be installed at Koeberg, north of Cape Town,
by a French group. The French stipulated that all reprocessing of
fuel from the reactor would take place outside South Africa; the
United States was committed, in connection with the Koeberg development, to produce low-enriched (3 percent level) uranium
from South African supplies. The total cost of the power station
and fuel contracts is estimated to be about $1 billion by 1984. A
French banking consortium is providing the financing in the
form of a buyer's credit.[16]

Instead of light-water reactors, South Africa could have
opted for the heavy-water type, in which it could have burned its
own raw uranium oxide without having had to depend upon
others for enriched fuel. Heavy-water reactors are admittedly
more expensive, by a factor of about a fifth, than light-water
ones. But the main reasons for what now appears to be a controversial decision were the then good relations with the United
States; the efficiency and presumed greater reliability of light-
water reactors; a political reluctance to depend upon Canada,
the chief manufacturer of the heavy-water reactors; and—most
of all—the expectation that substantial economic and political
advantages would inhere to a country capable of self-sufficiency.
If South Africa could mine uranium, refine it, and enrich it
(which South Africa intended to do on a large scale), South Africa could dramatically reduce its dependence on the West. It
could also profit by exporting a portion of the enriched fuel (for
which there would be no need if a heavy-water reactor were constructed). This dream of vertical integration and consequent

16. *Nuclear Engineering International*, XX, 262 (September 1977), 48.

profit and advantage has since been postponed, probably indefinitely.

Compared with a 2,000-megawatt coal-fired station, Koeberg will save 16,000 tons of coal a day, and 200 million tons of coal over its operating lifetime. This will release massive amounts of coal for export or for internal consumption in the form of petroleum products (after the completion of SASOL III). When Koeberg becomes operational in 1982, it will help meet the need for electrical power in the Cape Province without expensive new transmission lines from coal-fired generating plants in the Transvaal. Additional nuclear stations have been discussed, one Escom executive predicting that South Africa's coasts will one day be lined with nuclear generating facilities.

Koeberg will also produce an estimated 507 to 881 pounds of plutonium, obtainable from reprocessing the spent fuel, per year. In 1978 South Africa had no publicly acknowledged facilities capable of undertaking reprocessing, but recovering plutonium for weapons-grade materiel was not beyond South Africa's technical or economic capacity. Indeed, a secret facility for the handling of plutonium may have been completed as early as 1976 (although it is unlikely), making it theoretically possible to assemble as many as fifty city-destroying nuclear bombs a year from the by-products of Koeberg.[17] But to do so South Africa would have to violate all safeguards written into the fuel-supply treaty and to expel the International Atomic Energy Agency inspection team.

New Technology

The enrichment of uranium is a second area of concern to those who seek to understand and curtail South Africa's weapons-making capability. In 1970 South Africa announced that its own scientists had discovered a process "unique in concept" that could enrich uranium more economically and efficiently than others available to South Africa. The South Africans had apparently modified the so-called nozzle method used by the Germans, but allegations of intensive German cooperation with the South Afri-

---

17. *Washington Post,* May 15, 1976; *New York Times,* June 1, 1976; Rogers and Cervenka, *Nuclear Axis,* 198.

cans before about 1972 remain unproved. Based on the general principle of a high-performance stationary walled centrifuge, the South Africans had managed to enrich uranium by a simpler process than the gaseous diffusion techniques used in the United States. The South African method is thought to involve flowing streams of UF_6 in a carrier gas such as hydrogen with some special means being utilized to take advantage of minor differences in light and heavy uranium hexafluoride in the flow field.[18]

Since the nozzle-based modification required a smaller initial capital investment but heavier ongoing electrical-power costs, it was well adapted to South African conditions. With coal supplies that were relatively inexpensive (given transport subsidies and labor costs) and abundant, South Africa was in a position to supply electricity to the enrichment facility at about one-fourth the cost of comparable American power.

South Africa completed a pilot enrichment plant to employ the new method in 1975.[19] Nearly all of the construction work was performed by 235 local firms. The relatively small plant is owned by the Uranium Enrichment Corporation of South Africa (UCOR) and is capable in principle of producing 40,000 separative work units (SWU) per year. (The SWU is the unit of measure of enriched uranium services. Most large power reactors require about 100,000 SWU per year for their operations.) The South African enrichment plant has not, in practice, functioned at its design capacity on any regular basis.

Weapons Capability

A simple nuclear weapon requires about 2,000 to 4,000 SWUs; a more sophisticated weapon can be constructed with about half of this amount. Therefore, South Africa could in theory produce up to twenty nuclear bombs a year if its pilot plant operated at full capacity to produce highly enriched uranium and if it used the output of the pilot plant primarily to supply

18. Nelson Sievering, assistant administrator for international affairs, Energy Research and Development Administration, statement before the House Subcommittee on Africa, unpub. (June 30, 1977), 4; Robert Gillette, "Uranium Enrichment: With Help South Africa Is Progressing," *Science,* CLXXXVIII (June 1975), 1090-92.

19. *Cape Argus,* January 6, 1978.

weapons-grade materiel. In the early 1970s the responsible South African minister promised to expand the pilot plant into a full-scale enrichment facility with a capacity of 5 million SWUs, or 1,000 tons of reactor fuel, per year by 1986.[20] Escom even announced plans to construct two coal-fired stations in order to provide power for the enlarged facility; preliminary contracts were drawn up in 1977 for about $2 billion to $3 billion worth of construction.

South Africa has since been compelled drastically to revise its plans for a new facility. The United States refused to supply the necessary components and prevailed upon other (mostly European) potential manufacturers to do likewise. Without this ability to procure the necessary mass-produced pumps, compressors, and so on (uranium hexafluoride is exceptionally corrosive), South Africa learned that the construction and operation of a large-scale plant would, given prevailing American attitudes, prove excessively expensive. Since the local recession and the attitudes of foreign lenders also made finance difficult, South Africa was compelled to scale down the size of the proposed plant from an output capacity of 5 million SWUs to 250,000 SWUs a year.[21] Yet South Africa's light-water power-producing reactors will require reloads (in addition to initial core requirements) in the 1980s of about 200,000 SWUs per year. Although the large-scale facility would have produced an excess of millions of SWUs a year, for either export or weapons production, the modest facility will thus generate an excess of only 50,000 SWUs a year. In theory South Africa could have produced up to two thousand bombs each year from a 5 million SWU excess.[22] The 250,000 SWUs per year output would, given the level of technology probably available to South Africa, make possible the production of about

20. *Yearbook for South Africa* (1976); U.S., Department of Energy, "Republic of South Africa, Atomic Energy Program," unpub. (July 1977).

21. *Economist*, February 25, 1978. German researchers, however, claim that the decision to scale down the enrichment facility expansion was but a cover for the secret construction of a separate, large plant associated with the SASOL II project in the eastern Transvaal. West German technical and French financial involvement is alleged. See Rogers and Cervenka, *Nuclear Axis*, 192.

22. Ronald H. Siegel, "The South African Nuclear Program," unpub. (1977), 4.

twelve, rather than a theoretical twenty-five, bombs. For its nuclear strike force, however, France needed about 400,000 SWUs. Yet even one or two bombs could be a powerful threat in South African white hands, and—unless its surplus amounts of enriched uranium are exported, which carries its own dangers— South Africa will surely have the requisite supplies soon, if it does not now, to make such a threat credible.[23]

Throughout the 1970s South Africa has refused to place its pilot plant under international safeguards. It has taken the position that inspection by the International Atomic Energy Agency would endanger the secrecy of its technology. South Africa has also adamantly refused to sign the Nuclear Non-Proliferation Treaty, presumably because the white minority government has long wanted ostentatiously to reserve the right to develop nuclear weapons as a last defense against external pressures to accede to black rule. The reason given officially, however, is that the inspections required under the treaty would expose the secrets of the country's enrichment process to the pirating gaze of commercial rivals.

As a result of South Africa's failure to sign the treaty, and despite the potential conflict with the objectives of simultaneous, delicate bilateral and multilateral negotiations over the future of Namibia and Zimbabwe, the United States has attempted a variety of strategems to move South Africa from obstinacy to cooperation. It ceased fulfilling contracts calling for the supply of highly enriched uranium to the experimental reactor. It became coy about its willingness to carry out the provision of the 1973 contract that calls for the supply of low-enriched fuel rods to the Koeberg power station. It successfully prevailed upon American and European computer manufacturers, as well as suppliers of other critical components, to stop providing equipment or facilities that directly or indirectly could enhance South Africa's ability to enrich uranium or develop explosives.[24]

The absence of South Africa's signature on the Nuclear

23. *Financial Times,* August 24, 1977. South Africa has signed contracts for the supply of enriched uranium with West Germany, Switzerland, and Japan. See Rogers and Cervenka, *Nuclear Axis,* 153.

24. *Nuclear Engineering International,* XXII, 261 (August 1977), 12.

Non-Proliferation Treaty was of no little concern because of its potential capacity to produce bombs. Even before 1977, there had been widespread suspicion of South Africa's ambitions in the nuclear weapons field. Indeed, a long-overlooked official report indicates that South Africa may have begun attempting to further these ambitions as early as 1972, when its Atomic Energy Board admitted that it was investigating what it called the possible peaceful applications of nuclear explosions.[25]

As special emphasis was placed by the new administration of President Jimmy Carter in 1977 on preventing the proliferation of nuclear capability throughout the world, so South Africa, a uranium supplier subject to major internal cleavages and a tendency to national paranoia, naturally became one among several objects of special scrutiny. This incipient suspicion turned to alarm in mid-1977. In August the Soviet Union reported that its satellites had discovered nuclear testing facilities on the southern edge of the Kalahari Desert, in the northern marches of the Cape Province. Photographs taken by American satellites quickly confirmed that structures above ground bore a close resemblance to those constructed elsewhere to detonate nuclear devices in an experimental setting. The governments of the United States, France, Britain, and West Germany demanded explanations and reassurances; in response, Prime Minister B. Johannes Vorster denied that a test site existed. He said that South Africa had not been about to explode a nuclear weapon. Above all, Vorster pledged that South Africa (whatever it may have been doing, or contemplating) had no plans to build a bomb in the future.[26] Either because of premature discovery, or because of difficulties with and the costs of its own manufacturing processes, the veracity of Vorster's pledge was enhanced in June 1978. Satellite photographs disclosed that South Africa had dismantled its suspicious

25. Republic of South Africa, Atomic Energy Board, *Sixteenth Annual Report, 1972* (Pretoria, 1973), 17. *Seventeenth Annual Report, 1973,* carried a further report on this project, also on p. 17, but *Reports* after 1973 make no references to it. By then it had become impolitic, in view of the changing world attitude toward the dangers even of peaceful explosions, for the Atomic Energy Board to refer to its experiments, no matter how benign.

26. *New York Times,* August 24, 1977; Daan Prinsloo, *United States Foreign Policy and the Republic of South Africa* (Pretoria, 1978), 115.

structures in the Kalahari. Whatever they were, they were no more.

The question of whether or not to accept South Africa's disclaimer of its bomb-making intentions at face value is still open. Knowledgeable observers believe, without being able to be certain, that South Africa has the means to assemble a relatively unsophisticated bomb within a year from the time a political decision is made to produce it. South Africa can (if it has not already done so) bring together the required components and use locally produced enriched uranium to make and then test the bomb. But, given the reaction of the West to such a decision, and given the value South Africa still places on its ties to the West, the political and economic consequences of making a bomb cannot lightly be ignored. Nor can three key questions: A bomb for what purpose? Upon which nation could a bomb be dropped? Would there be any point in destroying Maputo or Luanda? Using a bomb internally would accomplish nothing except self-destruction. The leverage which would flow from possession of a bomb is thus limited, if not negative.[27] South African policymakers doubtless considered this point in 1977, when Vorster proclaimed his country's innocence, and in 1979, when Botha was as reassuring.

Uranium and Bargaining

As a major supplier of uranium in a world rapidly depleting its comparatively inexpensive sources of energy, South Africa may be well placed toward the end of the present century. Together with immense deposits of coal, uranium will give South Africa a comparatively high level of self-sufficiency in energy. A large exportable surplus will also be available. Even if this surplus is preenriched, it should find a ready, profitable market. It if does, and if the needs of the northern hemisphere are great enough, South Africa will possess an important weapon of incalculable importance in the international arena. Under certain circumstances as yet unforeseen, South Africa might even be in a

27. Richard K. Betts, "A Diplomatic Bomb for South Africa?" *International Security,* IV (1979), 91-115, discusses the extremely unlikely case of direct Soviet intervention in southern Africa and American uninvolvement. In that combination of circumstances, a South African *force de frappe* could have some utility. Betts soberly analyzes other rationales for South Africa's nuclear arming.

position to convert its role as a supplier into important political leverage. This aspect should not be overdramatized; equally, it ought not to be ignored.

South Africa's twin abilities—to generate power from nuclear fuel cells and to enrich uranium as well as mine it—give it an enviable new degree of flexibility in the energy field, but that flexibility is accompanied by dependence upon Western suppliers, particularly the United States. With its soon-to-be-realized ability to generate electricity from uranium instead of coal, and to convert coal into petroleum, South Africa may manage to make itself less dependent, in the medium term, on oil. Having technological knowhow also enhances its status and its bargaining capacity. It enables South Africa to offer assistance to other pariah and to nonpariah states. It gives South Africa a critical regional-level role in the field of atomic power as well as that of enrichment. When those capacities are coupled with its role as a major supplier, South Africa becomes capable of applying some countervailing weight of its own (though the amount should not be overestimated) to a range of international disputes.

By demonstrating the capacity, if not the willingness, to enrich uranium effectively and to build a bomb—if it has not already done so—South Africa also bolsters its own credibility as a determined regional power. It may never wish to try to solve its own internal problems by using nuclear weapons, but the mere possession of, or the ability to construct, such weapons may well have a deterrent effect upon black African states by discouraging hostility. (In late 1979 an American satellite detected a light flash characteristic of a low-yield nuclear explosion, but no other forms of surveillance provided conclusive additional evidence that a device had been detonated in the vicinity of South Africa.) Certainly South Africa's demonstrated technological capacity makes the United States ever more anxious as it strives to reduce nuclear proliferation and the worldwide spread of enrichment and reprocessing facilities. The United States will maintain its pressure on South Africa, possibly even refusing to supply enriched fuel for the Koeberg reactors, but at some point South Africa may become free of the United States in this realm.

6 | Reconciling the Past with a Future

SOUTH AFRICA ENTERS THE 1980s with two key questions as yet unanswered. First, how can the government of the Republic ensure the kind of future for the black and white people of the country that minimizes conflict and maximizes reconciliation and harmony? Second, by what means, in what form, to what extent, and how soon is the political participation of the majority of South Africans to be achieved?

Both of these two questions and satisfactory answers to them are mutually dependent. The questions are at last beginning to be posed privately and publicly within all South African circles; yet leaders of white as well as black opinion despair at the failure of Prime Minister Pieter W. Botha's government to be bold, imaginative, and decisive in seeking answers to the key questions (and to subsidiary ones). Critics claim that only by rigorously analyzing the components of the South African dilemma, clearly enumerating the available options, and firmly accepting the consequences of the best options can the government preserve South Africa from rending conflict and economic destruction. These critics fear political paralysis and remind outsiders that South African whites (and blacks, too) are basically resilient, pragmatic, and resourceful. They also aver, with some reason, that whites want security and expect their government to chart the course that will guarantee it even, if necessary, at the expense of privilege.

It is evident to those who would seek such security that no simple perpetuation of the policies that make up the status quo can reconcile South Africa's future with its past. Virtually no one of prominence in South African public life argues otherwise. In that regard, the debate proceeds from very different premises than it did either one or two decades ago. This is not to imply that there is a consensus about the logical progression of events either within South Africa or between South Africans and the West. Rather, there is a generalized groping for agreement or compromise on a series of propositions. It is only from a discussion of these propositions, and by building upon the results of the discussions, that some kind of common program of action can be articulated.

It is not necessary to subscribe to historical determinism—to assume that societies dominated by minorities cannot endure indefinitely—to believe that the tide of worldwide decolonization has eroded and sooner or later will undermine even the most elaborately constructed bulwarks that a white-ruled South Africa can throw up. Depending upon the circumstances, erosion can be a long-term, gradual process or, as a product of sudden, violent tropical tumults, swift and catastrophic. Whether gradual or catastrophic, erosion is less often reversible than it is capable of being minimized, deflected, and—in the world of nature—prevented. In nature, to prevent is usually to alter the ecology—to construct massive breakwaters, to dredge channels and clear streams, and, above all, to modify the manner in which men utilize their available resources and respond to the anticipated determination of an environment that is capable of being both cruel and capricious. Non-South African analysts are by heritage uncomfortable with approaches for policymaking purposes that assume a static, repetitive world.

Many South Africans take very seriously the African view that there is a new, somber mood in the black cities and townships. The relative quiet in the urban areas during most of 1979 could well be merely the lull in a shifting storm, for the young—the unemployed and the underemployed, the many who have come of age in the three decades since the National party victory of 1948—more than their elders seem as a result of the violence in Soweto since 1976 to have accepted the consequences of renewed militance. It may be mere bravado, or a false abandoning of the careful calculation of inherent risks, but reports that Africans have adopted new modes of thought and new ways of handling what they view as the problems of change in South Africa persuade foreigners, as well as white South Africans, that the internal dimension of the problem will be ignored only by those who are willfully blind.

The Pressures on South Africa

In estimating the near- and middle-term pressures on the South African predicament, outsiders are bound to consider the impact of prolonged systemic, if low-level, violence; various levels of industrial unrest and, possibly, sabotage; and renewed rioting leading to insurrection. If these and other similar manifestations of black discontent are possible, then they must form a part of the overall equation. Nothing persuades observers that the potential for internally generated protest and violence has disappeared.

South Africa has the security apparatus and military might to contain and repress internally generated insurrection and, for the foreseeable future, to withstand attack from without (assuming the absence of direct involvement of the superpowers). It has a reasonable level of self-sufficiency in armaments manufacture. There is also the question of South Africa's nuclear weapons plans. But South Africa is not invulnerable, nor has its all-out determination ever been tested.

The question of vulnerability is complex. South Africa is no more than partially independent of imported petroleum (see chapter 4). The present method of storing oil in unused mines could guarantee supplies for months if not years. Rationing—even draconian measures to eliminate private consumption entirely—can extend existing resources. Furthermore, short of a concerted blockade by superpowers, and the threat of clashes on the high seas, there is likely to be sufficient pirated oil worldwide to fuel a fighting force. Yet, even with such caveats there must be concern about diesel fuel, and about the continuing supply of aviation spirit.

More damaging is the price that civilian South Africa will have to pay. The usual fears of an antiwhite holocaust are probably overdrawn; there is no sustained African example of black genocide against whites (although of black genocide against blacks there are several). Yet to put white South Africa on a footing of all-out war would both strain an already fragile economy and place a crushing psychological burden on a white population the confidence of which has been undermined by several years of tension. Emigration has begun to be a factor, no matter how minor now, in the South African equation. All-out hostilities could but intensify flight and destroy the economic confidence that is the country's lifeblood.

South Africa can outgun most combinations of likely African invaders. It certainly has the means to overwhelm revolutionaries in small groups, or whole townships. But can South Africa sustain for more than a brief period simultaneous internal and external conflict, labor unrest or industrial sabotage, or widespread, multiprovincial internal hostilities? Can it fight two different kinds of wars at once? Can it afford to repress with brutality in the political and emotional climate of today's world? What levels of internal dissent can be tolerated by any government before it becomes unable to govern, losing legitimacy in white as well as black eyes and in the eyes of the international community?

Largely because of its position as an important supplier of strategic minerals, South Africa is not devoid of countervailing levers of its own. Europe is much more dependent than the United States upon South Africa as a market and a supplier. Equally, South Africa remains vulnerable to a variety of internationally imposed constraints short of and also including sanctions, boycotts, and blockades. It will ultimately be unable to sustain a position as an outcast. South African whites cannot cut themselves adrift economically, politically, or culturally from the West, to which, white tribe or no, they remain tied.

South Africa will want to reconcile its future with its past. As a white state it has a brilliant future behind it; as a nation capable of fruitfully linking black and white, it may have a future far surpassing any that can presently be imagined for whites alone.

Toward the New Future?

One of the striking lessons of South Africa in the late 1970s was how its diverse communities had begun to grope toward a

new future. This process was glimpsed in the changing rhetoric
—the discarding of pejorative appellations and the devising of
new, if imperfect, terms; in the slow erosion of racial separation
in the discotheques, the banks, the international hotels, even —
illegally and sporadically—in a few urban residential districts.
Dan Jacobson, the novelist, caught the sense of these changes in
1978: "To an outsider," he wrote, "the changes that have taken
place . . . may seem pitifully inconsequential; but anyone who
remembers the South Africa of even five years ago will be startled
to see black children swinging on swings in the public parks, or an
Indian family eating a meal unhindered in an open-air restau-
rant."[1]

More significantly, these changes were apparent in the ways
in which the leaders of the cabinet, and their foremost civil servants, conceptualized the overriding problem. They sought ways
of remaining true to the old formulas while, in fact, altering —
sometimes dramatically—the fabric of South African life as
whites had long known it. The oligarchy was saying one thing and
doing another: "They now speak," wrote Jacobson, "with lofty
disapproval of *rassisme* and *geskeidenheid* (discrimination), and
announce with a curious mixture of pride and ill-disguised reluctance that they are taking this or that step to 'normalize' (their
word) this or that sporting event or public facility."[2]

South Africans justly complain that foreigners too rarely
recognize the extent to which the nature of the debate within the
country was transformed during the 1970s. That there was much
Afrikaner criticism, for example, of the harm done by the Mixed
Marriages and Immorality Acts, that there was an awareness of
the damage done by the rigid enforcement of pass laws and in-
flux-control regulations, and that there was an attempt to
provide a new means of giving political representation to Indians
and Coloureds were all indications of an incipient, if tentative,
flexibility. They demonstrated that the clock had not stopped.

But others may be forgiven if they also see these initiatives as
too restrained and too limited. These and similar opportunities

1. Dan Jacobson, "Among the South Africans," *Commentary,* LXV (March 1978),
33.
2. Ibid.

appear unequal to the challenge of the overriding problem. They seem to lag behind, not to leapfrog the existing levels of concern. Most of all, the debate within the government remains too muted, and the leadership given to the public too limited, to provide the consistent, bold charting of the kind of new alternatives that offer white South Africa its only realistic influence over the future.

Political Representation

The overriding issue of political representation simply cannot be subsumed or avoided by clever legerdemain, by the devising of new categories of citizenship, by the creation of so-called independent homelands, or by the rewriting of South Africa's social charter. This point of view is often expressed in moral terms or as an imperative of human rights. But it is not necessary to be normative. In cold, analytical terms, resolution and reconciliation are not possible without attention to the political issues. The numerical superiority of Africans in South Africa, however defined, is impossible to erase. After all, today's 19 million Africans include at least 9 million who are integrated into and essential to the white-run economy. They live in the urban industrial and farming areas controlled by whites. The remainder reside most of the year in homelands; but the homelands are vastly overcrowded and, under foreseeable circumstances, can absorb additional numbers only at the expense of living standards of Africans already there. African numbers in the urban areas cannot shrink and in the year 2000 are expected to be four times those of whites, whatever the policy of separate development may mandate. Whites will remain a minority in every urban and rural area.

Aware as all analysts must be of the demographic time bomb, they look for a variety of initiatives that would begin to ease its impact. In the short term, they see the importance of major changes in the social fabric. They presume that the most effective way of boosting morale and deescalating tension would derive from a bold approach to, for example, the manner in which the pass laws are now enforced. Any reconsideration of the continued utility of pass laws would obviously lead to a reevaluation (tentatively explored in 1979) of the policy of influx control,

squatter settlements, and so on. Once the social fabric is recon-
sidered in a thorough manner, the pragmatism that could be
South Africa's political salvation becomes applicable in other
areas.

Increased expenditures on African education and African
control over educational policy would be welcomed as an earnest
of serious intent. A retired senior white South African educational official has called for an end to the isolation of black
schooling policy, which he said needs to be "brought in from the
cold." Policies need to be made in consultation—for the first
time—with leading Africans of "all types." Only by gaining the
backing of the black community, he has said, can confidence and
credibility be restored in this area.[3]

Any successful evolutionary restructuring of South Africa
will require careful and assiduous preparation and the kind of
leadership skills that are rare in South Africa's public life. South
Africans nowadays propose a model for this kind of restructuring
that proceeds from the assumption that public debate is less
effective in dealing with such issues (particularly if any radical
departures are to be made from existing approaches) than is a
policy conceived in a caucus of the few and stamped with the im-
primatur of the ruling oligarchy. Many go farther and assert that
South Africa may be unable to devise and implement the kinds of
changes that will be effective unless and until there is a shift away
from parliamentary democracy either to the authoritarianism of
a strong presidential system or—and many speak of it as a real alternative—until the military, with or without the acquiescence of
elected officials, imposes a solution upon the country.

This belief in the efficacy of policy change by fiat runs deep.
It draws upon models of change in such disparate places as post-
Ottoman Turkey, Pahlavi Iran, and the major Marxist and the
prewar Fascist countries. It certainly is a strand that it would be
unhelpful to misunderstand or to dismiss cavalierly. Yet it is clear
that policies of change—particularly the momentous ones that
could be anticipated—will be unworkable unless they have been
developed by leadership representative of the full spectrum of

3. H. L. Hartshorne, quoted in *Eastern Province Herald,* July 7, 1978.

South African life. Obviously, this is not a suggestion that only the simple model of a national convention of all races will work; the leaders of white South Africa will need to prepare their own electorate to accept the legitimacy of some kind of consultative process, whether a convention or the much more likely and rather prolonged dialogue that could consist of a series of meetings over months. The process of change will be legitimated by, and will preempt other kinds of alterations, only as a conclusion to such a process of consultation. Events often spin out of control; speed is therefore more essential than ever before.

Certainly the structural problems of the South African economy provide little comfort to those who would defer new initiatives or who deny the need for thoughtful haste. Many analysts lack confidence in the ability of South Africa to attract the large amounts of new capital that it needs until such time as the logjam is broken politically. The vast numbers of unemployed young Africans will, in any event, depress the confidence of outsiders. That view reflects perceptions about the costs of security, the rising cost of petroleum, and the likely absence of any dramatic near-term upturn in the world economic picture.

Those who seek a permanent solution to the South African problem — one that is fair to all South Africans and to Africa in general, and one that strengthens South Africa's regional and international roles — believe that it is as important to commence the debate as it is to arrive at answers. Where the code words of many South Africans are caution and care, their counterparts for many analysts are courage and charisma. No one assumes charity. No one requests supine concessions. All talk of realities, but whereas some South Africans ask for assurances, many outsiders suggest action based on a clear canvas of all available alternatives.

Those who seek to reconcile the Republic's future with its past seek solutions that work. They are of one mind in their insistence that nothing that substitutes new for old injustices, that lessens or destroys the quality of life, that sabotages the economy, or that creates new class, social, or ethnic conflicts can contribute to a reconciliation that will succeed. The choices are stark. As much as they may be concerned humanistically and strategically about the fate of whites in South Africa (a South Africa deprived artificially of its white talent would be a poorer, less viable country), they view the long-term security of the position of whites as achievable only in the context of a progression to some kind of new arrangement arrived at by bargaining with fully representative Africans.

A Response to the Pressures

One of the hallmarks of South Africa in the late 1970s was the search for new politicogeographical frameworks. There was a tacit awareness that a unified, white-run South Africa might not necessarily prove durable politically. Sometimes timidly, sometimes assertively, Africans and whites thus suggested rearrangements of the land mass, and hence of peoples, in order to improve the durability of the whole. These suggestions included outright partition; a redrawing of the boundaries of the existing homelands in order to improve their size and viability and eliminate fragmentation (a variety of partition); confederalism arranged between both equal and unequal blocs of power; a cantonalism of some kind based loosely on the Swiss example; and—again inexact—a centralized federalism. No matter how general or vague the present conceptualization of these various terms and ideas is within the South African framework, none deserves to be dismissed without an examination of its potential contribution both to the ongoing debate and to the practical search for answers to the country's dilemma.

What is more certain, however, is that few share the National party's belief in the efficacy of separate development as elaborated by and through the homelands. Were they consolidated, economically robust, resource-rich, and at least potentially independent of South African largesse, outsiders might see the homelands in a more favorable light. But when 70 to 85 percent of the general budgets of the homelands is supplied by a vote of the South African parliament, when all are too small, too impoverished, and ecologically too wasted to provide for the millions who theoretically are assigned there, and when the urban question is avoided by the fiction of homeland citizenship, then the government's homeland policy may not be seen to embody a helpful approach to the more central problems of South Africa. The homelands have provided training grounds and platforms for Africans. But they have not introduced Africans to thoroughgoing participatory democracy, nor to the kind of entrepreneurial opportunities (through the imaginative management of mineral or agricultural resources) that have been productive of real growth elsewhere in the Third World. It is difficult to understand precisely in what ways the homelands — as presently conceived, arranged, used, and assembled — can provide real answers for the South Africa of the 1980s.

Beyond geographical gerrymandering, there have been suggestions for various forms of qualified franchise and for restricted or weighted varieties of proportional representation. In some senses both alternatives would be more reminiscent of earlier South African practices than would the proposed geographical rearrangements. Cecil Rhodes himself espoused equal rights for all civilized men. Whether advanced before 1978 by the Progressive Federal party or more recently by National party mavericks, a qualified franchise would be based on property or education or both; it would — unlike the Rhodesian franchises of the 1930s, 1940s, and 1950s — be immune to reevaluations upward in order to put a cap on Coloured, Asian, and African voting totals. The constitutional proposals of the National party may also assume a kind of qualified franchise for the indirect as well as any direct elections to the proposed Asian and Coloured councils. If this concept is extended at some point in the near future to Africans, then it too may depend electorally on arrangements short of universal franchise.

These political and sociopolitical proposals, and variations and improvements upon them, may form the basis of a debate that has not yet fully begun. It may soon begin, and if so will flow out of the kinds of processes that have already been discussed, but not if there is an attempt to avoid focusing upon the central issue of South Africa's future: political representation of Africans.

South Africans, when asked to bargain credibly with blacks, often aver either that leaders are difficult to discover or that some method must be devised for selecting appropriate representatives of the people and peoples of South Africa. To argue thus is mere sophistry, however, for the jails of South Africa are filled with persons who have been incarcerated because of their leadership activities. Or they are banned because of their outspokenness on behalf of a group or a cause. Then there are those who have been jailed or banned and released, such as the Soweto Committee of Ten. Chief ministers of the larger homelands must also be presumed to be representatives of their people, as must the officers of the South African Black Alliance and Inkatha, the largest political parties in the country's history. Coloureds and Asians are divided, but they can name their leaders. It is willful obfuscation to deny the existence of black leaders of various kinds and of various backgrounds, urban and rural. It is true that they have in many instances achieved positions of eminence and authority in their diverse communities in unorthodox ways, but they have had few other, more regular opportunities.

The dimension of time is important, too. What might prove acceptable in certain constituencies today may seem limiting or irrelevant tomorrow. Even those who know South Africa well, and over many decades, cannot understand why the discussion of the issues that rightfully absorb South Africans has not begun, and in public.

White South Africans provide at least one level of explanation. It begins with the notion that the white electorate is resistant to massive change and will abort the development of any plan of action if it is introduced too abruptly. The National party, this explanation continues, having successfully unified Afrikanerdom and redressed the losses of the Anglo-Boer War and the discrimination that Afrikaners endured after Union, would suffer a fatal schism or series of schisms if the ruling electorate within the overall white electorate should find itself presented with stark choices: one comfortable, the other dangerous. Afrikaner leaders fear such splits and abhor the kinds of divisions that could permit decay, and the loss of control. Behind these perceptions of political reality usually lurks an unstated assumption about the reactions of Afrikanerdom to the kinds of escalating demands that might be made of them. Will they acquiesce in the compromises expected of them only grudgingly, and up to a definable point? Is there such a point beyond which they will not budge, and will

demand to do battle instead? Or can they be led (and manipulated) indefinitely?

South Africa has a parliamentary system that, even with its
restricted franchise, offers only a minimal level of participation.
An oligarchy makes decisions and is largely immune from pressures from commerce, trade unions, and nowadays perhaps even
from the church. When it chooses, the oligarchy conveniently ig-
nores criticism even from within committed Afrikaner circles
and the back benches of the National party. (From the far right,
the Herstigte Nasionale, or Reformed National, party is no
threat.) This it appears to do with impunity. After a change of
government, a major scandal, Botha's new verbal assaults on
apartheid, and a late 1979 by-election loss, the ability of an oligarchy to shape the destiny of the nation seems unimpaired.

There is skepticism about the real significance of the many
electoral and ideological constraints that are said to limit the
maneuverability of South Africa's white leaders. The lesson of the
American South is too clear. There responsible leadership
everywhere was decisive. Where the community leadership — admittedly the men of commerce, cloth, and journalism, as well as
the politicians — led, accommodation was swift, change relatively
painless, and subsequent relations between white and black acceptable.

Many South Africans claim that Afrikaners are psychologically unique — that compromise is foreign to their nature, that
they would rather fight than trade, that the lessons of the frontier
have, in the face of adversity, not taught adaptation and re-
sourcefulness as well as immovability. Given the movement of
Afrikaners off the land and into the cities, from the farms into
business and the civil service (and state employment generally),
many of the old assumptions about Afrikaner behavior are bound
to need reassessment. Today they are certainly less independent
economically, given the decrease in the numbers of Afrikaners on
the platteland, or farmlands, but they are also more modern, and
much more a part of the Westernized economy of South Africa
and the world. Is it therefore at least a reasonable assumption
that Afrikaners, and whites more generally, will consent to the

charting of a new future, particularly if that future is articulated by the leaders to whom they have already given support, in whom they presumably have some faith, and for whom they can realistically substitute no others? If the articulation of the future is also to evolve, as a process, with final goals as yet undetermined, then the acceptance of such a route seems less than impossible.

It is the logic of such a position that seems inescapable. Strong leadership is not only needed, but available, and could be exercised. An ordered, leadership-influenced, evolutionary resolution of the outstanding issues between white and black South Africans may not remain possible indefinitely. That is the inescapable message of today's South Africa.

Namibia

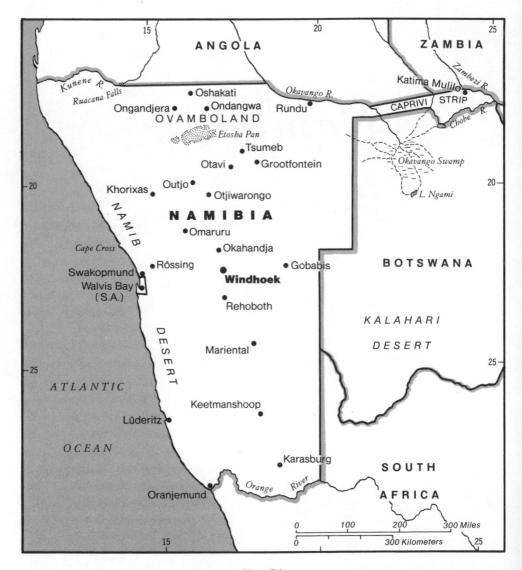

Namibia

7 | The Framework of Society

NAMIBIA IS SPARSELY POPULATED, ecologically fragile, and agriculturally limited. The territory has no industrial base and, in purely African terms, is administratively primitive. Yet Namibia is mineral-rich, enjoys the advantages of an Atlantic coastline, and has a ratio of blacks to whites more nearly in balance than that of neighboring Zimbabwe. It is a country by accident rather than design, betraying its origins in ways more economically and politically limiting than other countries of black Africa.

Before the modern period the harsh terrain of southern and central Namibia played host to dark-skinned Damara, to San, or Bushmen, and to nomadic Khoi, or Hottentot, groups that periodically crossed the Orange River from the Cape Colony. The Herero, a Bantu-speaking people heavily involved with cattle, occupied much of central Namibia before the eighteenth century. They took land from the Damara, subjugated them, and consigned many to decades of serfdom. Later the Ovambo, another Bantu-speaking collection of peoples, probably followed the Herero in time, crossing the Kunene River in the north to occupy the arable grasslands of northern Namibia.

Although Portuguese explorers had sailed along the Namibian coast and set anchor in its harbors, European interest in the area before the late nineteenth century was limited to guano and the Gospel. As early as 1842 beds of guano, sometimes as much as 66 feet deep, which covered a chain of small islands off the Namibian coast, were being excavated for their natural supplies of fertilizer. These diggings changed hands in 1861 and again in 1866, when the British Cape Colony twice annexed the twelve islands. Off the coast of Namibia, British and South African sailors were also killing whales and seals, catching fish, and shipping the products to Cape Town. But Britain was otherwise only mildly interested in extending its control over the Cape Colony to what was beginning to be known as South-West Africa.

True, representatives of both the London Missionary Society and the Wesleyan Methodist Missionary Society had crossed the Orange River in the early years of the nineteenth century; they had established missions among the various Khoi and Nama (descendants largely of white and Khoi liaisons) groups that had settled north of the Orange, and a few of the missionaries had even traveled as far as Windhoek by the 1830s. But this constituted no more than a temporary English beachhead. Only after 1840, when the London Missionary Society transferred its territory to the Rhenish Missionary Society, did men of the cloth begin to play an important role in opening up the territory. It is because of this early missionary interest, too, that Germany came to play such a formative role in colonial Namibia. The Rhenish Missionary Society tried to work among both the Herero and their Nama antagonists. Other missionaries followed. As early as 1870, the Finnish Mission Society began taking the Gospel to the Ndonga branch of the Ovambo; English Anglicans and German Roman Catholics later opened stations elsewhere in Ovamboland.

Conflict in Early Namibia

The major conflicts during these early years were not between the indigenous inhabitants and the Europeans. Instead, from 1840 to 1892 Namibia was the scene of fierce battles between new waves of white-influenced Nama and the Herero. They competed, as Afrikaners and Africans had begun to do in the Transvaal, for grazing lands. The Herero suffered their first major defeat in 1840, when they were driven back north of the Swakop River. There were bitter wars between 1863 and 1870 and after a period of calm, during which the Basters, a peaceful people of mixed black and white ancestry who had been ousted from the Cape Colony, settled on good grazing lands near Rehoboth, and new warring Nama groups pressed against the fragile north-central Namibian frontier, the Nama and Herero locked themselves into another exhausting series of wars between 1880 and 1892.

During episodes of peace Herero cattle were exported by sea, and ostrich feathers and ivory were sent overland to Cape Town. This burgeoning commerce, the nascent activities of the German missionaries, and the convulsive wars of the interior began attracting European attention. Small groups of Boers trekked north and west from the Transvaal, hoping to find hospitable lands on which to establish new settlements. The British government of the Cape, partially in response to requests for assistance from the paramount chief of the main branch of the Herero and partially because of its fear of Afrikaner designs on Namibia, sent an emissary to Okahandja in 1876. He concluded agreements with the Herero and recommended annexing all of South-West Africa. The British government, however, limited its territorial ambitions to the 969 square kilometers of Walvis Bay and its environs; it annexed Walvis Bay in 1878 and incorporated it and the twelve islands into the Cape Colony in 1884.

The Coming of the Germans

In 1880 Britain explicitly told Germany, worried about its missionaries in a land torn by war between African groups, that it did not intend to extend its administrative aegis beyond Walvis Bay. In 1884, a year after Adolf Lüderitz, a young, adventurous merchant from Bremen, had established a trading outpost at Angra Pequena on Namibia's southern coast, the Germans undertook to move into the area themselves. By late 1885 Germany had extended its "protection" to all of what is now Namibia except the Caprivi Strip, which was recognized as part of South-West Africa by the terms of the omnibus Anglo-German agreement of 1890. Lord Salisbury, the British foreign minister, and Count Georg von Caprivi, his German counterpart, traded the strip—a thin wedge of land providing Germany with access to the Zambezi River—for unfettered British control of Zanzibar, Uganda, and Kenya.

Even so, in spite of their building a first fort in Windhoek in

1890, the German initiative altered Namibia little until 1893, when the Germans had become strong enough to rout the Nama and exchange their own for Nama harassment of the Herero. The eastern branch of the Herero revolted in 1896, but were easily defeated. In the next few years Germans began to buy land from the Herero; railways were constructed from Swakopmund to Windhoek and from Angra Pequena toward Keetmanshoop; the flow of German settlers and the harsh enforcement of German law added to tension between Herero and Germans in the center of the colony and between Nama and Germans in the south. The populous Ovambo were effectively still outside of the German sphere.

In late 1903 the Bondelswarts branch of the Nama revolted and German troops rushed from Windhoek 400 miles to the south. A month later, while the military was still fighting in the south, the main body of the Herero rose up against the Germans, and in late 1904, the northern Nama joined the fray. More than 100 whites died, and the German repression led to the annihilation of the Herero and Nama peoples. Of about 60,000 Herero in 1903, only 16,000 survived to benefit from the armistice of late 1905. Of about 15,000 Nama, only 9,000 remained. Although Herero and Nama were killed in battle, along with nearly 14,000 German troops, much of the loss of life occurred in prisoner-of-war camps. Both the pastoral Nama and Herero also forfeited their cattle, without which life was worth little for many.

The results of these revolts dramatically altered the population balance between southern and northern Namibia. Socially and economically, the revolts also had a lasting impact. Thereafter, Herero and Nama were regimented and segregated; they were compelled to carry identity documents, or passes, and to labor — under harsh conditions — for whites.

Herero and Nama were increasingly employed on the extensive German sheep and cattle ranches. After diamonds were discovered in the south in 1908, Africans were recruited to gather and process the stones. The Germans completed the railways to Keetmanshoop and from Otavi to Grootfontein in 1908, and in 1911 they began, however tentatively, to draw upon Ovambo labor. But both the predatory and the developmental aspects of this early German rule were brought abruptly to an end in 1915, when South African troops conquered and began administering the colony. From the revolts until that time, about 15,000 Germans had ruled, under a form of self-government, a vast territory with only 80,000 indigenous inhabitants, the majority of whom were now Ovambo, not Herero.

South African Control

Although the new occupiers wished simply to incorporate South-West Africa into what was then the Union of South Africa, at the peace conference after World War I United States President Woodrow Wilson refused to approve such an annexation. After much bargaining, South-West Africa became a Class C mandate of the League of Nations and, in disregard of the intent of that form of mandate, from 1920 South Africa began to administer the former colony as if it had been annexed. (Walvis Bay and the twelve islands had in 1910 become part of the Cape Province. From 1922 on, however, they were treated in local law and practice as if they were a part of South-West Africa.) The government placed the interests of whites above those of the local population, promoted white immigration, gave limited self-government to the white minority in 1925, and signally failed — in the opinion of the Permanent Mandates Commission of the League of Nations and a 1936 report by a South African investigatory commission — to advance the welfare of the indigenous inhabitants.

South African managed under the mandate to take the good grazing land that remained in African hands and give it to whites. It erected social and economic barriers to black (African, Nama, and Coloured) advancement, and it applied South African laws that made those barriers irksome. It compelled African laborers to become migrants and thus disrupted indigenous life. "The crux of the matter," Wellington wrote, "is surely that the mandatory, having been directed to make the welfare of the Natives its chief concern, and having been given the power to carry out this policy effectively, seized the best land for its own (white) subjects, relegating its wards, who were 'not yet able to stand by themselves under the strenuous conditions of the modern world,' to areas too small for their sustenance, or else, as in the case of the Herero, to land far worse than they were accustomed to."[1] When the Bondelswarts again rebelled in 1922, the South Africans literally bombed them into submission. The Basters revolted in 1925, too, but were repressed without the use of air power.

South-West Africa was considered a white province, the African inhabitants as contract workers for whites or as subsistence agriculturalists and pastoralists on circumscribed reserves. South Africa made vagrancy an offense and punished offenders with enforced labor for whites. In 1920 a Masters and Servants Proclamation made it illegal for Africans to leave white employment under most conditions. Pass laws were introduced in 1922: Africans could not enter or leave Namibia or leave their home areas without permits. Curfews were enacted and enforced, and the apparatus of what later became known (on the South African model) as apartheid was erected. Meanwhile, only paltry sums were being expended on educational and medical care for Africans and on the agricultural development of the African areas; vastly greater efforts and funds were directed to the betterment of whites.

The Ecological Deficit

An examination of a rainfall map quickly indicates the harsh limits of Namibian economic reality and some of the parameters of future foreign assistance. Only the swampy easternmost portion of the Caprivi Strip and a small section of northern Namibia west of the strip receive, on the average, more than 24 inches of rain a year. Moreover, when the rain comes, it falls in short, sharp bursts during the summer months. Britain usually survives on 24 inches distributed evenly over twelve months. Namibians, like most of the other African peoples affected by the southern intertropical convergence, see their best rain wasted be-

1. John H. Wellington, *South West Africa and Its Human Issues* (Oxford, 1967), 307-308. In 1936 the South West Africa Commission, which had been appointed by the government of South Africa and included a member of the South African judiciary, was even harsher in its criticism of the way in which African affairs had been administered by South Africa. According to the commission, the government of the territory had been a failure; South Africa had aborted its sacred trust.

cause of its usual concentration in fierce, brief storms during three or four months. Since it falls in the summer, too, rates of evaporation are high and much is lost. The hard or sandy soils of Namibia also encourage runoff rather than penetration.

Namibia's rainfall pattern extends in five bands from the 24-inch level in 4-inch intervals steadily southwestwards across the territory. Most of Ovamboland, in the north, receives an average of 20 to 24 inches a year. A thick band of terrain, mostly in the country of the Herero, receives 16 to 20 inches of rain, and Windhoek and its surround is in the 12- to 16-inch band. Proceeding south and west, through the lands of the Damara and the Basters toward South Africa, the rainfall gradually becomes nonexistent. The western coast of Namibia, like much of the Somali coast, is a desolate, totally arid anomaly. It constitutes about a fifth of Namibia and boasts the highest desert dunes in the world—a feature of interest only for the development of tourism.

Of the 318,261 square miles of Namibia (equal to Texas and Louisiana combined, two-thirds of South Africa, four United Kingdoms, four Liberias, or nine Netherlands), only about a third—mostly in the north—is at all hospitable to settled agriculture. Only on the extreme northern and southern borders of the country, for example, are there perennial rivers and streams. Between this region and the Namib Desert on the coast, from which the country takes its name, is a crumpled, elevated plateau between 4,000 and 8,000 feet high. Mostly semiarid, this central region also includes lands overlaid with thick layers of terrestrial sand and limestone of the westward-creeping Kalahari Desert. In much of this central area there is only very limited surface water.

Much of the eastern Caprivi Strip is well watered. To its immediate west is inhospitable desert; westward still is Ovamboland, with rains that, in good years, turn a flat sandy country intersected by a network of broad, shallow watercourses into a series of submerged flood plains (in the manner of Zambia's Bulozi). When not covered with water, these flood plains provide good grazing for cattle and sheep.

Only 1 percent of Namibia is suitable for continuous dryland cropping. Another 30 percent is suitable for grazing, but because of the low carrying capacity of the soils and their characteristic moisture deficit, these lands must be used in an extensive fashion if they are to survive. Beef cattle ranching is concentrated in the northern and central sections of the interior, and karakul sheep are grazed in the central south and south. In 1978 5,000 white-owned commercial farms or ranches exported about 400,000 head of cattle (either on the hoof or in the form of canned beef) to South Africa; these products were worth $90 million in 1977, and karakul (Persian lamb's wool) exports were worth $61 million. Blacks and other indigenous nonwhite groups own about 25 percent of the territory's 10 million domestic cattle and sheep. Africans grow millet, sorghum, beans, pumpkins, watermelons, gourds, and peanuts in Ovamboland; maize is also grown in the richer Kavango and eastern Caprivi areas.

The few substantial towns in the territory either are ports on the coast or else are near Windhoek, in the center, or Keetmanshoop in the south. Their distribution broadly reflects the artifact of colonization, which came from the direction of the white south in the nineteenth and twentieth centuries, and the salubrious climate of the high central plateau. Their location bears no relation to indigenous centers of population, which are mostly in the north, or to the territory's agricultural capability, which is also concentrated in the north. Namibia's 2,000 miles of paved highway and 1460 rail miles link the white towns and farming centers, but poorly serve the parts of the country occupied by Africans.

Walvis Bay, Namibia's only substantial port and its main trade window on the non-South African world, has long been integrated administratively and economically into Namibia. Until 1977, the routine affairs of the town, Namibia's second largest, were controlled by a council responsible to the administration in Windhoek, not Cape Town, and the area elected a member to the South-West African as well as the South African parliament. Throughout the twentieth century, Walvis Bay has shipped and landed the bulk of the territory's cargo; nearly all of Namibia's minerals, fish, and livestock products are moved from Walvis Bay. The territory's oil requirements are met by tankers from the Middle East, the oil being transferred into the interior by rail. Overall, Walvis Bay in the early 1970s was the fifth largest port administered by South Africa in terms of cargo tonnage. In 1976,

2 million metric tons of cargo were loaded and unloaded. Moreover, Walvis Bay was the center of Namibia's lucrative offshore fishing industry, second in value to minerals. Fishmeal and fish oil were processed there, and pilchards were canned for export.

Lüderitz, formerly Angra Pequena, the territory's only other port, is indisputably Namibian. But important though it was in the nineteenth century, when the Germans used it as a port of entry, it has little significance today. Loading facilities and communications at Lüderitz are inferior to those at Walvis Bay, and the port is patently unable to handle Namibia's current level of international trade. The town itself has declined economically, and the harbor has been allowed to silt up. In January 1976 it handled 1 percent of the total metric tonnage of cargo handled during the same month at Walvis Bay; in that month five ships called at Lüderitz and 97 at Walvis Bay.

The People and Their Surroundings

The human endowment of Namibia is both limited in total number (making possible the future achievement of high per capita incomes) and overwhelmingly of a single ethnic group (providing potential future problems for the country). The total population of Namibia is about 1 million. Sixty percent of that number live in the north, where the availability of ground water and tolerably good soils has permitted settled agriculture. This is the area inhabited by the Ovambo, who number nearly 500,000; the Kavango, 56,000; and the Caprivi, 30,000. Elsewhere, the lack of water, the sands of the Kalahari, and a harsh climate have limited the carrying capacity of the land and given to the population of Namibia an unusually dispersed character. Villages in all areas are usually small (there is nothing in Namibia reminiscent of the large Tswana settlements in Botswana), and the overall population density is about two per square mile on the average.

The Ovambo live within a well-watered, palm-dotted triangle of savannah 40 miles from Namibia's northern border with Angola. This is the only part of the territory that is at all heavily populated; it is also the only area with important potential for intensive agriculture, given present rainfall patterns. Theirs is also the part of the territory that historically has been neglected. Until the 1970s, when hostilities turned Ovamboland into a war zone, there were few roads, only limited forms of communication, hardly any sources of power, and a pervasive sense of isolation.

A Bantu-speaking, matrilineally organized people who have traditionally kept stock and grown subsistence crops, the Ovambo were until very recent times the least well integrated into Namibia of all the peoples of the territory. Their ethnic identity, which distinguished them from all but the Kavango; their physical isolation, their nonpastoral quality; and their total number (half of all Namibians are now Ovambo) kept them socially and economically separate from the rest of the country. Many Ovambo lived, as 100,000 or more still do, in Angola, and this factor may have added to the distinctiveness of the Ovambo.

In the early years few white administrators dealt with the Ovambo. Missionaries there were, but governmental disinterest contributed to the relative impoverishment of the Ovambo, and hence to an exodus of migrants to South Africa or to the towns of Windhoek and Walvis Bay. Since World War II, Ovambo have worked as contract laborers elsewhere in Namibia. Without their labor the machinery of industry, mining, and the ports could not have functioned. Their importance was demonstrated best in 1971 and 1972, when a strike by 73,000 Ovambo and Kavango paralyzed Windhoek and Walvis Bay. They demanded better working conditions, higher pay, and improvements to their contractual arrangements — all of which they received, after months on strike.

Because the Ovambo are by far the largest ethnic group within Namibia, and because the leadership of the South-West Africa People's Organization (SWAPO) — the territory's main nationalist group — is predominantly Ovambo, Ovambo are likely to play a major role in shaping the future of their country. Like the Kikuyu in Kenya, however, the Ovambo are less a cohesive polity than a loose congeries of linguistically and culturally associated subethnic groupings that have lived together under South African-imposed governmental arrangements but that, in the precolonial past, refused to acknowledge any single, all-tribal hierarchy. In the nineteenth and early twentieth centuries, conflict between the subethnic groups was common, arms being introduced into the area by one of the subethnic chiefs in order to settle disputes over water and grazing rights. Echoes of these antagonisms remain, as does a heritage of authoritarian rule that was common to each of the Ovambo subethnicities and that remained a feature of local Ovambo rule under the hegemony of South Africa.

The Ovambo comprise seven peoples. The Kwanyama straddle the northern Namibian border and are the largest, about a third of the total. Linguistically and culturally related to the Ovimbundu of Angola, they are proportionally underrepresented in the movements of modern nationalism in Namibia. The Ndonga, the other large Ovambo subethnicity, make up a second third of the total. More acculturated than the Kwanyama because of their greater exposure to the Finnish Lutheran and English Anglican missionaries, the Ndonga are well placed to play a significant role in any battle for political preeminence that may ultimately be fought among the Ovambo. The other five Ovambo peoples, the Njera, Kwambo, Kaluudhi, Mbalantu, and Kolonkadhi, are smaller in population and historically less influential. None controls exceptional natural resources, although the Kwanyama and the Ndonga would benefit the most from supplies of irrigation water from the Angolan-controlled Kunene River; each has a stake in the outcome of any competition over the spoils of victory. Thus, as any new government of Namibia attempts to draw the Ovambo closer to the peoples of the south and as it moves toward modernization and centralization, it may find the Ovambo politically less one people than a still loosely related amalgam capable under stress of demonstrating the fissiparous tendencies that have often been evident in Africa during post-independence struggles for power.

The remainder of the vast emptiness that is Namibia is populated by smaller groups of great cultural and racial diversity. The Herero, who number 65,000, rival the Ovambo for territorial primacy only by virtue of their heritage, their heroic stands against both the Nama and the Germans, and their intense involvement with modern South Africa. Although predominantly pastoralists who in recent years occupied eleven sections of a scattered homeland, the Herero early were influenced by German missionaries, who established stations among the Herero beginning in 1845. After their heavy losses to the Germans, the Herero turned to Christianity in large numbers and adopted many of the accoutrements of modernity. In the 1970s Herero held lower-level positions in the civil service, were active in commerce, and raised stock.

The other indigenous groups exerted less influence during the colonial and mandatory periods. The 85,000 Damara, thought to have descended from the earliest inhabitants of Namibia, now live northwest of Windhoek. Traditionally, they lived in a decentralized fashion and offered largely unskilled labor services to the Ovambo, the Herero, the Germans, and the Afrikaners when they arrived.

The Kavango live along the southern bank of the Okavango River, one of the most favored reaches of the territory. There they farm, fish, and hunt with success. They speak a Bantu language and are associated with the Ovambo as migrant laborers as well as in political contexts. The Subia and Mafwe peoples of the eastern Caprivi Strip, settled agriculturalists, are physically separated from the remainder of Namibia by an arm of the Kalahari Desert. They speak Silozi, a Sotho-influenced Bantu language used widely in western Zambia. Their wage-earning has usually been restricted to Caprivi, and they have not worked in large numbers in Namibia proper.

Several of the smaller population groups, the Nama (34,000), the Coloureds (30,000), and the Basters (20,000), have long sought to defend their claims of intermediate status as part-whites in the evolving context of a South African-controlled Namibia. The Nama, the collective designation of the various Khoi and Khoi-related groups that invaded Namibia from the south, raise stock in scattered settlements in the south and central sections of the country. The Coloureds, mainly immigrants from the Cape Province of South Africa, are active throughout Namibia (as in the Republic) in construction, in fishing, in schoolteaching, and in the civil service. Although Coloureds who lived in African areas carried passes until 1977, they could own land. The Baster community, defined according to the South African system of classification as Coloured because of their mixed origins on the Cape frontier, are almost exclusively raisers of cattle and sheep. They hold title to freehold farms and are, as a people, remarkably cohesive.

Namibia's population also include 26,000 San, 7,000 isolated herdsmen, called Kaokovelders, who live in the arid coastal northwest part of the territory, and 5,000 Tswana.

More numerous than any of the other non-Ovambo peoples are the whites of Namibia. They total about 100,000, but about half are South Africans working within Namibia for the government, for public services, or in business. The other 50,000 whites include 21,000 Germans, 12,000 of whom hold West German passports, and about 20,000 Afrikaans-speaking "Southwesters." The Germans, about two-thirds of whom raise sheep and cattle, have their own newspapers and their own culture; they have historically been less well integrated into South Africa's Namibia than have the Afrikaners. The English-speaking whites number about 10,000 and include as many missionaries as settlers.

Geopolitics

Namibia's ties to and future involvement with South Africa overshadow its links to Botswana and Angola, countries with which it shares long land borders, and to Zambia, with which the border is far shorter. By rail and air, Namibia has been tied to the well-developed South African transportation network. Since Walvis Bay remains a South African enclave, Namibia's main port is also controlled by its large neighbor. Sixty percent of Namibian exports and imports have, in any event, traditionally been destined for and come from South Africa; the most important are 90 percent of all beef exports and 70 percent of all wool. And South African Railways and Harbours controls all of the rolling stock. The postal, telephone, and telegraph systems have been run by South Africa.

The Infrastructure

In contrast, the electricity supply system is locally based. The generation of power along the northern borders of the territory, especially from the Kunene River, will provide a separate source of hydroelectricity for the nation. But the main dam, at the Ruacana Falls, lies within Angolan territory and its use has been and will continue to be a subject of negotiation between Angola and Namibia.

According to a 1969 agreement between South Africa and Portugal for the development of the Kunene's hydroelectric potential, South Africa agreed to finance the project in return for control over the dam and others that might be built (fourteen were projected). The total capacity of the first stage of the scheme, the Ruacana dam, was 240 megawatts; its cost was roughly $250 million. According to the original plans interrupted by the war in Angola, generation was to begin in 1977, and power was to be channeled south to the mines and towns of Namibia. Whenever the dam is allowed to be used to full capacity, the shortage of cheap power that has hindered the development of mining in Namibia should be eliminated. At present, power is generated by stations at Walvis Bay, Windhoek, and Tsumeb from coal imported from South Africa.

Because Namibia has for so long been treated as a fifth province of South Africa, it lacks even the rudimentary separate technical services or tradition of local individualism that characterized many poor African countries at the times of their independence. Until 1977, fundamental decisions were made in Pretoria, not Windhoek; personnel owed their loyalties to South Africa. However, the high quality and thorough coverage of the infrastructure (Namibia has the second-highest number of telephones per person in Africa in the cities and towns, for instance) holds out the hope—given a reasonably satisfactory transitional arrangement—that on independence Namibia will have the kind of efficient, well-run transportation and communications system that is essential for its modernization.

The expertise of the existing technical staff could be needed for some time. Africans help run the railways and the airways; the Ovambo, in particular, provide the muscle for the main port at Walvis Bay, but South African practices have limited their advancement into positions of responsibility. Under favorable circumstances, the handover of power from South Africa to Namibia will be accompanied by a fair division of South African Railways and Harbours staff and maintenance facilities (as well as rolling stock and aircraft); likewise, the staff of technical services like water resources management, and of the postal and telephone systems, will be divided and transferred. Such a base would make possible the kind of expansion needed to integrate Ovamboland and northern Namibia with the hitherto white-dominated plateau. Yet, under less than optimal circumstances, Namibia could find itself the inheritor of a splendid railway and one or more harbors, landing fields, airbases, hydroelectric transmission lines, and other technical facilities and resources, with but limited human means to run or maintain such a splendid gift. In this case, outside assistance would prove essential.

Namibia and Its Neighbors

Just as Namibia's present and future are inextricably intertwined with South Africa, its involvement with its other neighbors is a fact of the future far more than the present. With Zambia there would be virtually no dealings were it not for the accident of the Caprivi Strip and for the fact that SWAPO guerrillas based in Zambia used that terrain as a base for attacks upon South African control of Namibia and as a land route into Ovamboland and the central plateau. Until 1977 there were a dozen SWAPO bases in western Zambia; more recently, SWAPO militants were based in southern Angola.

With independence, given the underdeveloped quality of western Zambia and the isolation of the eastern Caprivi Strip from most of the economic activities of Namibia, relations between Namibia and Zambia could become unimportant to both countries at any level other than the macropolitical. However, at this level they ought to be important, and the presidents of both countries will doubtless maintain the support relations now common between Botswana and Zambia and others. As far as intrinsic national interest or economic involvement, however, interactions with Zambia will be important primarily to ethnic or other subgroups of the Namibian population. Only the Lozi-speaking peoples of the eastern Caprivi will retain, and possibly strengthen, their ties. If sensible border realignments were thinkable in Africa (which they generally are not), Namibia would probably wish to cede this area to Zambia.

San, Herero, and small groups of Tswana straddle the border between Botswana and Namibia, which is merely another colonial artifact. Nevertheless, with Botswana's independence and the general impoverishment of western Botswana, the border area has never developed strategic or significant economic importance. If Botswana constructs an east-west railway, about which there have been a number of discussions and some planning, and if copper and nickel deposits are exploited south of Lake Ngami in Botswana along the border, then the presently limited involvement between Botswana and Namibia could alter radically. If the railway is in fact constructed, Botswana will want to continue the tracks to Windhoek in order to link the existing line to Walvis Bay. Such a decision would give Zimbabwe its long-dreamed-of westward shortcut outlet to the Atlantic, and would also assist Zambia in solving its transportation problems. Without the railway, however, Botswana has too little common interest with Namibia for relations between them to be of more than diplomatic importance in the short term.

Angola and Namibia have much more in common. They share the hydroelectric potential of the Kunene River and the essentially unresolved problem of the Ruacana dam. Probably of equal significance is the fact that the Ovambo straddle the border and — at present — are among the peoples most antagonistic to the government in Angola. With independence Angola and Namibia may need to cooperate economically, whatever the politics of each.

The Mechanisms of South African Control

Until 1969, despite the protestations of the League of Nations and later the United Nations, South Africa maintained its mandatory control over Namibia. But it did so through a fictitiously separate administration of the territory. Although the whites of the territory, then numbering 27,000, gained autonomy for their own affairs and a legislative assembly of eighteen members in 1925, the South African-appointed administrator could veto legislation and retained legal control of all nonwhites. In 1949 the whites gained six seats in the South African House of Assembly. In the same year, many of the rights vested in the governor-general of South Africa (and of Namibia) were vested in the South African parliament. In 1954 "native affairs" were transferred completely away from South-West Africa and into the hands of the new South African minister of Bantu administration and development. Finally, in 1969, the South-West Africa Affairs Act abolished the autonomy of the South-West African legislative assembly and transferred its power to Pretoria.

That was the high-water mark of South African domestic imperialism. Subsequently, in response to pressure from the United Nations and in line with the South African government's gradual shift in the direction of pragmatism, the integration of South-West Africa into the Republic lessened and Africans began very slowly to regain a portion of their premandatory and precolonial rights, dignity, and self-esteem. The Development of Native Nations Act of 1968 authorized the creation of homelands and the transfer to them of enumerated powers of taxation, control over education, and welfare services.

From 1969 to 1979 the fundamental nature of South African control over the future of Namibia remained unchanged. Major decisions of consequence for the future of the territory were being made in Pretoria, not in Windhoek, where there was no significant autonomy, even for whites. Virtually none of the leading policymakers were South-West Africans. The important posts in the civil service not only were filled by whites but were filled by nonlocal whites whose first loyalty was to Pretoria, not Windhoek. (Africans — about 21,000 of 30,000 workers in the civil and teaching services — remained in the lower ranks; as late as 1978, none had reached the middle levels. There thus was a great administrative deficit on the black side.)[2]

Until 1977 even the towns of the territory, all of which have substantial black populations, were run by white Municipal Councils or Village Management Boards. Legislation passed in 1949 restricted the membership of these councils or boards to whites, and only whites were allowed to vote for their members. These boards and councils were in turn subordinate to the South African minister of local government. The separately administered company towns like Tsumeb and Oranjemund were run by the corporations concerned under the same ministry.

2. Wolfgang H. Thomas, *Economic Development in Namibia* (Munich, 1978), 205.

Education

In the 1970s Namibia had, for blacks, 10 secondary schools
that went to matriculation level and 291 primary schools that
went up to the secondary level. In 1977, 97 blacks successfully
passed the matriculation or graduation examination that marked
the completion of their high school educations. Of the total, only
2 were Ovambo. Expenditure per capita on education was R 63
for Africans, R 163 for Coloured, Nama, and Basters, and R 613
for whites. In the past many black secondary-school graduates
went on to train as teachers. Only a few continued on to universities, and in 1978 Namibia's 28 African graduates of universities
included one who had obtained a doctorate in politics at the University of Oxford. In 1978, 107 of Namibia's 112 physicians were
white, four were Baster, and one was African. Of Namibia's lawyers, three were black. Namibia will begin its independence with
the kind of educational deficit among blacks that created difficulties for Zaire, Zambia, and Botswana during their first years of
self-rule.

Justice

Justice for blacks in Namibia was administered in two forms
until 1977. In the north the chiefs and councils of headmen had
full civil and criminal jurisdiction in accord with tradition. The
indigenous jural system consisted of district courts, a tribal court,
and a court of appeal advised by a Bantu commissioner. Serious
crimes (murder, rape, and treason) were dealt with in the South
African courts. In the south Bantu Affairs commissioners' courts
held concurrent jurisdiction with the courts of magistrates; both
were run by whites and heard civil disputes in accord with black
custom and with the assistance of black assessors. Ultimately,
Roman-Dutch common law prevailed, as it did in South Africa.
This judicial feature may be significant in arranging the kinds of
external assistance that could become helpful after independence.

Armed Forces

Beginning in 1915, South African control over Namibia was
maintained by armed might. At the lowest level were the tribal

police, some of whom have been armed and trained by South Africa. A national police force operated in the white areas, and, as a result of SWAPO insurgency, a buildup of regular military troops in the north to a total of at least 25,000 began in 1966. In addition to air-force and army bases near Windhoek, Gobabis, Keetmanshoop, Grootfontein, Katima Mulilo, and Walvis Bay, bases were established along the Kunene River, near Ondangwa in Ovamboland, near Bwambwata along the Okavango River, and at Ohopoha in the Okaoko region.

The Administration of African Areas

In late 1976 the government altered its plans for the creation of independent black homelands, similar to Transkei, in Namibia. Until then Africans had political representational rights only through and in their homeland legislative bodies. The homelands conformed to the territorial bounds of the indigenous reserves as supplemented in the 1970s by comparatively large stretches of, for the most part, arid terrain. As a result of the report of a South African commission in 1964, the administration of South-West Africa began to grant measures of autonomy, leading to internal "self-government," to the indigenous peoples of the territory.

Ovamboland

The first to be granted the status of a homeland was Ovamboland, for which a legislative council was established in 1968. The council was initially composed of twenty-two tribal chiefs from the seven subethnic groups of the Ovambo and twenty commoners—following the South African homeland pattern first seen in the Transkei in 1963. An executive council, with one member from each Ovambo group, administered the homeland and elected a chief councillor. It created cabinetlike departments and received a variety of governmental functions as they were transferred from the administration of South-West Africa. In 1973 this devolution was sufficient for Ovamboland to become self-governing, as defined by South Africa. The legislative council was enlarged to fifty-six members: five chiefs from each of seven tribal authorities and three elected from each of the same ethnic divisions. The resulting council elected a chief minister who in turn appointed six cabinet ministers.

The elections of 1973 were the first test of popular opinion in indigenous Namibia. SWAPO and the Democratic Cooperative Party (DEMCOP) were not allowed to campaign, however; thus Chief Filemon Elifas's Ovambo Independence Party (OIP) was the only contending organization, and SWAPO and DEMCOP proclaimed a boycott. Only 2.5 percent of the Ovambo voted, and Elifas became chief minister.

The central government granted Ovamboland a new constitution in 1974; it provided for a legislative council of thirty-five appointed and forty-two elected members. South Africa agreed to permit SWAPO to campaign, but because of the continued existence of emergency regulations dating from 1966, SWAPO again urged a boycott. Elifas's government had meanwhile declared its intention to join with the 120,000 Ovambo in southern Angola to form an independent Ovambo nation. In early 1975, with a 55 percent voter turnout, the OIP again triumphed, and Elifas was reelected as chief minister despite the warnings of outside observers that the exclusive support of traditionalism (and the effective intimidation of voters by SWAPO and DEMCOP organizers in the weeks preceding the election) would prove a source of future instability. During the next few months, assisted by an embryonic local civil service largely made up of white South Africans, Elifas acted more and more autocratically—in the manner of Ovambo chiefs—and tried to eliminate the power of SWAPO within the homeland by means of imprisonment and floggings. He also continued to make preparations for a separate Ovamboland. In August 1975, Elifas was killed by bullets from a passing car, presumably on the orders of SWAPO. He was succeeded by Cornelius Ndjoba, a Lutheran pastor.

Kavangoland

The second self-governing homeland—that of the Kavango—was established in an analogous fashion. After the official recognition of five tribal authorities (the subethnic groups of Kavangoland) in 1970, a legislative council and an executive committee were established. Chief Linus Shashipoppo became chief executive councillor. In 1973 Kavango was given "self-government," with a capital at Rundu and a legislative council consisting of fifteen chiefs (chiefs of the five tribes and two members nominated by each of the five tribal authorities) and fifteen commoners, three elected from each tribe. The executive council was composed of five ministers elected from each of the five tribal caucuses within the legislative council; its members elected a chief minister.

In contrast to Ovamboland, politics in Kavango was still in its infancy in 1977. In the local election of 1973, 66 percent of all eligible Kavango went to the polls. There were no political parties, and a commoner, Alfons Majavero, emerged as chief minister. He continued to reject the notions of internal independence espoused by Elifas. At the same time, the Kavango agreed in 1976, like the Transkei, to develop a local defense force — a small army. Majavero, along with other homeland leaders in Namibia and South Africa, depended for technical assistance, parliamentary direction, and budgetary aid on the territorial government and ultimately on the government of South Africa.

Other Areas

In the eastern Caprivi, at Ngweze near Katima Mulilo, the two dominant Lozi-speaking peoples of the area were amalgamated in 1972 into a nonself-governing territorial authority with a twenty-eight-member appointed assembly, a small executive council, and a chief councillor — Chief Josiah Malba Moraliswani. Four (later six) departments were created to be run, in effect, by white officials transferred from South-West Africa and the Republic. In 1975 this region was elevated to the status of a self-governing homeland with the same arrangements as Ovambo and Kavango. In addition to the chiefs, twelve members of the legislative council were elected. Chief Richard Mamili, a Mafwe, became chief minister.

The other indigenous peoples of Namibia had more traditional forms of home rule. The Damara, lacking historically legitimated chiefs and notions of Damara hierarchy, hardly advanced beyond ward councils. There were eleven within the Damara homeland; together these eleven headmen formed the Damara Advisory Council under Senior Headman Justus Garoeb, also the president of the Namibia National Front. The advisory council had influence but no governmental authority. The advisory council, however, often expressed itself truculently against racial discrimination and in favor of United Nations supervision. It was abolished in 1975 and was replaced in 1977 by the South African-sponsored Damara Representative Authority, a homeland-type regional government, which has been ignored by most Damara. Indeed, the advisory council, which since 1975 has been called the Damara Council, continued to function unofficially.

Within the nascent Nama leadership, hitherto of eight headmen without an advisory council, there was a struggle for primacy in 1975. Three of the headmen supported SWAPO and refused to accept any kind of ethnically based arrangement. The other five disagreed and, in mid-1975, the central government created a Nama advisory council, subordinate tribal authorities, and a variety of village management boards. The council consisted of all chiefs or headmen of the tribal authorities, a chairman chosen by them, and six councillors appointed by the South African Minister of Coloured Affairs.

The Basters of Rehoboth have long enjoyed a form of self-rule. Since 1928 there has been an advisory council of seven members elected according to the Basters' own notions of patriarchal respect and affiliation. This council traditionally espoused home rule within a multiracial Namibia. Such separatist sentiment led to a political split in 1975, however, when five of seven councillors publicly supported SWAPO. In 1976 a Kaptein's Council was created. The first election was won by a pro-South African alliance led by Dr. Ben Africa; the second (in 1979), by Hans Diergaardt, who opposed South African influence in Namibia.

The Coloureds have had an advisory council since 1961. It was first composed of six elected members and five government appointees under Chairman A. J. F. Kloppers. In the elections of 1974 the Federal Coloured People's party, led by Kloppers, won three seats; the Southern Group, led by Charles Hartung, won two; and an independent was elected to the sixth seat. In 1978, however, Kloppers lost control to L. J. Barnes.

Like the Nama council, the activities of the Coloured council, and therefore the activities of the Coloureds and Nama themselves, were supervised until 1977 by the South African minister of Coloured affairs. The Basters, however, refused to be guided by a ministry of Coloured affairs; a separate Ministry of Rehoboth Affairs and a Rehoboth Investment and Development Corporation were formed in 1973.

Not until 1975 did the people of Kaokoland fall under the homeland rubric devised by the central government. In that year, the territory of the former reserve was divided into twenty-eight wards, each with a headman and a council.

In Hereroland, despite its relative modernization and its people's long tradition of following Western models, the homeland model was not accepted. From 1975 to 1977 there were two community authorities and seven headmen functioning with traditional councils, as before. Until his assassination in 1977, the unquestioned leader of the Herero was Paramount Chief Clemens Kapuuo. A teacher turned storekeeper, Kapuuo was born in 1923 in the Okahandja district. Educated locally by Anglicans, he trained to be a teacher in Johannesburg. Later he was president of the South-West Africa Teachers' Association from 1950 through 1953, served as a member of the Herero Chief's Council, and interpreted for Chief Hosea Kutako, one of the first Namibian petitioners at the United Nations. Kapuuo, whose opposition to South African dominance of the territory was widely known as early as 1955, became paramount chief after Kutako's death in 1970. In the 1950s and 1960s he supported the efforts of exiled nationalists, but in the 1970s he grew critical of them, and began cooperating with South Africa.

In general, indigenous personnel gained a significant measure of administrative experience only in the Ovambo and Kavango homelands. In those areas, whites controlled most of the day-to-day administrative decisions, as distinct from policy making. Three of the peoples were directly administered by a Coloured affairs bureaucracy; the others were overseen or advised by personnel seconded by South African departments or those in Windhoek. This was the practice in the South African homelands, too, where all of the major subcabinet positions were in white hands. There was too little time for local Africans to gain experience, and the qualifications required in both the Republic of South Africa and South-West Africa served as a barrier against African advancement, thus limiting promotion into the higher administrative grades. Politics in the homelands was left far more in black hands than was administration; technical services were predominantly run by South African whites. For example, the Department of Water Affairs, so critical to the future of Namibia, was an exclusively white service — even in the home- lands.

Preparing for the Transfer of Power

The homelands provided a conceptual base for the constitu- tional deliberations that later took their name from a converted German assembly hall, the Turnhalle, in Windhoek. There an exercise in the elaboration of ethnic politics was developed from late 1975 through early 1977. Under the aegis of South Africa, the eleven ethnic groups of the territory — both those with ac- knowledged homeland administrations and those without — met together in massive plenary sessions and in smaller meetings of the three principal delegates from each ethnic group for weeks at a time throughout the three years.

The object of the exercise was a formula — a new constitu- tion — that would permit the devolution of power by South Africa to a newly constituted government elected by the eleven ethnic groups. In the discussions — which proceeded by consensus only — each ethnic group had equal weight. Thus the three Tswana, representing a mere 5,000 people, theoretically had a say equal to that of the representatives of the 100,000 whites and the 500,000 Ovambo. In discussions, however, the whites (led for much of the time by Dirk Mudge), the Herero (led by Kapuuo), the Ovambo (led by Ndjoba), and the Basters (led by Dr. Ben Africa), emerged as the groups of major political influence. Mudge had South Afri- can backing and was the most farsighted of the whites. He en- couraged concessions aimed at giving the black and brown popu- lations more meaningful stakes in the new Namibia. For much of the time, he had to drag his unwilling white colleagues, and sometimes South Africa, into compromise. He also played a ma- jor role in keeping the black and brown delegates focused upon long-term rather than short-term objectives.

Except for Mudge, the whites wanted a new government that would appear to represent all racial groups but that would effectively be run by whites, with strong long-term ties to South Africa. The other groups wanted an effective and broadly representative multiracial government. The arguments were detailed and tortuous, and progress was at first slow. Later, as the administration of President Jimmy Carter took charge in the United States and external pressure intensified, the Turnhalle meetings made more progress. South Africa's growing flexibility encouraged such progress. So did Mudge's determination and persistence about the possibility of merging white and nonwhite interests for the good of Namibia.

Ultimately the Turnhalle delegates agreed upon a complicated formula that, for a time, was meant to provide the basis for a transfer of power in Namibia by the end of 1978. After a final, formal session in late 1976, the delegates were persuaded to adopt a constitution calling for three tiers of government. At the first level, local governments would be elected by their own ethnic groups. So, in effect, would regional governments, the second level. At the third level, a national government would be selected by the regional governments and would be responsible for defense, foreign affairs, finance, and similar matters. Education, health, agriculture, and other functions closer to individual communities would be the responsibility of the regional tier. The regions, furthermore, were to correspond to ethnic territories as of 1976; that is, whites would remain sovereign in the bulk of the country. Homelands would continue to exist and would be called regions.

The central government was intended to be run by an executive president, who would be advised by a ministers' council chosen by the territorial National Assembly. This council was to be composed of one minister from each ethnic group and a chairman; its decisions would be made by consensus, thus permitting ethnic vetoes. The National Assembly, in turn, was to be composed of members elected by the individual ethnic groups voting separately. After some hard bargaining in the Turnhalle the Ovambo were given twelve of its sixty members; the whites, six;

and all others, five. On a straight demographic basis, the Ovambo should have received thirty.

These policies had the advantage of administrative tidiness. They were also designed to perpetuate white control over the kinds of governmental functions that most affected whites. Housing, educational and medical segregation would, in effect, continue. Moreover, because voting for the central government would be based on ethnic parity, the whites would have much more say about Namibia overall than they could be expected to have under a "one man, one vote" constitution. The objects were clear: to limit the impact of the larger numbers of the Ovambo and other northern peoples and to match the peoples of the south against the numerically superior northerners. The southerners were expected to be more closely allied in their interests to the whites. (At one point Mudge and others even talked about a central government with two parliaments—one for the north and one for the south—with legislation requiring agreement between the two for enactment.)

In February 1977, the Turnhalle conference completed its deliberations by formally approving the proposals that had, in effect, been accepted the previous December. The stage was set for a South African-sponsored transfer of power by means of an ethnic-based election and a subsequent request for independence from an interim, multiracial government in which the local whites, led by Mudge, would presumably have a major say. Such an arrangement, however, would not automatically have attracted international approval. Quite the reverse, Nor could it have ended the border war in which SWAPO guerrillas regularly attacked South African forces from Zambia and Angola or eliminated the threat of Cuban and Soviet involvement on the side of SWAPO. The Turnhalle solution thus proved of only transitional value. Although it might have been realizable in full a decade before, in the 1970s it did not provide a meaningful way of setting Namibia on the road to an independence that needed to be both internationally acceptable and peaceful.

8 | Achieving the New Nation

T HE FIRST GOVERNMENT of a new Namibia will benefit from the unusual process of decolonization that, since mid-1977, has, with unexpected swiftness, given prior South African obstinacy, brought the territory to the edge of or at least the contemplation of independence. During the thirty-one years before 1977, South Africa steadfastly refused to acknowledge that its administrative authority had lapsed with the demise of the League of Nations and that it had passed, in the eyes of most other countries, to the United Nations. South Africa rejected the authority of the Trusteeship Council. It fought a running, ultimately acrimonious, and juridically complex battle to prevent the United Nations from diminishing its hegemony over Namibia. In 1976 the United Nations established a special Council for Namibia as a formal administrative authority in exile. The existence of the council, however, and every resolution pertaining to Namibia passed by the General Assembly or the Security Council have been ignored by South Africa.

Long before 1969, Namibia, as South-West Africa, had become a de facto fifth province of South Africa. Following the National Party electoral victory of 1948, as noted in an earlier chapter, Namibia was absorbed more and more closely into the Union (later the Republic) of South Africa. Whites living in Namibia elected representatives to both houses of the South African parliament. Laws made in Pretoria were applied automatically to South-West Africa. Even Walvis Bay was integrated into the fifth province. By 1970 no separate administration even sat in Windhoek; instead, the supposed province was run departmentally from Pretoria.

Negotiating the Future

The collapse of Portuguese power in Africa in 1974 signaled the need to rethink South African strategy for Namibia. The Turnhalle meetings were an initial response. A second was the journey of Secretary of State Henry Kissinger to southern Africa in 1976; during this visit American concern for the future of Namibia was made known to the government of South Africa, virtually for the first time. But it was the victory of Jimmy Carter in the presidential election and the movement of a new group of Africa-oriented foreign-affairs specialists into positions of influence that translated this concern into determination. Kissinger was prepared to respond sympathetically to South Africa's internal dilemmas if it in turn were willing to assist in promoting the devolution of power in Rhodesia and Namibia. Vice President Walter Mondale, United Nations Ambassador Andrew Young, and, notably and effectively, Ambassador Donald McHenry, then Young's deputy, went farther. They demanded the end of South Africa's attempt to pass power to the ethnically based, white-controlled government negotiated by the delegates to the Turnhalle.

Many perceptive South Africans had already realized that the exercise in cooptation set in motion by the Turnhalle agreement would not necessarily resolve the riddle of South-West Africa satisfactorily. General Hendrik van den Bergh, director of the Bureau of State Security and a principal advisor to Prime Minister B. Johannes Vorster, Foreign Minister Roelof F. Botha, and other members of the cabinet had come to appreciate that it was profoundly in the self-interest of South Africa to transfer power in Namibia only in such a way as to attract international acceptance. Creating a second Transkei would hardly count as a permanent solution. Retaining control intransigently would be certain to encourage continued international animosity. Although SWAPO's guerrilla forces could probably be contained indefinitely by the far superior military capability of South Africa, continued hostilities might result in the direct participation of the Soviet Union and Cuba and the kinds of escalated combat that conceivably could contribute to added tension and conflagration within South Africa's cities. It was far wiser to purchase time for internal readjustment by selling peripheral space, particularly the kind of space to which South Africa had no indisputable claim and for which it had no overriding need. From a military point of view, too, shorter perimeters were easier to defend, even if closer. Many argued that new black governments characteristically were weak regionally and tended to be concerned primarily with strengthening their own internal control; such a government in Namibia would be unlikely to sponsor adventuresome aggression on the part of anti-South African guerrillas. South Africa could also gain credit with the West, whatever Young and McHenry might say in private, if South Africa cooperated on the issue of Namibia (and Rhodesia). Of the two, Namibia provided the better opportunity, for there South Africa — not a local white electorate — had control, and the white population numbered less than half, in absolute terms, of the Rhodesian total. There were also only half as many Afrikaners in Namibia as in Rhodesia.

For these reasons, as well as because of his own calculation of South African self-interest, Vorster met in May 1977 with McHenry and representatives of Germany, Canada, Britain, and France (collectively known as the Contact Group), abruptly annulled the Turnhalle agreement, halted the momentum toward a simply conceived home rule, and acknowledged the standing of the United Nations with regard to the future of Namibia. This was a major breakthrough; South Africa was at last prepared to negotiate. It made no promises, and for another year Vorster threatened to continue with the internal solution while bargaining briskly and sharply with McHenry and his colleagues. South Africa seemed to be hoping throughout 1977 and 1978 that it could somehow persuade the Contact Group and the United Nations to accept or otherwise validate a Turnhalle-like solution. South Africa's troops also kept up their military assault on SWAPO.

Whether out of self-interest, realism, fear, or duplicity, in April 1978, South Africa finally agreed to the then final version of the Western plan. SWAPO had tried hard to avoid commitment and had frequently raised new obstacles, but never had any other viable option; finally, in July 1978, it rewarded the Contact Group with an agreement to the same plan that had been accepted by South Africa. Despite accusations of bad faith, SWAPO's frequent unwillingness to negotiate, the antagonism of the Soviet Union, and the opposition within South Africa of Pieter W. Botha, then the minister of defense, a calculated preemptive strike by South Africa against a SWAPO base in Angola in May, and hot and heavy propaganda on all sides, an agreement was nonetheless signed and later accepted by the United Nations.

The plan had a number of controversial components. South Africa was to reduce its armed forces on Namibian soil to 1,500 six weeks before the first internationally supervised election. SWAPO wanted them to be based in the far south. McHenry never accepted this argument; the troops were permitted to be stationed in the north at two South African bases. South Africa was to retain control of the police forces in the territory. Together with the administrator-general whom South Africa had appointed in 1977 to run Namibia, a representative of the secretary-general of the United Nations was to organize, supervise, and control territory-wide elections for a constituent assembly (leading to an independent local assembly). The special representative was to be assisted in his functions by 2,000 civilians and 7,500 troops recruited by the United Nations. (In the negotiations leading up to these mid-1978 agreements, the juridical anomaly of Walvis Bay was deferred until after independence.)

Judge Marthinus T. Steyn had been appointed administrator-general immediately after Vorster's dramatic shift of policy in May 1977. Yet even the selection of an individual such as Steyn was a breach of McHenry's private understanding with R. F. Botha and Vorster. Steyn, a judge in the Orange Free State, was empowered to run Namibia without the need to consult any body other than the government of South Africa. This was a mandate that he accepted enthusiastically; the happy combination of his initial instructions and an effective personal approach rapidly transformed Namibia from a province into the beginnings of a nation. By mid-1978 he had repealed most discriminatory legislation and had taken under his aegis all of the departments hitherto directed from Pretoria (except the police, defense, and foreign affairs). In most areas he also replaced the South African parliament as the legislative authority for Namibia. In the process he demonstrated his independence from local whites, promoted social change favorable to blacks, and spoke earnestly of the need to prepare all of Namibia socially and economically, as well as politically, for ultimate independence and integration. At times, however, his hand was as heavy as those of previous South African administrators. In 1978, and again throughout much of 1979, he detained most of the leaders of SWAPO's Namibian wing without trial for months. He deported whites who were alleged to be friendly to SWAPO and therefore presumed to be security risks. Throughout 1978 and the first half of 1979, Steyn showed as much determination to maintain order as to promote meaningful social change.

The Liberation Movement

The Byzantine origins of nationalism in Namibia are of less importance today than the extent to which the animosities of those early years suggest the ethnic and sectional conflict that might emerge with the assumption of control by a transitional and then an independent black government.

The charge that SWAPO is no more than an Ovambo organization reflects its beginnings, the backgrounds of some but not all of its leaders, and the numerical superiority of Ovambo within SWAPO outside Namibia, especially among the guerrillas; it also reflects the antagonism of the Herero and the other less populous black groups of the territory toward Ovambo and their natural fear of Ovambo domination. But this charge is also an inescapable result of the sheer mass of Ovambo within Namibia now and in the future. Since more than half of all blacks and Coloureds are Ovambo, and since for geographical reasons it has always been easier to recruit guerrillas from the Ovambo than from other groups, it would be extraordinary if Namibia's main nationalist organization were not closely allied to the ethnic group that dominates Namibia. Further, the charge must also reflect to some important degree the animosity and distrust instinctively felt by traditional rulers who have stayed home and worked for reform within the South African-dominated system toward exiles who have chosen the path of violence and who espouse the kind of rapid change that cannot help but be anathema to any indigenous ruling class.

In the 1970s the Ovambo have been in the vanguard of organized protest against the rule of Namibia by outsiders. But the Herero bore the brunt of militant anticolonial activity against the Germans, and southerners opposed South Africa during the early years of the mandate. Otherwise, anti-South African political activity was limited within the territory until the Trusteeship Council of the United Nations attempted to assume supervision of Namibia.

At first, in the late 1940s and throughout the 1950s, Namibians and their white allies presented petitions to the United Nations in forlorn attempts to prevent the rapid administrative integration of Namibia into South Africa as a fifth province. This effort elicited a healthy cooperation between younger and older, more traditionally oriented, opponents of South African control. In Tanganyika (now Tanzania) during the same years, petitioners before the Trusteeship Council included chiefs and educated commoners; similarly, an Anglican missionary, South African-educated university graduates, and aged, mostly Herero, chiefs were the initial petitioners for Namibia. In part this alliance drew, for a time, on the energies of the South-West Africa Student Body, formed at Fort Hare University College in South Africa by Namibians who were close to that country's African National Congress and its Youth League. Later, in 1955, this student organization became the South-West African Progressive Association under the leadership of Jariretundu Kozonguizi, a Herero student at Fort Hare. Kozonguizi, born in 1932, was the son of a farm laborer; he attended primary school in Windhoek and then was sent by his brother to South Africa. There he was employed by the Department of Native Affairs, attended a Dutch Reformed Church high school in the Transvaal, and went on to Fort Hare, where he graduated with a bachelor's degree in 1956. He obtained a Diploma in Education from Fort Hare in 1958 and much later received legal training and opened a practice in Britain.

In the mid-1950s the Progressive Association had effectively joined the Reverend Michael Scott in his pro-Namibian petitioning activities at the United Nations. Kozonguizi had designated Mburumba Kerina (formerly Eric Getzen), a part-Herero student at Lincoln University in Pennsylvania, as the association's petitioner. The Herero, under Paramount Chief Hosea Kutako, and the Nama under their Kaptein S. H. Witbooi, were also active in sending petitions to New York. By the late 1950s, however, when large numbers of petitions were being submitted from throughout the territory, it was clear that the United Nations was powerless to alter the direction of South African policy. For this reason, as much as because of the growing political frustration and agitation within South Africa itself, Namibians began to create political movements to carry forward their struggle with South Africa.

The Ovambo People's Organization

In the late 1950s a number of politicized Namibians were living and working in Cape Town. The foremost was Herman Toivo ja Toivo, an Ndonga born about 1924 and educated by Finnish Lutherans, who had served loyally in the South African Native Military Corps during World War II. After the war he resumed his profession as a schoolteacher; worked briefly as a railway policeman, a clerk at a manganese mine, and a gold miner; and then moved to Cape Town, where he found employment in a furniture factory in nearby Woodstock.

Another was Andreas Shipanga, also an Ndonga. Trained at the Finnish Lutheran mission school in Ondongwa and its teacher-training institution in nearby Onipa, he taught primary school in Ondongwa, the principal town in Ovamboland, from 1951 to 1954. In that year he traveled north through Angola to Lobito, where he found work as a clerk. In 1955 Shipanga began a long journey through the copperbelts of Zaire and Northern Rhodesia (now Zambia) to Bulawayo, in Southern Rhodesia (now Zimbabwe), where he was employed as a clerk through 1956. In Bulawayo he was in contact with Joshua Nkomo, George Nyandoro, and James Chikerema, three of the leading political figures of the colony. He then traveled to Johannesburg and tried underground mine work, but, disliking it, he found a job in a mill in Randfontein before going to Cape Town. There, from 1957, he passed as a Coloured, using an assumed name, and thus found employment more in keeping with his aspirations. Shipanga was a member of the crew of a deep-sea trawler for a short time and later worked as a clerk in an insurance company. Politically, he had matured. In 1957 he promoted the Ovambo People's Congress, which was never formally organized, however, for fear of attracting the attention of the South African security police.

In 1958, with Toivo and Solomon Mifima, a Kwanyama, Shipanga established the Ovambo People's Organization (OPO). It was opposed to the contract (migratory) labor that had already helped undermine Ovambo family life. OPO was antagonistic to South African control but, at these initial stages, did not support immediate independence for a territory not yet called Namibia. (Other early members of OPO were Emil Apollus, a Nama who was then at Athlone High School; Kozonguizi; and Isaac Newton, a Coloured worker in Cape Town.)

Toivo had meanwhile sent a tape-recorded petition to the United Nations, an action that resulted in his prompt deportation, in late 1958, to Namibia. There he and others attempted to mobilize support for OPO. He spoke on its behalf in Windhoek and then, on his way home to Ovamboland, was detained in Tsumeb. Until 1961 Toivo was confined to his house in the Ndonga district. In 1966 he was arrested and tried under South Africa's security laws, being sentenced in 1968 to twenty years on Robben Island.

Kozonguizi had accompanied Toivo home. After Toivo's detention, he and a number of fellow Herero, particularly Chief Clemens Kapuuo, Uatja Kautuetu, and Jacob Kuhangua, formed the South-West African National Union (SWANU), Namibia's first truly territory-wide political body. Later in the year it expanded from its narrow Herero base to include Nama and Damara leaders and Ovambo, notably Sam Nujoma, an Njera.

Nujoma was also trained by the Finnish missionaries. The son of a farm worker who lived in Ongandjera, the capital of the Njera district of Ovamboland, Nujoma left school early to live with relatives in Walvis Bay during World War II. In 1949 he moved to Windhoek, where he learned English from Anglican missionaries. Until 1957 he worked for the South African Railways. First as a sweeper and then as a junior clerk, he saw service throughout the territory. Subsequently, he was employed as a clerk in the offices of the Windhoek municipality and as a clerk in a wholesale store. His political awakening took place about this time, and in a multiethnic, not strictly Ovambo, setting.

SWANU's first major initiative, late in 1959, was the organization of a mass protest against the forced removal of black and brown Namibians from a residential township within Windhoek (the Windhoek Old Location) to the new town of Katutura on the outskirts of the capital. The campaign, in which Nujoma played a major role, included a boycott of public buses, movie theaters, and beer halls, as well as demonstrations. In a notorious clash with the police, eleven Namibians were killed, buildings were set on fire, and Namibia came dramatically to the attention of the world press.

SWANU was also active internationally from early 1960. Under Kozonguizi, its president until 1966, who left South-West Africa after the Katutura troubles, SWANU opposed South African rule of Namibia from its offices in Cairo, Dar es Salaam, Accra, London, New York, and, eventually, Stockholm. SWANU was closely tied during the early 1960s to the exile politics of post-Sharpeville South Africans and was aligned with the African National Congress (ANC). SWANU was widely assumed to be linked increasingly strongly to communism because of its membership (until 1967) in the Afro-Asian People's Solidarity Organization and its recognition by the Organization of African Unity. That recognition was, however, rescinded in 1968. Kozonguizi also began visiting Peking in the early 1960s and made known his antagonism to the West. SWANU was unable, despite its strength outside the territory, to mount an effective guerrilla campaign against Namibia. By the 1970s, it maintained several offices overseas but had otherwise emerged primarily as an active, if small, political party within Namibia. By 1975, as a Herero organization, SWANU was allied with several smaller political groups in the Namibia National Front against both the Turnhalle initiative and SWAPO.

The South-West Africa People's Organization

Neither Toivo's arrest nor the formation of SWANU had halted the growth in Ovambo political consciousness and the process of political mobilization. The alliance between Nujoma, representing OPO, and SWANU was uneasy during those few months at the end of 1959 and early in 1960 when Africans were opposing the razing of the Windhoek Old Location. After Nujoma went to the United Nations in 1960 to present a petition, ties between OPO and SWANU effectively ceased. At the same time, Kerina, who was representing OPO at the United Nations, was struggling for primacy with Kozonguizi on the international circuit. Their rivalry led to the transformation of OPO into the South-West Africa People's Organization (SWAPO) in mid-1960. Nujoma joined Kerina in this effort when he arrived in New York. The shift in name was clearly essential if their efforts were not to be derided as merely tribal. At first, the panethnic pretensions of SWAPO were bolstered by support from the Herero Chief's Council, which feared the radical tendencies of SWANU, especially after Kozonguizi was received in China.

Nujoma assumed control of SWAPO in 1962, after arranging Kerina's expulsion. In that year, and again in 1964, Nujoma and Kozonguizi tried to merge their two organizations, but personal and ethnic antagonisms prevented any meaningful compromise on the status of the leaders or the approach of the parties. Moreover, from about 1964, the Soviet Union began to take an interest in SWAPO thanks to Kozonguizi's flirtations with China. The Soviet involvement, at first very tentative, was stimulated by SWAPO's growing realization that Namibia would never be liberated by petition. Young Namibians were recruited for training as early as 1962 and more intensively up to and after the first attacks on Namibia were launched in 1966. Yet SWAPO was recognized as the authentic liberation group for Namibia by the Organization of African Unity only in 1968 and by the United Nations only in 1973.

Shipanga had remained in Cape Town, where he had joined a Maoist study group that included members of the Congress of Democrats, a South African clandestine political body. In early 1963, he returned to Namibia to work for SWAPO. Later that year, when the Coloured members of the study group were apprehended in Cape Town, Shipanga escaped into neighboring Botswana (then the British Protectorate of Bechuanaland), where the South African police pursued and ambushed him on the lonely road from Ghanzi to Lobatse. Returned illegally to Namibia, he spent twenty days in jail before being released through the legal pleading of a white Namibian lawyer and the intervention of British diplomats. By October 1963, Shipanga was in Dar es Salaam, where he rejoined SWAPO; he became its representative in Cairo until 1969, then served as its information secretary and the third-ranking SWAPO leader.

From 1966 to 1979, first with Algerian and Soviet and more recently with Soviet and Cuban assistance, SWAPO attempted to infiltrate small groups of trained guerrillas from Zambia into the Caprivi Strip and thence into the main part of Namibia, and from Angola directly across the border into Ovamboland. Its successes were intermittent; they were for the most part limited by numbers (SWAPO forces were estimated in 1978 to number between 3,000 and 5,000), training, weapons, and the extent and effectiveness of South African surveillance, intelligence, and firepower (South African troops numbered 25,000 in the same year). Nujoma and a military commission have guided and coordinated the attack.

The military directorate has had its political counterpart in the SWAPO national executive and central committee, both of which nominally operate under the guidance of a national congress. However, SWAPO stopped calling congresses after 1969. In the 1970s Nujoma controlled the sixteen-member national executive and the thirty-five-member central committee. Decisions were made by him and his close associates.

SWAPO's organization within Namibia took its policy direction during the 1970s from Nujoma and the executive in Lusaka.

But, for practical reasons, it also had to function somewhat more autonomously within the territory than such external direction would imply. Sometimes there were differences of emphasis, based on local factors, but no attempt was ever made to secede from SWAPO or to devise a separate negotiating or military strategy for the liberation of Namibia. Yet many of the leaders of the internal wing, like many of the SWAPO representatives abroad, have been non-Ovambo.

Nujoma began receiving steady Soviet support in 1970. Since then his hold on SWAPO has been challenged only once, unsuccessfully. In 1976, after months of grumbling in guerrilla camps in Zambia by new, youthful recruits from inside Namibia, Shipanga became the focus of an anti-Nujoma movement. The young guerrillas complained of the inefficiency and corruption of the military and political leadership of SWAPO. The charges of corruption were supported by detailed lists of arms, ammunition, and medical supplies that Shipanga and the guerrillas alleged had been appropriated by local commanders responsible to Nujoma. Shipanga said that this materiel had been sold for private gain. As a result, the war could not be prosecuted properly, nor could the wounded receive adequate medical attention. Shipanga and the guerrillas argued that a national congress would have to be held to discuss the question of SWAPO's leadership in accord with a constitutional provision requiring such a meeting every four years.

Whatever the merits of the charges, Nujoma and the Zambian police arrested Shipanga in April 1976, along with nine other senior SWAPO leaders and nearly a thousand disaffected recruits. In 1977 Shipanga and the other nine were flown secretly to Tanzania (with official cooperation from Zambia and Tanzania) on the eve of a habeas corpus hearing in the High Court of Zambia. Shipanga was held in close confinement in the Dodoma Central Prison in Tanzania; he was released only in mid-1978, along with the other nine prisoners. By then his thousand supporters had been freed from detention and dispersed to remote refugee camps in Zambia.

In mid-1978 SWAPO was the only Namibian political body or nationalist organization recognized by the United Nations or the Organization of African Unity. With the ouster of Shipanga, Nujoma reigned supreme. Within Namibia, Daniel Tjongarero, a Herero, and Mokganedi Thlabanello, an Ovambo, were in the vanguard, but they acknowledged their subservience to Nujoma. SWAPO Vice President Mishek Muyongo, a Caprivian, and internationally well-known figures like Peter Katjavivi, a Herero, followed Nujoma's lead.

SWAPO's Political Opponents

In addition to the Turnhalle delegates, who had formed themselves into the Democratic Turnhalle Alliance (DTA) under Dirk Mudge and Kapuuo, the other main political group in Namibia in 1978 was the Namibia National Front (NNF); this was an amalgam of SWANU, the Federal party, and the Damara Council. SWANU in the 1970s had come to be based in Windhoek and was no longer Marxist; it had a distinct Herero orientation. The Federal party, led by Bryan O'Linn and John Kirkpatrick, was the tiny remains of a quasi-liberal white group from a decade before. The Damara Council, led by Justus Garoeb, was the largest political group among the Damara. Individually and as a collective, the constituent groups and the NNF were opposed to South African control of Namibia, contemptuous of the ethnic politics of the Turnhalle, and anxious about the radical economic and social policies of SWAPO. The NNF represented a middle force, but a middle force prepared to compromise and cooperate with SWAPO.

After his release from prison and a few weeks in London, Shipanga returned to Namibia and established SWAPO-Democrats, a new party. He allied it with the NNF but maintained separate offices and a separate identity. Its policies were very similar to those of the NNF; it was anti-SWAPO but equally antagonistic to South Africa and South African clients within Namibia.

Despite Shipanga's secure ethnic base among the Ndonga, and despite the qualities of men like Garoeb, Cornelius Ndjoba, and Tjongarero, by 1978 Namibian nationalism had produced only one figure who could match or surpass Nujoma's claims to leadership. Of all Namibians, only Toivo ja Toivo rivaled him in popular imagination; only he was said to possess the charisma that Nujoma may lack. Toivo, a man of religion, had a large following among the Lutherans of Namibia. Above all, as an Ndonga, Toivo automatically possessed a far broader constituency among Ovambo than did Nujoma, an Njera.

Toivo ja Toivo

Toivo is known mostly by reputation. His stature is large in hearsay and has been accentuated by the long years on Robben Island. This is natural, and it is likely that his devotion to authentic nationalism has been strengthened by the experience. Persons who have recently emerged from the prison, or have talked with others who have seen him, report his continued dedication to the cause of Namibian independence. Information on his views is derived almost exclusively, however, from his remarkable speech from the dock after being convicted of terrorism in 1968. On that last appearance in public he questioned the very basis of South African authority in Namibia:

> We find ourselves here in a foreign country, convicted under laws made by people whom we have always considered as foreigners. We find ourselves tried by a Judge who is not our countryman and who has not shared our background . . .
>
> You, my Lord, decided that you had the right to try us, because your Parliament gave you that right. That ruling has not and could not have changed our feelings. We are Namibians and not South Africans. We do not now, and will not in the future recognise your right to govern us; to make laws for us in which we had no say; to treat our country as if it were your property and as if you were our masters. We have always regarded South Africa as an intruder in our country. This is how we have always felt and this is how we feel now, and it is on this basis that we have faced this trial.
>
> I speak of "we" because I am trying to speak not only for myself, but for others as well, and especially for those of my fellow accused who have not had the benefit of any education . . . The South African Government has again shown its strength by detaining us for as long as it pleased; keeping some of us in solitary confinement for 300 to 400 days . . . It has shown its strength by passing an Act [The Terrorism Act of 1967] especially for us and having it made retrospective. It has even chosen an ugly name to call us by. One's own are called patriots, or at least rebels; your opponents are called terrorists . . .

We have felt from the very time of our arrest that we were not being tried by our equals but by our masters, and that those who have brought us to trial very often do not even do us the courtesy of calling us by our surnames . . .

It suits the Government of South Africa to say that it is ruling South West Africa with the consent of its people. This is not true . . . Your Government, my Lord, undertook a very special responsibility, when it was awarded the mandate over us after the First World War. It assumed a sacred trust to guide us towards independence and to prepare us to take our place among the nations of the world. We believe that South Africa has abused that trust because of its belief in racial supremacy (that White people have been chosen by God to rule the world) and apartheid. We believe that for fifty years South Africa has failed to promote the development of our people. Where are our trained men? The wealth of our country has been used to train your people for leadership and the sacred duty of preparing the indigenous people to take their place among the nations of the world has been ignored . . . To us it has always seemed that our rulers wanted to keep us backward for their benefit . . .

I do not claim that it is easy for men of different races to live at peace with one another. I myself had no experience of this in my youth, and at first it surprised me that men of different races could live together in peace. But now I know it to be true and to be something for which we must strive. The South African Government creates hostility by separating people and emphasizing their differences. We believe that by living together, people will learn to lose their fear of each other. We also believe that this fear which some of the Whites have of Africans is based on their desire to be superior and privileged and that when Whites see themselves as part of South West Africa, sharing with us all its hopes and troubles, then that fear will disappear. Separation is said to be a natural process. But why then is it imposed by force, and why then is it that Whites have the superiority . . .

Your Lordship emphasised in your judgment the fact that our arms come from communist countries, and also that words commonly used by communists were to be found in our documents. But my Lord, in the documents produced by the State there is another type of language. It appears even more often than the former. Many documents finish up with an appeal to the Almighty to guide us in our struggle for freedom . . .

We do not expect that independence will end our troubles, but we do believe that our people are entitled—as are all peoples—to rule themselves. It is not really a question of whether South Africa treats us well or badly, but that South West Africa is our country and we wish to be our own masters . . .

Is it surprising that in such times my countrymen have taken up arms? Violence is truly fearsome, but who would not defend his property and himself against a robber? And we believe that South Africa has robbed us of our country . . .

My Lord, you found it necessary to brand me as a coward. During the Second World War, when it became evident that both my country and your country were threatened by the dark clouds of Nazism, I risked my life to defend both of them . . .

But some of your countrymen when called to battle to defend civilization resorted to sabotage against their own fatherland. I volunteered to face German bullets, and as a guard of military installations, both in South West Africa and the Republic, was prepared to be the victim of their sabotage. Today they are called our masters and are considered the heroes, and I am called the coward . . .

I am a loyal Namibian and I could not betray my people to their enemies. I admit that I decided to assist those who had taken up arms. I know that the struggle will be long and bitter. I also know that my people will wage that struggle, whatever the cost.

Only when we are granted our independence will the struggle stop. Only when our human dignity is restored to us, as equals of the Whites, will there be peace between us.

We believe that South Africa has a choice — either to live at peace with us or to subdue us by force. If you choose to crush us and impose your will on us then you will not only betray your trust, but you will live in security for only so long as your power is greater than ours. No South African will live at peace in South West Africa, for each will know that his security is based on force and that without force he will face rejection by the people of South West Africa.

My co-accused and I have suffered. We are not looking forward to our imprisonment. We do not, however, feel that our efforts and sacrifice have been wasted. We believe that human suffering has its effect even on those who impose it. We hope that what has happened will persuade the Whites of South Africa that we and the world may be right and they may be wrong. Only when White South Africans realise this and act on it, will it then be possible for us to stop our struggle for freedom and justice in the land of our birth.[1]

1. Quoted in J. H. P. Serfontein, *Namibia?* (Pretoria, 1976), 379-384.

Economic Prospects

To the victorious groups in Namibia will go both the problems and the opportunities of a new country emerging from decades of economic as well as political colonialism. Since the 1920s Namibia has supplied raw materials to the world through South Africa, purchased consumer and heavy duty goods there, and been powerless to influence the investment decisions of its suzerain. Industrially, Namibia has been unable to hide behind tariff walls or compete, in the crucial mining sector, with South Africa with regard to wages, conditions of employment, or attractiveness to investors. Nor, since the structure of apartheid was applied to Namibia in all of its complexity, has the territory been permitted to rival South Africa in nonmaterial benefits.

The territory's infrastructure has been developed with a natural emphasis on long-term connections with South Africa. Its road, rail, and air services are all focused upon that country. It has access to South African technical knowledge and skills, but is nearly isolated from its power grid, and from its water-supply system. Yet Walvis Bay, administratively reunited with South Africa in 1977, is Namibia's major port. Without its incorporation into the new country, Namibia's economy could be seriously damaged.

Minerals

Namibia's future lies less with its plateau grazing lands — although the success of the raising of beef in Botswana belies such an assertion — and little with its long and supposedly strategic if craggy, dry, and inhospitable south Atlantic coastline. Fishing may contribute substantially to the economy, especially if Walvis Bay becomes Namibian, and there is potential for the development of agricultural self-sufficiency in the north. But it is Namibia's minerals that provide the most promise. In 1978 the total export earnings of minerals were more than R 700 million; about half the total was in diamonds and uranium. The diamond deposits at Oranjemund in the arid extreme southwest are the largest in the world. They are mined from vast alluvial deposits by Consolidated Diamond Mines, a wholly owned subsidiary of the

De Beers Corporation. Production in 1978 was about 2 million carats, worth more than R 200 million. Oranjemund contributed about 21 percent of the profits of De Beers, a South African concern, in 1978.[2]

Namibia's reserves of low-cost uranium oxide were estimated at about 100,000 tons before the discovery of new deposits near Swakopmund in 1977 and 1978. Exploration is continuing, and prospectors expect to locate substantial additional sources of uranium. The existing uranium mine at Rössing, 40 miles northeast of Swakopmund, is at last producing near its rated capacity of 5,000 metric tons a year. Although it reached that level in 1979, about two years behind schedule, and after significant cost overruns due to severe technical problems in the separation and concentration phase, Rössing has now begun contributing to the resource base of Namibia as well as to the balance sheet of its parent companies. In 1978 Rössing's gross earnings were $173 million. Rio Tinto Zinc owns 48.5 percent of the one-third equity capital (two-thirds of the $300 million development cost was in the form of loans) and manages the project. A Canadian subsidiary of Rio Tinto owns 10 percent. Total has 10 percent; General Mining (of South Africa), 6.8 percent; the South African Industrial Development Corporation, 13.2 percent; and other private investors, the remaining 11.5 percent.

A Swiss subsidiary of Rio Tinto, not South Africa's NUFCOR, markets uranium from Rössing. The Swiss subterfuge was necessary to satisfy Japanese and other customers who were embarrassed to buy directly from Namibia in the face of United Nations prohibitions against such traffic. Japanese utilities have apparently agreed to purchase more than 8,000 metric tons and a single Japanese firm has contracted to take another 15,000 metric tons by 1984. There are French, German, and Italian contracts and a 7,500-metric ton contract with British Nuclear Fuels, Limited, for the period from 1976 to 1982.

For about fifty years, Namibia has also supplied copper from mines at or near Tsumeb in the north-central section of the territory. Tsumeb, which was barely breaking even in 1977 because of

2. Figures for the Namibian economy are from Economist Intelligence Unit, *Quarterly Economic Review of Southern Africa* (April 1979).

the low world price of copper, made a profit of $17 million in 1974, when copper prices were high, and had a net income in 1978, when copper prices had begun to recover, of approximately $12 million. In 1978 Tsumeb produced 46,000 metric tons of blister copper. (Yet two relatively new copper producers shut down their operations in 1977 and 1978.) Tsumeb also produces 40,000 metric tons of refined lead and 79,000 kilograms of refined cadmium. Tsumeb once produced zinc, but in recent years the smelting of zinc has become uneconomical. The Tsumeb mine complex is owned by Newmont Mining of New York, Amax Incorporated, Selection Trust of London, and the O'Okiep Copper Company, Union Corporation, and South West African Company, all of South Africa.

Zinc, lead, and vanadium have been mined in Namibia from 1922. The Berg Aukas mine, owned by the South West African Company (a subsidiary of Gold Fields of South Africa, Limited), has produced intermittently since that time, especially from 1947 to 1950 and again since 1955. Vanadium output from the mine, which is located near Grootfontein, was once important internationally. Now that the richest part of the ore body has been consumed, however, only about 1.5 million pounds a year of vanadium pentoxide are produced, along with zinc and lead concentrates. Vanadium is also known to exist in the tailings resulting from uranium production at Rössing; given sufficiently high prices, vanadium will be recovered from this source and may also be mined along with newer uranium ventures in Namibia. Presently, tin is another of the base metals mined in Namibia, but it, along with lead, zinc, and copper, plays but a small part in the world supply picture.

The greatest wealth of Namibia is thought to exist, as yet unexplored, in the ground. Diamonds and uranium will remain the key earners in the medium term, and prospects for base metals are also bright. However, the extent to which the future of the territory rests upon the mining of minerals will depend in large measure upon the attitudes of its future government to foreign investment, mineral producers, and mineral and petroleum prospectors. Neighboring Botswana and Zambia provide dissimilar patterns, the first encouraging, the second not.

Economic Organization

SWAPO, for its part, may introduce a radical approach to the development and reorganization of Namibia. Its leaders repeat hoary promises to deprive foreign investors of their mineral rights or, at a minimum, to renegotiate those rights on terms more favorable to the state. Some, if not all, of the existing mines are apparently slated for nationalization, not necessarily with compensation, and there is a generally accepted idea within the SWAPO hierarchy that large agricultural and grazing holdings (primarily cattle and sheep ranches) in white hands should also be transferred to the state. As usually set out, these and similar expectations by the present leaders of SWAPO seem to be repetitions of rigid formulae, rather than parts of a well-thought-out program. There is little differentiation between multinational investors and local karakul raisers. SWAPO officials may not have thought sufficiently about how, if and when it governs, it will differentiate between various alternative economic ideas in order to maximize postindependence productivity while retaining control of national resources and their allocation. Even so, SWAPO seems to have a wise awareness of how arbitrary and illusory were the economic and social goals set by Frelimo for Mozambique. SWAPO wants to stop short of the economic anarchy that was perceived as being (whether or not it in fact was) the motivating force behind the flight of the Portuguese from Mozambique in 1975-1976. SWAPO expects and wants whites to stay, obviously on its terms, but to stay nevertheless. There also seems a tendency to welcome new investors even if wholesale nationalization of extractive industries proves to be the ruling dogma.

Inherent contradictions are either brushed aside, at this stage, or rationalized. It is possible to suspect that the economic and social attitudes of the SWAPO leadership are not yet well thought out or not yet shaped for a Namibian election and for the assumption of rule. Furthermore, it is only comparatively recently that SWAPO assumed a pro-Soviet, rather radical-sounding posture. For a long time the organization was bourgeois in rhetoric while militant in action. Only since 1971 has it followed an avowedly socialist approach. Should we question SWAPO's dedication to socialism?

The other parties of Namibia all espouse private enterprise and future cooperation with South Africa. They oppose SWAPO's version of socialism, however it may finally be moderated or mediated by events. The DTA is the most fervent proponent of strengthened ties with South Africa, but the NNF and the SWAPO-Democrats also say that they recognize what they refer to as an unpleasant reality.

None of the contenders for power in Namibia appears adequately to have thought through how each will organize a government. Each has leaders of ability sufficient to fill a cabinet and make policy for the country; at the same time, there is a dearth of educated Namibians capable at this point of staffing the middle levels of the bureaucracy (until now filled exclusively by South Africans) or the middle and upper levels of the technical establishment.

There is little doubt that any discussion of the reconstruction of postindependence Namibia must begin with the reality of South African economic and administrative involvement. Clearly, South Africa's all-pervasive domination (through integration) of the territory's economy will have to cease at independence. But the process of disentanglement will not be easy; nor will the mere substitution of foreign technocrats for South Africans prove sufficient unless and until a new government wishes to begin afresh or to decree a radical restructuring of the economic basis of the territory. Namibia is presently organized for growth and stands ready to absorb investment from outside; its first problem will be how to transfer the organization and administration of the infrastructure from South African to local hands without disrupting a well-run economy. How to replace South African subsidies (especially of the Namibian railways and airlines) will also be a crucial question.

Given these problems, if Namibia is to manage an economy and a society arranged roughly as they are at present and to cope with the usual pressures felt after independence by any country, the new government may want for a few years to rely on assistance from overseas or from South Africa. It will want to decide the extent to which South Africans will be asked to continue to administer and perform technical tasks; it will—of necessity—think of contracting the servicing of its infrastructural needs to foreign managers or finding ways to work with South Africans. Even raising such questions is anathema, but the high level of development of modern Namibia, the aspirations of SWAPO and others for growth from this base, the sheer size and small population of the country, and its vast potential, all suggest that an independent Namibia will either be organized imaginatively—with a flair similar in inspiration to Botswana—or become a zone of stress and internecine conflict.

Certainly economic and social dislocation, stemming, inter alia, from plummeting productivity, mismanagement of the infrastructure (and the ports), and conceptual rigidities, could— given the length of time Namibians have been linked to South Africa and the implicit economic expectations which that association has raised—encourage political disagreement and, if political control (by means of patronage) follows ethnic lines, engender resentment rooted in ethnicity.

Like Botswana, Namibia is blessed with diverse mineral riches that have yet to be fully exploited, unrealized potential wealth in livestock, and a sparse population. In addition, Namibia, more than Botswana, could become agriculturally self-sufficient. It will take sensitive and popular management to realize Namibia's potential. Equally important, a government with a limited vision could easily squander Namibia's human and material patrimony. The ultimate result will reflect decisions made in 1980.

The Ongoing Political Battle

The forward motion that had been achieved toward solving the problem of Namibia internationally was suddenly arrested in September 1978. A few weeks after the secretary-general of the United Nations had drafted a plan that differed in a few respects from that which had been accepted by South Africa and SWAPO, Vorster suddenly resigned as prime minister. The resignation probably had much to do with the unfolding information scandal in South Africa, but Vorster coupled his resignation with a vigorous denunciation of the hard-forged agreement over Namibia. Pieter W. Botha, who succeeded Vorster as prime minister, immediately threw further vitriol on the agreement; he seemed ready to let Namibia proceed to some kind of internally arranged independence. Moreover, despite the protestations of the Contact Group and a hurried visit to Pretoria by Secretary of State Cyrus Vance, South Africa scheduled constituent assembly elections for December 1978; the West considered this an act of effrontery. Weeks later South Africa backed down; even though elections would be held, it was hinted, they would only count as a kind of interim poll to demonstrate the strength of the non-SWAPO political groups — that is, to demonstrate that the DTA was the most powerful of the internally based organizations.

The 1978 Elections

The election in December was boycotted not only by SWAPO but also by the other two anti-South African parties, the NNF and the SWAPO-Democrats. The only contestants were the DTA; Aktur (the Front for the Retention of the Turnhalle Initiative), an outgrowth of the right wing of the National party in Namibia; and three newly formed parties with mostly personal followings. The DTA, which had been holding lavish political rallies throughout the year, and spending unheard of sums on mass barbecues, employed its South African-supplied funds to mount a splashy American-style campaign. More than 80 percent of voters who had registered earlier in the year cast ballots over several days — for parties only, not for constituency-based representatives. The result, based on national returns, was a sweep by the DTA. Of the fifty constituent assembly seats, the DTA won forty-one by receiving 268,000 votes. Of the forty-one seats, eight ethnic groups (including whites) received four seats each, while the smaller Baster, San, and Tswana groups received one seat each. Aktur received 38,000 (presumably white) votes and six seats. The newly formed Namibia Christian Democratic party (which received 9,000 votes), the Herstigte Nasionale, or Reformed National, party (6,000 votes), and the Liberation Front (4,500 votes) each received a single seat. The Herstigte party is a branch of the extreme right-wing white group in the Republic of South Africa. The Liberation Front represented Coloureds who had been forced out of the DTA.

The election itself led nowhere. During the last days of 1978, South Africa reaffirmed its acceptance of the Western plan, spoke of its satisfaction with a redrafted version of the United Nations document, and promised to join the United Nations in sponsoring the kind of international election that had been anticipated earlier in the year and that would meet the requirements of Security Council Resolution 435. Thus, for a few months in early 1979, the prospect that the fall of the Shah of Iran and the loss of his oil, Western pressure, and new South African analyses of its options, would combine to bring about the peaceful transformation of Namibia from a lapsed mandate to a self-governing state was once again real. The West contemplated the happy task of testing the claims of SWAPO and other anti-South African parties against those of the South African-backed DTA at an internationally arranged and run national election. The West, at least, viewed such an election as the fitting conclusion to the second phase of the modern political transformation of the lapsed mandate, as well as to the country's liberation struggle.

South Africa had other ideas. In March it rejected the modified United Nations plan for preelectoral arrangements. A desultory meeting in New York between R. F. Botha and the Contact Group was inconclusive. Then South Africa (and the DTA) began promoting a possible new internal, interim solution, with power removed from Steyn and given to the DTA. The Rhodesian elections intervened, and prospects for an internationally valid election in Namibia in 1979, and some form of progress toward a recognized independence, looked increasingly grim, especially after South Africa permitted the DTA in May to transform its interim constituent assembly into the national assembly of Namibia. The assembly was permitted to make laws and to repeal or amend South African legislation. Provision was made for the appointment — from the ranks of parties not represented in the constituent body — of up to fifteen members more than the fifty elected in December. Shipanga, for whom this method was designed, refused to let the SWAPO-Democrats thus be coopted.

But O'Linn and Kirkpatrick, for the Federal party, and R. V. Rukoro and Dr. Zedikia Ngavirure, the leaders of one faction within SWANU, considered trying to work for change within the assembly.

Theirs may have been the politics either of optimism or of despair. Only unfolding events would decide. But for Aktur, the passage by the assembly in July 1979 of the Abolishment of Racial Discrimination (Urban Residential and Public Amenities) Act demonstrated decisively that the South African authorities controlling Namibia were serious about implementing Steyn's program for desegregating the territory. The act, made effective in August despite bitter verbal attacks by the leaders of Aktur and scattered violent incidents perpetrated by right-wing whites, ended urban housing segregation and color bars in hotels, restaurants, bars, holiday resorts, and similar establishments. Aktur had been pleading with little success for a halt to the steady annulment of social apartheid in Namibia. It had threatened to use its close connections to right-wing thinking within the National party of South Africa to embarrass Prime Minister Botha at home. Passage of the Abolishment Act enraged Aktur and stirred its leaders to heights of rhetoric, to the mounting of unsuccessful legal challenges to the existence of the assembly and its right to make laws, and to thinly veiled threats to take control of Namibia through some form of a putsch.

Pretoria's answer was dramatic. Without warning, Botha removed Steyn and replaced him with Professor Gerrit Viljoen, an urbane classicist who was then serving as rector, or president, of the Rand Afrikaans University in Johannesburg but whose real influence stemmed from his position as head of the Broederbond, the secret Afrikaner political and cultural organization. Viljoen was known for his comparatively liberal views about the need to dismantle social apartheid within South Africa (while keeping political separation). He was an advocate of negotiating a way forward with Africans (perhaps even of holding an omnibus national convention), and he was known to be among the more flexible, supple, and thoughtful Afrikaner intellects. But his position as the leader of the Broederbond also gave him unassailable credentials among right-wing whites in Namibia. Their own leaders

were members of the Broederbond. As late as September, shortly
after Viljoen had taken up the reins of office, Aktur was still refusing to acknowledge its defeat. But South Africa had amply
demonstrated that it would not readily waver from its support of
Mudge and the DTA, risen as they were from the phoenix of past
South African policy.

Viljoen had another asset. He was expected to be able to
help R. F. Botha negotiate effectively with the Contact Group.
The stalled discussions between the group and South Africa were
reopened in August after R. F. Botha promised the British government that his government was at least willing to talk. Earlier
McHenry had helped to develop a plan agreeable to Angolan
President Agostinho Neto, which called for the demilitarization
of a 35-mile-wide swath on both sides of the Angolan-Namibian
border, this buffer zone to be patrolled by troops of the United
Nations in order to prevent SWAPO infiltration—and, inciden-
tally, to weaken the forces of the Union for the Total Independence of Angola (UNITA), which since 1975 had been opposed
to the Angolan government. If South Africa were to agree to the
new proposal, perhaps Namibia could be put back on the path
toward a validated independence. But there was little optimism
in late 1979, even after the contending parties met in Geneva,
that South Africa wanted to find a solution satisfactory to both
sides.

Political Realities

Negotiations could not alter the underlying political com-
plexion of Namibia. Despite the success of the DTA in the 1978
elections, the partial breakup of the NNF due to the decisions of
the Federal party and part of SWANU to cooperate with the
DTA-controlled assembly, and the inability of Aktur to prevent
change, the control of Namibia's future remains a contest between South Africa and the DTA, on one side, and the United
Nations, the Soviet Union, and SWAPO, on the other, with both
the Contact Group and the African front-line nations attempting
to arbitrate. That contest might be continued on the battlefield,
where there was more action, and more white and black deaths,
in 1979 than in previous years, for some time to come. But it

còuld also be decided in the polling booth. If the latter, then SWAPO still remains a promising competitor against the DTA in a full and fair contest, with the remnants of the NNF and the SWAPO-Democrats unable to be completely discounted.

If the experiences of late colonial Zambia, Malawi, Kenya, and Tanzania provide an appropriate analogy, the masses of Namibia are likely in the future to follow leaders with historical legitimacy, like Toivo and Nujoma, in preference to those who belong, as do Mudge and Ndjoba, president of the DTA, to a transitional alliance of convenience. No matter how sensible and sober the appeal of the DTA may be, or how successfully the NNF may elaborate its anti-South African, non-Marxist attributes, experience elsewhere in southern Africa suggests that such multiracial, moderate efforts will fail to provide a credible alternative for most voters. This conclusion discounts the ability of the DTA ultimately to persuade traditionalists (and Namibia is in many ways a strikingly conservative land) that its policies provide valid options for the future. It also assumes that the appeal of Shipanga's SWAPO-Democrats will remain modest and that its alliance with the NNF will not materially improve its electoral potential.

Ethnic arithmetic supports such an analysis. Given SWAPO's origins as an Ovambo organization and its close ties to Ovambo, as well as its leadership, it is reasonable to assume that SWAPO's legitimacy among Ovambo could be transformed into votes by the thousands. Since the Ovambo turnout at an election will at least equal that of all other groups together, SWAPO has the kind of ethnic base that can only be the envy of its rivals. Its base is proportionally larger than that of the late Jomo Kenyatta's in Kenya in 1962, and far more impressive than Kenneth Kaunda's in Zambia in the same year and again in 1964. The base is unlikely to be eroded by the efforts of Ndjoba, the leading Ovambo collaborator with South Africa in the 1970s. The threat represented by Shipanga and his associates, notably Mifima, is much stronger. But, rightly or wrongly, their legitimacy is suspect; unless they can gain standing as a credible and worthy alternative to SWAPO, they should not seriously detract from the appeal of SWAPO to its historic ethnic fold.

One of Shipanga's problems is that the ethnic appeal of his party is blurred by its links to the NNF, which is perceived within

Namibia as a party dominated by Damara and Herero. Admittedly, the NNF has also been backed by the Westernized black élite, which seeks a realistic alternative to SWAPO outside the DTA. But this élite is small and is apt to remain so.

The DTA has not strayed from its roots in the Turnhalle. Many of the leaders who achieved prominence and some wealth through their appointment to that forum, and others who filled roles of importance as chiefs, teachers, physicians, or businessmen before the meetings, naturally continue to favor a reconstructed society in Namibia that will enshrine their own values and esteem their own contribution. Those in this broad category still fear exchanging South African control and assistance for a black government possibly unfriendly to South Africa and with ties to countries of the socialist bloc. The smaller ethnic groups also worry about Ovambo domination; a few, like the Basters, have fixed communal views rooted in a neo-Victorian approach to morality. Much as they want to be freed from South African discrimination, they, and other traditionalists throughout Namibia, remain suspicious of precipitous changes in the organization of personal and public life.

Unlike many other African countries, Namibia has a markedly bourgeois, religious cast. Such generalizations are true for the south, and also for much of the north of the territory. As generalizations, they also promise to endure in the face of egalitarian secularism. African voters in much of Namibia appear to be less radical in their aspirations for modernity than their counterparts in such countries as Kenya and Nigeria. Socialism, however defined, may have less appeal to many Namibians than it would have had to a comparable electorate in other African nations in the 1960s. When they come to vote, however, the overwhelming mass of Namibians may disregard ideology and concentrate on nationalism, ethnicity, and legitimacy as sanctified by the long black struggle against South Africa. On those grounds, SWAPO may claim the loyalties of the Ovambo, and of most other Namibians.

SWAPO and the DTA are both well organized, but SWAPO's organizational roots are particularly deep. Although SWAPO has been a military and political body operating from bases outside Namibia since 1966, it has also been represented inside Namibia by an above-ground internal wing with widespread contacts, branches, and cells. In 1979 Steyn feared this network sufficiently to detain up to seventy-two leaders of internal SWAPO for months at a time. The full capacity of SWAPO inside the territory, insofar as it rests upon the long-standing effort of the internal wing of SWAPO, can never be known precisely. But the network that successfully engineered the massive Ovambo strike of 1971-1972 has not been permitted to decay. Ovambo still work throughout the country in a number and variety of strategic locations — from Oranjemund in the south to Tsumeb in the north. SWAPO has direct ties to these work forces. In less sure but equally significant ways, it also has ties to clusters of Damara, Nama, and Herero.

The nature of elections in black Africa may also influence the decisions ultimately made in Namibia. Where there is little experience with and little understanding of the electoral process, voters can be stampeded, if not coerced and intimidated, indirectly and with little effort. For these reasons, and because the security of a secret ballot is regarded skeptically and fear of retaliation is real, Africans often demonstrate a capacity to vote for expected winners. Whoever leads it at the time, SWAPO will be well placed to take advantage of such circumstances. When combined with the fact that voters in first elections in Africa have typically rejected moderate or middle-of-the-road alternatives, and have instead turned in overwhelming numbers to the party or leader perceived as legitimate, SWAPO's advantage could well prove sufficient to counteract the achievements of the DTA in office during 1979.

The transformation of Namibia from a lapsed mandate to an independent multiracial nation may not prove easy. Conflict there was endemic through 1979, and efforts to resolve that conflict rapidly were bedeviled by the concerns and needs of South Africa, the fears and hopes of SWAPO, and tension between the great powers. All that was certain was that the less open and internationalized the process of political transformation, the more delayed would be the achievement of a new Namibia. Moreover, the longer that achievement is delayed, the greater will be the potential for interethnic conflict in postindependence Namibia.

Zimbabwe

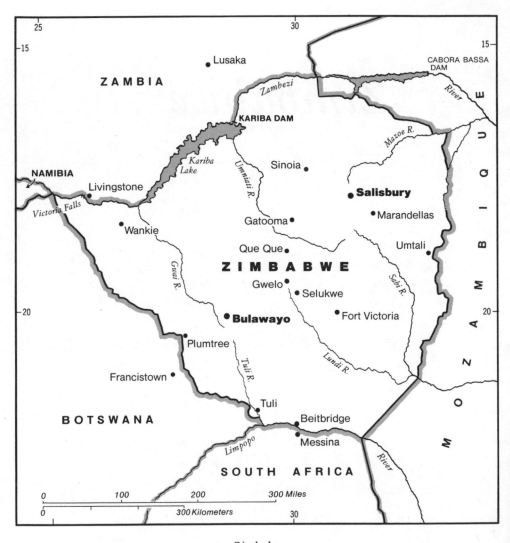

Zimbabwe

9 | The Social and Economic Setting

T HE FUTURE ZIMBABWE may still be poised on the brink of unparalleled prosperity. After enjoying decades of growth for whites, Zimbabwe may now be capable of using its abundant resources for blacks as well. Over the decades since the white conquest of 1890, white capital and black labor have together constructed what, in 1965 and again in 1975, was a well-developed country making much of its natural ecological endowment as well as its subsoil mineral resources. Unlike so many other African economies in 1975, Rhodesia (the colonial name for Zimbabwe) had a healthy balance among reliance upon primary crops and raw materials, industry, and the contributions of tourism, banking, and the like. Certainly Rhodesia, in white hands, had made as much as it could of its special position on the border of the tropical and temperate zones of Africa, and as the last defensive bastion against the movement southward of black autonomy.

The Bounty of the Land

Zimbabwe is blessed with a beneficial combination of soils and climate. Together with modern farming practices, this combination has made Zimbabwe an exporter of food staples, such as maize, and—in good times—high-earning cash crops such as tobacco and sugar. Under an internationally recognized independent African rule Zimbabwe could continue to feed its own population and earn foreign exchange from export sales if sound farming practices were continued and the country's excellent infrastructure were maintained.

In 1978 white-farmed land, accounting for 50 percent of the aggregate land mass of the territory (and by far the most arable land) produced about 75 percent of the maize crop and 95 percent of all cash crops. Nearly 90 percent of white-owned land in 1965 was concentrated in Mashonaland North and South, two of the seven Rhodesian provinces. Most of these provinces consist of Highveld (a 4,000 to 5,000-foot high plateau) extending from Bulawayo 400 miles northeastwards to Salisbury and Marandellas. In precolonial times this was savanna grassland occasionally interrupted by rocky hills, or *kopjes*. This is the region of the mineral-rich Great Dyke, an extrusion of ancient lava. It has a comfortable tropical climate without extremes and enjoys 24 to 32 inches of rainfall. Given reasonably abundant use of fertilizer, this amount of rainfall has permitted the cultivation of maize, tobacco, beans, and vegetables in what is otherwise a soil of only moderate fertility. Well-fed cattle also graze on unfertilized sections of this region.

A more fertile area exists in the northeast, where the highlands rise to more than 8,000 feet. Cooler than the Highveld and wetter (with 40 to 70 inches of rainfall per year), this area is suited to specialized farming and the cultivation of hardwood for timber. Most of the accessible areas of this region are in white hands. The Middleveld rises to about 3,000 to 4,000 feet above sea level. Most of it lies to the west of the Highveld and is primarily in African hands. Its annual rainfall is about 16 to 24 inches, too little to sustain intensive cropping without irrigation and large increments of fertilizer. The Lowveld (less than 3,000 feet above sea level) comprises land on the northern and southeastern peripheries of Zimbabwe. Here rainfall is less than 16 inches per annum, temperatures are torrid in summer, and rates of evaporation are extremely high. About 20 percent of Zimbabwe is classified as Lowveld. Most is nominally in African occupation. Only expensive irrigation (from the Sabi and Limpopo Rivers) permits dependable farming; sugar and cotton have been grown commercially in this region on a few white-owned estates.

White farmers numbered only 5,400 in 1979. In contrast, about 700,000 Africans grew maize and Turkish sun-dried tobacco, and grazed undernourished cattle on the poorly watered, overworked Tribal Trust Lands, or African reserves. Only about 10 percent of the production of these farmers was in the cash sector. Nearly 9,000 Africans had freehold farms in the African Purchase areas, or extensions to the reserves. In 1978 they produced about a third of all the crops—maize, millet, sorghum, peanuts, rice, and beans—grown for cash in the African sector. In 1969 fewer than 65 percent of all Africans lived on the Tribal Trust Lands. Only 3 percent lived in the African Purchase areas.

Ethnicity and Sectionalism

Traditional Zimbabwean ethnic cleavages have been exacerbated by colonial/settler rule and by the fratricidal conflict of recent years. Moreover, when an internationally recognized black government is inaugurated—whether on the battlefield or after elections—these ethnic realities will hinder the easy articulation and implementation of a national policy of development.

For centuries before the mid-nineteenth century, Cishona-speaking Africans of diverse clan backgrounds practiced settled agriculture and some minimal stock raising on the high and medium veld of Zimbabwe, a name used by the Cishona-speakers for their capitals, or "big houses." As an offshoot of the Nguni Mfecane, Sindebele-speaking Africans invaded Zimbabwe from the south in the 1830s and, with their short stabbing spears, modern ideas of warfare, hierarchical forms of organization, and wealth of cattle, dominated the Shona. Today, however, the warrior Ndebele number only 16 percent of all Africans, and about half of the 16 percent are Sindebele-speakers of Shona extraction. They live for the most part in the southwest, around their traditional capital of Bulawayo.

Of the 7 million Africans in today's Zimbabwe, 70 percent speak Cishona. The largest of the groups that make up the Shona population is the Karanga, about 40 percent of the total. The Karanga live within an 80-mile radius of Fort Victoria in the south. The Zezeru, of the central Mashonaland area (near Salisbury and Sinoia) number 35 percent; the Manyika of the highlands in the east, about 14 percent; the Ndau of the southeast, about 6 percent; the KoreKore of the Zambezi River valley, about 3 percent; and the Kalanga near Gwelo, about 2 percent.

In colonial times the Zezeru, Manyika, and the Ndau received more attention from missionaries and the settler government than the other ethnic groups. They—especially the Zezeru—were therefore more closely associated with modern life. Many were educated and acculturated and today dominate the African intellectual elite. The Karanga, on the other hand, received proportionally less attention from settlers and fewer of the colonial benefits. Part of today's ethnic antagonism among Shona reflects this past leadership of Shona by Zezeru, Manyika, and Ndau. Karanga seek a status reversal beneficial more to themselves than to other Shona.

In precolonial times the Shona shared cultural and religious bonds but lacked strong political ties. The chiefdoms were locally based and held together by kinship rather than by notions of a centralizing hierarchy. The power of the chiefs was limited and depended upon their popularity with their constituents. Since 1965 the chiefs have been government nominees—minor officials of the white administration of the Tribal Trust Lands. Under each are six to twelve ward headmen and, within each ward, *kraal* (or village) headmen, each in charge of several kraals numbering as many as 200 people. This colonially ordained administrative apparatus (directed by white district commissioners or magistrates) will have little carryover into the 1980s. Most officeholders have been discredited by their association with the settler government, and the legitimate nature of African chieftaincy has long been eroded. Only a few chiefs resisted the settler government and either fled into exile or were deposed. This conclusion is also valid for the Ndebele and the other indigenous peoples. Even the descendants of the Ndebele conquering paramountcy—the lineal descendants of the great nineteenth-century chiefs Mzilikazi and Lobengula—will have a diminished authenticity in the independent era, especially in a government dominated by Shona.

Other linguistic groups are unimportant in the Zimbabwean equation. The Sena and the Chikunda fled from Mozambique during the Portuguese period and live in the northern portion of Zimbabwe. Along the Zambezi River are Tonga related to the acephalous Tonga of Zambia. The Venda, of the Transvaal, live in southern Matabeleland (Ndebeleland) together with the Lemba, their clients. Along the Botswana border, again in southern Matabeleland, are Tswana-speaking peoples. In the southeast live Thonga and Hlengwe from southern Mozambique. In 1969, 337,000 Africans (7 percent) had been born outside Rhodesia, in Malawi, Mozambique, and Zambia. Most were farm laborers. In recent years the recruitment of Malawians for work on the isolated farms of the east and northeast has, for security reasons, intensified.

The white population of Rhodesia numbered about 230,000 in 1978. In the late 1960s and early 1970s it increased primarily because of the immigration of whites from what was then Portuguese Angola and Mozambique. Between 1969 and 1972 there was a net immigration of 30,000 whites. In 1974-1975, 20,000 Portuguese arrived. And 30 percent of all whites arrived between 1966 and 1972, approximately 50 percent since the white Unilateral Declaration of Independence (UDI) in 1965. But in 1976 the net outflow began to assume serious proportions. In 1977 and 1978 the exodus continued; a net total of over 1,000 whites left Rhodesia each month until late 1978, when 3,000 a month departed permanently; the 1978 total net loss was more than 13,700.

In 1969 about 70,000 whites held foreign passports. In the 1970s it was estimated that 20 percent of all white Rhodesians spoke Afrikaans. Possibly another 17 percent came originally from South Africa; 22 percent had been born in Britain, and 41 percent in Rhodesia. In general, white Rhodesia can claim only a minor proportion of adults who know no other home. If 50 percent are post-UDI immigrants, another 25 to 30 percent are post-1950 immigrants. Under conditions of turmoil, a white exodus could be sudden and widespread.

In 1969 Rhodesia had only 9,000 Asians, 70 percent of whom were born in Rhodesia and 9 percent elsewhere in Africa. They still hold a monopoly of retail trade in the African townships. Of the 18,000 Coloureds (as defined in South Africa), 91 percent were born in Rhodesia. Some claim descent from the pioneers of the 1890s; they are predominantly in manufacturing, trade, and service occupations.

Zimbabwe is less heavily urbanized than Zambia, only 17 percent of all Africans living (until recently in legally segregated circumstances) in the eleven major cities and towns. The Shona are more heavily urbanized than others. About 19 percent of all Africans live in the white-dominated rural areas, so a total of 40 percent of all Africans live (and have lived for a long time) in areas that until early 1979 had been designated "white."

If an independent Zimbabwe is dominated by Karanga, there may be a shift in developmental emphasis from the north and southwest to the south, and, perhaps, a concentration on agricultural improvement in the Middleveld; Africans may also be substituted for whites on the large holdings of the Highveld. The competition of the 1970s for ethnic preeminence is not apt to abate in the 1980s. Developmental priorities are likely to have a sectional bias and, in the short run, to tend to run counter to strict notions of efficient employment of investment capital and direction of developmental resources.

The Administration of Africans

The administration of Africans in colonial Rhodesia concentrated more on the maintenance of law and order than upon development. It devoted little attention to the training of African administrators and relied largely upon a class of untutored chiefs and white supervisors. Except for the continued control of the rural areas, the traditional and, in 1979, prevailing systems of administration for Africans have a limited relevance for the 1980s.

Early in this century a Native Affairs Department was established by the administering British South Africa Company. Powers belonging to chiefs were transferred to Native Commissioners, who controlled the movement of Africans into and out of the reserves that had been created for Africans in 1898. In 1910 the commissioners gained civil and criminal jural jurisdiction over Africans. The chiefs were effectively reduced to the level of minor civil servants. In 1927 the African Affairs Act made tribes administrative units. The governor of the colony was given the power to appoint or remove chiefs and to pay them salaries and allowances as determined by the government. At about this time, too, the Native Affairs Department was made responsible for technical services to Africans.

The separation of African and white spheres was made more complete in 1931, when the settler parliament passed a Land Apportionment Act. It prohibited Africans from purchasing land and ratified the existing division of land within the colony. Fifty percent was declared a white area, about 30 percent an African area (22 percent in the reserves and 8 percent in the newly created African Purchase areas, where Africans could, according to complicated formulae, buy land); 18 percent became Crown land; and 1 percent, forest. The white half comprised the more fertile, higher, better-watered land in the colony. Africans were subsequently removed from white-dominated rural areas.

An amendment, in 1941, extended the Land Apportionment Act to the urban areas. Separate African townships were established under the aegis of the white municipalities. Special arrangements had to be made in the late 1950s for the first African barristers and physicians to rent offices on the fringes of the white municipalities.

With the inauguration of the period of segregationist Rhodesian Front government in 1962, the system of native administration was modernized in terms of nomenclature and atmosphere without, however, altering the basic system of African subservience. Native Commissioners became District Commissioners, and the Department of Native Administration became the Ministry of Internal Affairs; the reserves were renamed the Tribal Trust Lands. The white government also tried to step back from its long direct rule so as to give more stature to chiefs. The new district commissioners were also charged with community-development responsibilities, but they were instructed to work through and preside over local community-development councils on which chiefs and elected Africans were expected to sit. (Many elections were, however, boycotted; the commissioners appointed Africans to fill the seats reserved for elected Africans.)

In 1978 the district commissioners still ran all of those councils. There were few responsible Africans involved, and African staff members were involved at the lower levels of policymaking only. Underneath the approximately 100 community-development councils were about 265 community-development boards, some of which had the potential to develop into full-fledged councils.

In 1978 Rhodesian chiefs occupied the lowest rungs on the white-arranged administrative ladder. Because the Rhodesian Front had tried to counter the effective attraction of the African nationalists, chiefs again, despite their lowly positions, received permission to allocate land and hear civil and criminal cases. Ten chiefs also sat in the old twenty-three-member Rhodesian Senate, or upper house, and eight in the lower. In the African Purchase areas, elected farmers' committees and councils ran their areas free from the interference of chiefs, but under the supervision of whites. In the urban areas, there were elected township boards, but they were for the most part advisory. Only a few were given responsibility for welfare and recreational services.

The way in which the Rhodesian government administered Africans promises little continuity for the future or, at least, hardly more than the nominal use of the existing hierarchies of chiefs for the dissemination of information and the control of rural Africans. The government over the years made chiefs irrelevant. Moreover, because of their collaboration with that government, chiefs as a class can expect little by way of support from any new nationalist black government.

The Administrative Reservoir

Although analysts have long had the impression that an internationally recognized, independent Zimbabwe could begin governing with the assistance of large numbers of well-trained indigenous civil servants, the actual figures question that assumption. Zimbabweans may be well trained, but their numbers (inside the country) may be proportionally greater in the upper echelons of the teaching rather than the civil-service ranks.

In Zimbabwe the central government is the largest single employer of whites. In 1972 it had 24,000 white and 24,000 black employees. (Together with their spouses, the white group constituted about a third of the entire white electorate.) This figure excluded whites in the employ of municipalities, the army, and the police. Of the 48,000 civil-service positions, 35,000 were so-called untenured, or non-executive, positions. The majority — 23,000 — were filled by Africans in 1972. Of the 13,000 tenured, or executive, positions, only 829 were held by Africans. And of those 829, only three were considered truly senior posts.

The Rhodesian civil service was no more Africanized in 1979 than it was in 1972, or even in 1953, on the eve of the establishment of the Federation of Rhodesia and Nyasaland. In respect to the authority and autonomy given Africans in the civil service, the extent of Africanization may even have been reduced, especially in relation to the numbers of available trained Africans. Clearly, graduates of the multiracial University of Rhodesia have not been absorbed into positions in the civil service. Figures for African bureaucratic employment do not include local governmental employment, the army, or the police. But none of the seven white municipalities (each governed by a mayor and a council elected by white property-owners), the four town-management boards, or the twenty-one white rural councils employed Africans in other than menial capacities. The exceptions were Salisbury and Bulawayo, where Africans were employed by the municipalities (which have jurisdiction over the adjacent African townships) as social workers and administrators for the townships.

A new Zimbabwe will doubtless have a large pool of underused black skills on which to draw. There are at least 5,000 black university graduates living outside Rhodesia; possibly another 3,000 live in the country. Each year about 1,100 Africans study at the University of Rhodesia in Salisbury; 500 of those usually receive bachelor's degrees in the arts and in technical subjects. The Bulawayo and Salisbury technical colleges are also multiracial, with substantial numbers of Africans enrolled. Whereas Zambia became independent with 102 university graduates, the Congo (now Zaire) could count two or three graduates, and Namibia now lists only 28 graduates, Zimbabwe is blessed with a large cadre of educated men and women anxious for the opportunity to serve their country in ways other than teaching school.

Despite the healthy number of university graduates, Rhodesia was reluctant to encourage the training and advancement of black skilled and semiskilled artisans. Although — with the need to replace whites called up for military service — there has been considerable improvement in recent years, only 814 of the 4,019 apprentices in training in 1978 were Africans. Overall, Rhodesian employers were slow to advance their black staff, especially into white-collar occupations. The exception is the mining industry, where employers have been farsighted.

The Economy

Because of sanctions and, more recently, a massive civil war, the structure of the economy of Zimbabwe has been greatly altered. From a sleepy colonial producer of unprocessed minerals and a few cash crops it became the lively financial, service, and minor manufacturing center of the Federation of Rhodesia and Nyasaland (from 1953 through 1963). After the local white Unilateral Declaration of Independence in 1965, and the resulting imposition of United Nations-mandated sanctions in 1967, there was a slump, preeminently because of the fall in tobacco export earnings and the cutting off of transit trade from Zambia. But in the succeeding seven years, through 1974, Rhodesia enjoyed an unprecedented period of boom; it coincided with years of high net white immigration, the comparative failure of British-sponsored diplomatic activity and of attacks by guerrillas, and the manufacturing of import substitutes as well as the security of medium-term investments.

Between 1968 and 1974, real output grew at a rate of 8.3 percent per annum.[1] Real income per capita grew at a rate of 4.6 percent per year, a level of growth unprecedented for Federal or post-Federal Rhodesia. The output of the manufacturing sector doubled, and employment in this sector grew from 85,000 to 153,000. Mining output nearly doubled, while tripling in value. The share of intermediate and capital goods in the manufacturing sector grew to 64 percent of the total. Together, these indicators testify to the permeability of the sanctions barrier; except

1. Elliot Berg, "Growth, Structure and Prospects of the Zimbabwe Economy," unpub. (October 14, 1967). Economist Intelligence Unit, *Quarterly Economic Report for Rhodesia and Malawi,* annual supplement, 1977, gives slightly different figures. Much of the discussion that follows is based on figures from these sources.

for tobacco in the early years, Rhodesia was able — at a price — to find buyers for its exports, and to obtain a range of imports from Eastern as well as Western suppliers. Despite the British blockade of the port of Beira, in Mozambique, ample supplies of petroleum were available through South Africa and through Mozambiquan approved transshipment facilities at Maputo (then Lourenço Marques). Even the British government was aware of this major breach in the sanctions wall, and connived at it officially. Exporting proved equally easy, with Rhodesians affixing false Mozambiquan, South African, and in some cases (involving peanuts to Singapore) even Botswanan declarations of origin. Malawi maintained its trade links and Zambia was compelled to continue buying coking coal for its mines and, on at least one celebrated occasion, maize to feed its populace.

The Rhodesian regime reorganized the country's economy in order to make the most of its assets and peculiar international position. The government controlled capital movements effectively, and the local formation of capital rose appreciably from an average gross domestic product (GDP) of 13 percent before 1976 to an average 20 percent per year from 1972 to 1974. The government conceived appropriate price, credit, import, and monetary policies, supporting those sectors of the economy that were temporarily vulnerable (like tobacco growing) until mechanisms could be devised to improve their competitive qualities. White farmers responded well to new forms of incentives, shifting from tobacco to other cash crops and increasing output while demonstrating a remarkable resilience. Most important, the manufacturing share of GDP grew from 17 percent in 1965 to 23 percent in 1976, a demonstration of the extent to which sanctions and intelligent governmental controls stimulated import substitution in new as well as traditional areas. Mining production also grew dramatically, especially after 1972, as a result of high world prices for nickel and copper and the congressionally approved (through the Byrd Amendment) American breach in the United Nations' chrome export barrier.

Overall, the gross national product per capita rose about 30 percent in real terms from 1965 to 1974. Average African earnings in wage employment grew an estimated 28 percent in real terms during the same years—from 238 to 304 Rhodesian dollars (R$238 to R$304). African employment in this sector also grew by about 50 percent, from 610,000 to nearly 1 million. It is estimated, too, that nearly 50 percent of adult male black Rhodesians were in wage employment in 1974, a percentage almost double that usually found in less well-developed countries. Even so, the positive impact of the wage sector on the traditional rural economy—still devoted to subsistence farming, stock raising, and petty trade—had been limited. The amount of remittances flowing back to the rural areas is unknown; one calculation of the negative impact of wage earning was that, of a population of nearly 3 million living in the rural areas, only 10 percent were adult males.

Since 1974 the civil war has taken its toll on the economy. In 1975 black and white per capita real incomes declined for the first time, falling by about 1 percent. They fell more than 3 percent in 1976, nearly 8 percent in 1977, and, in real terms, fell a further 19 percent in 1978. Black unemployment has also grown significantly, despite the shift of whites to part-time or full-time military service and the departure of 1,000 to 3,000 whites a month in 1977 and 1978. The war obviously was the biggest drag on the economy, costing about $1.5 million daily in 1978 and 1979.

Thanks to the growth and strength of the economy until 1974, and despite the war, Zimbabwe had hoped to enter the 1980s with an economy that was more highly diversified and had a larger industrial base than any other African country north of South Africa. The war will have eroded some of the strength of the economy, and dissipated some of its managerial and technical capability, but until 1979 it nevertheless had an underlying health that few Third World countries could boast on the eves of their own independence. Certain sectors, especially mining, where African advancement had been accelerated, entered the new era in better shape than others.

Agriculture

In 1978, on the eve of the abolition of the Land Apportionment Act, there were 680,000 black farmers and fewer than

6,000 white farmers. The black farmers sold only R$30 million in 1976 and R$25 million in 1977; the whites, R$393 million in 1976 and R$394 million in 1977. Moreover, production in both the subsistence and cash sectors of the black rural agricultural economy had dropped, because of population growth, overcrowding in the rural areas, population centralization in the rural areas (especially the Tribal Trust Lands), and the war, from 352 pounds per person in 1962 to 231 pounds per person in 1977. According to the rated carrying capacity of the Tribal Trust Lands (which make up 41 percent of the entire country, but far less than 41 percent of the fertile areas), fewer than 275,000 people should be deriving their support there. In fact, in 1977 these lands were being farmed by an estimated 675,000 cultivators. Ecologically, seventeen times as much land was being cultivated at any one time as was prudent. Obviously, too, there was little available arable land for young secondary-school graduates and dropouts and other aspirant farmers.

African agriculture supplied only about 10 percent of total cash production in 1978. Individual whites and a few agribusiness conglomerates were responsible for the remainder. Indeed, in 1976, 271 white-owned farming units (about 5 percent of the total) contributed 52 percent of the total taxable income attributed to agriculture. Most of these units were larger than 15,000 acres, since 50 percent of all white-owned farmland consisted of arable estates of that acreage or larger. A few agribusinesses owned units of more than 1 million acres. The average size of white-owned units was 5,300 acres. At the other end of the white spectrum, 32 percent of all white-owned farms were smaller than 1,000 acres and, in 1977, 30 percent of all white farmers (not necessarily those owning the smaller acreages) were insolvent. In 1976, two-thirds of all farmers were making too little to pay income tax. Pressure for land reform and land redistribution in the 1980s could, it follows, be satisfied without necessarily removing the most efficient white farmers, or the ones with the most extensive agricultural units. Alternatively, if Zimbabwe wanted to maximize productivity without counting the intense social costs, it could encourage the expansion of plantationlike agribusinesses.

Since 1965 crops previously grown only in small quantities

because of world prices, transportation costs, and Rhodesia's position in an overarching imperial economy have become central
to agriculture in the era of the sanctions. Cotton, once unimportant, has emerged as the first or second most significant crop both
for export and for vertical integration within the local textile industry, which grew dramatically as a result of import substitution. In 1976, Rhodesia produced 385.8 million pounds. Sugar
has been grown in the Sabi-Limpopo Lowveld area since the
1950s, but became important only as a result of sanctions. In
1976, 260,000 metric tons of raw sugar were grown. Production
of maize, primarily for internal consumption but also for export
to Zambia and Zaire, more than doubled from 822,000 metric
tons in 1965 to 2 million metric tons in 1974 as a result of the introduction of high-yield hybrid varieties. It fell to 1.4 million
metric tons in 1976. Virginia tobacco production, for which Rhodesia was renowned before 1965, dropped during the same period, from 246 million pounds to 188 million pounds, largely as
a result of compulsory reductions in acreage. The Rhodesian cattle herd has grown since 1965 to about 6 million head, of which
half are in African hands, but in 1979 the war was responsible for
the spread of tsetse-fly-borne animal diseases, which were taking
their toll, where guerrillas were not, of cattle numbers. As well-
diversified agriculturists, Zimbabweans also grow for sale wheat,
pyrethrum, peanuts, sorghum, soybeans, coffee (hard hit by the
war), tea, and grapes for wine. Overall, however, agriculture
contributes only about 17 percent of GDP, strikingly less than in
most nations of the Third World. The low level of this figure is an
asset in the future Zimbabwe. However, of the 17 percent, 12
percent is contributed by whites, and only 5 percent by the African cash and subsistence sectors.

Manufacturing and Mining

Rhodesia's manufacturers in 1976 accounted for the largest
portion, 23 percent, of GDP, up from 18 percent in 1966. Since
the cost of distributing goods has stayed constant at about 13
percent, it is obvious that sanctions have broadened Zimbabwe's
industrial base in ways that could greatly benefit the country.
Before 1965 the emphasis was on processing raw materials. Since

then Rhodesia has sponsored import substitution and industrial diversification. About 320 large firms (each with more than 100 employees) are responsible for 80 percent of the total industrial output. A local automobile-assembly factory was created in 1969, and there are now four; the manufacture of radios, textiles, and shoes and other leather goods has been expanded; and the Iron and Steel Company at Que Que has steadily increased its capacity to more than 400,000 tons of steel, tubes, chairs, doors, and mining and railway equipment, including rolling stock. Zimbabwe no longer needs to import tires and tubes, pulp and paper, beer, canned citrus products, canned meat, and much else. Only the Umtali petroleum refinery stands idle since the closing of the Beira pipeline in 1966. Indeed, the average import content of local manufactures is estimated at only about 25 percent.

Mining contributed 9 percent to total GDP in 1976, up from 7 percent in 1966. However, the mining sector has been diversified since 1965 and, with rising world prices for base minerals, the lifting of sanctions, independence, and the introduction of the kinds of technological advances that were largely denied to Rhodesia after 1965, the value of mineral exports could climb dramatically. Copper (3.5 million metric tons of which was produced in 1974) is the major mineral mined, but the government has recently opened low-grade gold mines to take advantage of price increases (about 33,000 pounds were extracted in 1974). Nickel is also important—two new mines were opened in 1976; there are new chrysotile asbestos mines—the quality of Zimbabwe's asbestos being among the best in the world; and the Union Carbide chromium-ore mines still produce the richest chrome oxide in the world. Silver and iron ore are mined, and coal deposits at Wankie are still plentiful and relied upon by copper and lead and zinc enterprises in Zaire and Zambia. However, in 1977 and 1978, hostilities compelled the closure of two copper mines. A nickel mine reduced its production for economic reasons, and a small chromium mine and smelter was mothballed.

Zimbabwe has inherited a highly developed infrastructure. There are more than 50,000 miles of road in the country, nearly 6,000 of which are paved. Since Mozambique cut the main rail lines to Beira and Maputo in 1975, Zimbabwe has relied upon its

old, government-run line through Botswana to Mafeking in
South Africa, which it operates on behalf of Botswana, and a new
link from Rutenga to the South African system at Beitbridge. In
1978 Zambia began importing fertilizer and exporting copper
over a line northward from the Victoria Falls, which had been
closed to Zambian traffic (but not to traffic to and from Zaire)
since 1972. Zimbabwean locomotives are old and in need of
replacement, as is much of the other rolling stock. Air Zimbabwe
still uses ancient Vickers Viscounts locally and Boeing 720 jets for
its South African flights. Since 1975 it has been unable to fly officially to Malawi and Mozambique. Flights to Zambia were prohibited in 1967.

Economic Decline

In 1979, despite its underlying strength, the Zimbabwean
economy was rapidly running down. The costly war was taking its
toll. There were two severe devaluations of the Rhodesian dollar
in 1977 and 1978, increasing the competitive posture of Rhodesian goods but making military imports more costly. Allocations
of foreign exchange to the business sector were reduced by 20 percent. Spare parts were becoming scarce as war-related needs
grew, and Rhodesian exports earned less. GDP declined by at
least 3 percent in 1978, an estimated 8 percent slide from its 1974
peak. One report indicated that real per capita income fell
between 1974 and 1978 by 25 percent, down to 1965 levels.[2] Nevertheless, because exports, led by mining — which had an unexpectedly good year in value terms — picked up toward the end of
1978 and imports were held down by sanctions, Rhodesia managed a small surplus on the balance of payments. Black, Coloured, and white employment figures fell, testifying to a continued reduction in total wage employment from 1974 highs.
There were layoffs in areas controlled by the government and in
the teaching and medical services areas. Inflation was over 11
percent and rising. Capital flight, legal and illegal, was a persistent phenomenon.

In 1978 Rhodesia's economy was notable for its low propor-

2. *Economist,* April 21, 1979.

tion of gross fixed capital formation originating in the public sector (only 40 percent), and for its strikingly low proportion of public to total employment (20 percent). The agricultural dominance of a handful of whites; the manufacturing importance of a comparatively few firms; the role of Anglo-American, Turner Newhall, and Union Carbide in the mining sector and Anglo-American in agriculture, manufacturing, and mining was obvious. Together these individuals and local firms had contributed to a remarkable degree of self-sufficiency—certainly a sanctions-induced self-sufficiency that most Third World nations could but envy. Even so, 23 percent of GDP in 1972 was due to imports, a proportion that may since have grown. Certainly the most unusual result of sanctions and isolation was an increase in the flexibility of the economy. Zimbabwe has reduced its imports and altered its exports, shifted from the manufacture of intermediate to the production of capital goods, and made other changes. But, mining aside, Africans were not well integrated into the managerial or technological sectors of the economy. The subsistence sector had given Africans little experience.

In 1979 bank analysts were predicting a further fall in Zimbabwean GDP: "The prospects for a return to meaningful real growth this year remain slim." At best, real GDP will show little change. At worst, there could well be a 4 percent further decline.[3]

Relations with Neighbors

Given its landlocked position, Zimbabwe must obviously depend for access to the sea on Botswana and South Africa (on which countries it now relies exclusively) and Mozambique (its traditional route of imports and exports). In the 1980s, these practical ties will limit its freedom of diplomatic and internal political maneuver and may make it more a hostage to its powerful neighbors than has been true hitherto. However, Zimbabwe will also be able to exert an influence on Zambia, the exports and imports of which flow conveniently through its arteries.

Of greater salience are the modern ties of industrial and con-

3. Standard Bank, *Review*, April 1979, 6.

sumer markets, hydroelectricity, and transportation. Together with Zambia, the colony of Rhodesia shared (if not equally) the flow of the Zambezi River, and therefore the hydroelectric power and tourist potential of the Kariba hydroelectric scheme on the river. Ideally, the Central African Power Corporation (controlled by Zambia and Zimbabwe) or a successor will operate in such a way as to reintegrate the power supplies of the various Zambian and Zimbabwean schemes for the benefit of the mines, industries, and consumers of both. Reopening scheduled air traffic between Zambia and Zimbabwe, as well as making road transport easier, would also end the isolation of Zambia and Zaire from the south and contribute to commercial development in the northern as well as the southern portions of Central and southern Africa. Most of all, Zambia (and to a lesser extent Zaire) requires access to ports in Mozambique, especially for the export of copper. In the medium term, this is no small matter for Zambia; the use by Zambia of the Zimbabwe railways will also be critical in terms of foreign exchange and other earnings for Zimbabwe. The Tazara Railway linking Zambia and Tanzania in no way lessens the importance attached by Zambians to their traditionally least expensive export and import route via Beira or East London and Port Elizabeth.

For Botswana, the continued control of Rhodesia Railways by a Zimbabwean successor is helpful. The Rhodesia Railways administration not only provides Botswana's only major import and export route. It also subsidizes passenger traffic within Botswana by keeping fares at an artificially low level. Overall, it also maintains and runs what would be an operation of great cost for Botswana alone. Therefore, an internationally recognized independence for Zimbabwe may well include a painful reassessment of railway arrangements between black governments with different national objectives.

Mozambique would welcome the resumption of railway, road, and air traffic from Zimbabwe (and Zambia) to Beira, now vastly underused, and Maputo. For Mozambique, an internationally recognized independence for Zimbabwe would permit the renewal of relations and thus the reopening of the border. Although it is likely that Mozambique will work with any black government, it may well exact more concessions of economic detriment to Zimbabwe from a moderate black government than from one with which the revolutionary government of Mozambique could feel secure.

Developments along this line could compel a future moderate black government to rely more than presently contemplated upon ties to South Africa. Indeed, whatever black governments come to power in Zimbabwe in the 1980s may find it economically expedient to maintain existing close relationships with a South Africa that now supplies most of Zimbabwe's military, industrial, and consumer imports. Certainly South Africa will try to encourage any future government to take advantage of South Africa's industrial and infrastructural capacity. Obviously, the extent to which Zimbabwe feels it can deal politically with South Africa will lessen its dependence upon Mozambique and Botswana; it might also—conceivably—contribute to the influence that it can exert upon South Africa, which may hunger after good relations with a new black neighbor. Potential for political leverage exists on all sides, and is bound to have an impact upon purely economic considerations.

10 | The Struggle for Majority Rule

ALTHOUGH THE AFRICANS OF ZIMBABWE have long and vigorously opposed the continuation of white rule, by 1979 that opposition had fractured, with several bitterly antagonistic black parties vying for primacy in the new Zimbabwe. They espoused distinctive nationalist philosophies and differed strikingly as to both strategy and short-term tactics. They were also separated ethnically, by personality, and by the impress of recent history.

The African Resistance

It was not always so. After the failure of the long and destructive Ndebele and Shona wars in the 1890s against white colonizers, Africans submitted to white rule — but not without continuous protest. Through the medium of voluntary associations, welfare groups, the churches, and other quasi-political organizations, Africans made known their dissatisfaction with the way white settlers disregarded their rights and discriminated against them socially, economically, and materially.

The catalogue of African grievances is long and difficult to exaggerate. Africans suffered legislative as well as personal denials of rights. Like the more deprived black South Africans and Namibians, they pleaded for a fair franchise, for equal employment opportunity, and for control over the soil in which they planted their subsistence crops and the grass on which they grazed their ill-fed cattle. But instead of improved treatment from the whites who controlled the colony from 1923, Africans received only privation. They forfeited their best land in the 1930s, on several occasions lost the opportunity to vote as a result of the revision of franchise thresholds, were segregated in the towns, and were consistently denied economic advancement. Laying petitions before the distant king, appealing to local politicians, pleading for consideration, and verbal protest at public meetings availed Africans little.

Political parties for Africans were formed in the 1920s, but these were élite bodies with little impact. Such bodies did oppose the imposition in 1953 of a Federation of Rhodesia and Nyasaland for fear that it would effectively bury African rights and aspirations. The Africans in Southern Rhodesia (as the colony was then called) were less energetic and organized in their protests, however, than their nationalist counterparts in Northern Rhodesia (now Zambia) and Nyasaland (now Malawi). In both of those protectorates, too, the anti-Federal agitation helped to consolidate the formation of the African National Congresses, or parties, which carried the struggle against white and British rule forward throughout the 1950s and 1960s to independence. In Southern Rhodesia, however, Africans gave the Federation a few years to prove itself. When, in their view, it failed to provide for effective black participation in either the Federal or the territorial government, and seemed simply to extend the white rule of the past into a segregated present and a similarly segregated future, Africans decided to follow the lead of their northern colleagues (and those in South Africa) and establish a modern political party to enunciate and work for change.

The Zimbabwe African People's Union

In 1957 a group of young men formed the Southern Rhodesian African National Congress (ANC) and invited Joshua Nkomo to become its first president. A Methodist educated at an American mission-run secondary school in Natal and later at the Hofmeyr School of Social Work in Johannesburg, Nkomo had been employed as a welfare officer on the Rhodesia Railways, as a trade union leader of the Railway Workers' Union, and as a shop-owner, insurance salesman, and auctioneer. He had also participated in negotiations in London over the establishment of the

Federation and had stood unsuccessfully for a Federal parliamentary seat. Of all existing educated Africans of national stature and mature age, Nkomo was expected to provide the kind of leadership that the indigenous majority in Southern Rhodesia had long lacked.

Originally there was only a single organization of Africans opposed to white rule. The ANC was proscribed and its main leaders jailed (Nkomo was out of the country, however) in 1959. It was succeeded by the National Democratic Party (NDP), which was also banned, in 1961. This was followed in 1962 by the Zimbabwe African People's Union (ZAPU), led by Nkomo. His principal aides were T. George Silundika, Robert Mugabe, Ndabaningi Sithole, J. Z. Moyo, and Josiah Chinamano. Throughout much of this early period, the movement of nationalism that these men headed had universal support among Africans throughout the colony. Ideological differences were muted and whatever personal disagreements there may have been over tactics and strategy were seldom voiced.

Nevertheless, Nkomo's judgment and leadership were increasingly a source of discontent within certain sections of the movement. In 1961 he temporarily lost favor by agreeing to constitutional changes proposed by the British government and supported by the white Rhodesian leadership of the day. In the next year some of his followers thought that they detected decreased militancy and determination in his approach to the liberation of the colony. By then the white electorate was turning sharply to the right, rejecting an accommodationist approach, and Britain was beginning the process of halting the Federal experiment and preparing for the independence of Zambia and Malawi. Just when progress and freedom seemed assured for their northern brethren, Rhodesian Africans realized that they were being thrown back into the cauldron to simmer or boil with a set of uncompromising white politicians, one of whom was Ian Smith, who became the leader of the right-wing Rhodesian Front in 1962. Action seemed essential; the African leadership began to wonder if Nkomo were still equal to the task.

Younger, more educated members of Nkomo's entourage began about this same time to accuse Nkomo of being too willing to compromise with whites, of being personally too easy for whites to seduce with promises of luxurious living, and of not being sufficiently ideological (in the sense that Nkomo then had little interest in debates over socialism, capitalism, Maoism, and so on). In the early 1960s, too, his critics felt that he accepted advice from and gave privileges to his older associates, most of whom spoke Sindebele, the minority but historically dominant language of the country. Many of the more recently trained men were from Cishona-speaking sections of Rhodesia. For them Nkomo's legitimacy, which originally stemmed from his involvement with striking railway workers and his leadership of the African National Congress from 1957, had been dissipated by years of easy living, egregious negotiating errors, and a generally flabby approach to what they considered the hard questions of nationalist strategy. Nkomo's failures in 1953 and 1961 contributed to their disenchantment with his qualities. When he fled to Tanzania in 1962 and 1963 to escape arrest and was unceremoniously sent home by President Julius Nyerere, they lost faith entirely.

The younger nationalists accordingly sought a leader more ascetic, more determined, and more willing to accept the argument that only violence could free Rhodesia from white domination. (Nkomo did not then approve of violence as a strategy). The fact that these younger men could never easily explain away Nkomo's support from the masses failed to interrupt their reveries of a future that excluded him and his still-loyal followers.

The Zimbabwe African National Union

For all of these reasons — ethnic, stylistic, ideological, and personal — Sithole, Mugabe, and a number of the younger militants broke away from Nkomo's ZAPU in 1963 and formed the Zimbabwe African National Union (ZANU). Sithole became its president, with Mugabe as its chief organizer and second-in-command. Antagonisms between ZANU and ZAPU quickly grew bitter, with the better-financed ZAPU at first remaining dominant in the internecine nationalistic struggles of the mid-1960s. But even before Ian Smith's declaration of independence in 1965, the white government banned both ZAPU and ZANU and imprisoned its top leadership. Nkomo and most ZAPU leaders spent the next decade at Gonakudzingwa, a remote, dusty detention center in the southeastern Lowveld (Silundika was in Lusaka, where he remained). There Nkomo's weight increased to nearly 300 pounds. His views hardened, as did his determination to triumph over whites. Mugabe, Sithole, and most of the ZANU hierarchy were simultaneously incarcerated in the maximum-security section of Salisbury Central Prison. Sithole was subsequently tried for plotting the assassination of Ian Smith, and sentenced to life imprisonment. Although years of deprivation, for some of the detained Africans they were also years of intellectual achievement. A number took law degrees and other professional courses by correspondence. One completed his university education and two law courses — all by correspondence. For most, too, they were years of planning and plotting, and years of testing the mettle of their jailed compatriots.

ZAPU was the first to mount guerrilla attacks from outside the country, but these were poorly led and reflected a lack of training; in exile, ZAPU was more shrill than energetic by 1970. ZANU, meanwhile, was only active overseas. But from 1972, after several years of training, its guerrillas made forays from Zambia and Mozambique, which was then partially controlled by troops of the Front for the Liberation of Mozambique, or Frelimo. These attacks were remarkably successful in the sense that Rhodesian whites became fearful and could no longer ignore the threat of guerrilla incursions. In terms of the rivalry between ZANU and ZAPU, these initial military successes seemed to promise a victory that would specifically exclude Nkomo and others of the "old guard" who had been too "soft" and too muddled to follow the model of nationalistic attack pioneered by Frelimo. After the coup in Portugal in 1974 and the availability of safe havens in Mozambique after it gained independence in 1975 under a Marxist black government, it seemed that ZANU guerrillas had a clear road to domination over ZAPU, if not Smith. Indeed, in the early 1970s, with Nkomo, Mugabe, and Sithole still in detention, President Kenneth Kaunda of Zambia and Nyerere largely backed ZANU, then led by Herbert Chitepo, a lawyer, and Josiah Tongogara, its field commander.

The Rivals

Another figure became prominent in 1971, when the then British government agreed to transfer power and legitimacy to Smith if he could obtain the consent of the black majority. To ascertain the views of these 6 million Rhodesians, Britain sent a large group (the Pearce Commission) of politicians and former civil servants (including some ex-colonial governors) to Rhodesia to hold meetings with urban and rural Africans. As a part of the Rhodesian-British agreement, a number of second-echelon ZANU and ZAPU leaders were released from prison. They formed the African National Council to mobilize African opinion against the proposed devolution of power to Smith. Two ex-detainees, Eddison Zvobgo and Edson Sithole, asked Abel Muzorewa, a Methodist bishop trained in the United States, to assume the mantle of leadership. He was then apolitical and secure mostly in religious favor. For them, he was an excellent choice who proved capable of giving the stamp of respectability to what was, sub rosa, a reasonably militant organization determined to frustrate the proposed transfer by encouraging Africans to offer a firmly negative answer to the opinion-seeking Pearce Commission. But, as a result of their ability to mobilize African sentiment against the handover of power to Smith, Muzorewa gained stature and, as the militants one by one left the country or were arrested, his credibility and leadership grew. Moreover, Muzorewa had not been party to the nationalist feuds of the 1960s, and that helped.

When Nkomo, Mugabe, Sithole, and others were released from prison and detention in 1974, Muzorewa was still a force with which to be reckoned. Although Kaunda and Nyerere tried to bring all of the leaders together in one common organization, the success of the ZANU guerrillas made them reluctant to play a secondary role behind a leader like Nkomo, for whom they had little respect, or Muzorewa, who had few credentials of militancy. Mugabe and Sithole had meanwhile grown personally antagonistic in prison, and Mugabe led the major portion of ZANU out of the old organization into the guerrilla camps in Mozambique.

Sithole lost his following, and retained only a minor constituency within Rhodesia. Thus, from the end of the long imprisonment until the Geneva negotiations of 1976, Rhodesia had not one or two, but four contending nationalist organizations.

The basis of their differences was personal and historical. But it was also tactical: Mugabe espoused violence and used more extreme language; the others were less militant. And the organizations were ethnically chauvinistic in a way that was new and more irreconcilable than ever before. Nkomo and many (but not all) of his lieutenants speak Sindebele. Only a very few, however, are of royal blood, or true Ndebele. Several are Cishona-speakers. Nkomo and ZAPU drew on a Sindebele-speaking base, and, accurately or not, ZAPU's appeal from about 1974 on has been largely based on its linguistic affinities. But by 1974 the bulk of the black soldiers in the Rhodesian army were Karanga; so were the ZANU guerrillas. Tongogara and Simon Mutuuswa (Rex Nhongo), their generals, were both Karanga. Many of the political leaders closely allied in Mozambique with the soldiers were Karanga.

Mugabe is not a Karanga but comes from the Zezeru area northwest of Salisbury. He has gained the backing of the guerrillas, however, and since 1975 has been their political spokesman and, less assuredly, leader. He is ascetic and dedicated, with a fervent streak that contrasts starkly with the personality of Nkomo. Yet without Karanga support, Mugabe would have no strong ethnic political base.

Mugabe was born at a Roman Catholic mission station near Salisbury in 1928. The son of a laborer, he was educated at the mission. Afterwards he taught primary school in what was then Southern Rhodesia before completing his secondary education and going on to Fort Hare University College, then the leading establishment of higher education in southern Africa, where he obtained a bachelor's degree in 1951. At Fort Hare, a center of student opposition to apartheid, he became politically active, joining the Youth League of the African National Congress. Back home, he taught in schools in Southern Rhodesia and obtained a B.Ed. degree by correspondence. In 1955 he taught at Northern Rhodesia's leading training school for teachers and, again studying by mail, obtained a B.Sc. degree from the University of London.

In 1958, a year after Ghana became independent, Mugabe joined a teacher training college in Takoradi, Ghana. As well as teaching in a noncolonial atmosphere, Mugabe married a Ghanaian. Together they returned to Rhodesia in 1960, where Mugabe became publicity secretary of the NDP, a post he retained in ZAPU. The Rhodesian authorities restricted Mugabe (that is, detained him without trial, but not in a prison) in 1962 for three months. In 1963 he was again arrested, but escaped to Tanzania, helping to establish ZANU. In prison in Salisbury from 1964 to 1975, he obtained London law and administration degrees by correspondence and earned the respect of most of his detained ZANU colleagues.

After the split with Mugabe, Sithole, an Ndau, likewise discovered that he had no important ethnic constituency. His Cishona-speaking followers are few and located largely in the east of the country along the border with Mozambique. Muzorewa, a Manyika, also speaks Cishona, but his version of the language is that of eastern Mashonaland—traditionally the politically most attuned part of the colony. Any assessment of modern Zimbabwean politics has to take into account these ethnic realities. The cleavages that they represent bedeviled attempts to promote the integration and stability of the country in the 1970s, and will endure into the future.

Toward Majority Rule

African cleavages, the skillful intransigence of Smith's white Rhodesian regime, and the failure of United Nations sanctions long upset British-sponsored attempts to put its colony on the path toward majority rule. By 1974, despite an economic boycott, which made the sales of tobacco and other export commodities difficult, despite a partial British blockade of Beira (then one of Rhodesia's two main rail outlets, the other being Mozambique's major port of Lourenço Marques, now Maputo), despite an internationally unacceptable currency, and despite its status as a pariah, the self-declared government of Rhodesia had maintained its usurped independence and had flourished economical-

ly. Confident of economic and moral support from neighboring
South Africa and the Portuguese colony of Mozambique, and
aware that the blockade of Beira and any number of international sanctions would not materially limit its supplies of oil or,
indeed, its ability to import virtually anything, even blacklisted
aircraft, Rhodesia had already turned itself into a Republic,
spurned reasonably favorable settlement offers from Britain, and
looked forward, bravely and confidently, well into the future. African discontent had, admittedly, thwarted the smooth ascent
into legitimacy that was expected to follow the Pearce Commission exercise. But that was merely a lost opportunity. Smith and
his followers were also confident that they could meet the challenge of guerrillas on their northern borders. Certainly, with
South African assistance, and the easy availability of petroleum
and the materiel of war, Smith feared little before a coup in Portugal in early 1974 profoundly altered the strategic picture of
southern Africa.

At various intervals Smith had agreed to talk about regular-
izing his regime. There had been talks about talks between Smith
and Muzorewa during 1973 and 1974, but they assumed no ur-
gency until the demise of Portugal as a colonial power. Thereafter, the prospect of an independent Mozambique, together
with the intensified guerrilla attacks in northeastern Rhodesia,
gave Smith greater reason than before to seek African cooperation. The realization that a Marxist Mozambique could deny its
harbors and other accustomed mercantile facilities to Rhodesia
was compelling. More worrying for the whites was South Africa's
patent refusal to intervene on the side of Mozambique's white
colonists. Its public willingness to accept a revolutionary-minded
government in Mozambique clearly altered the strategic context
of the struggle for control of Rhodesia and all of southern Africa.

Rhodesian whites suddenly became aware that they could no
longer count upon the hitherto unquestioned support of their pa-
tron to the south. As a client state, Rhodesia could be jettisoned.
Because South Africa was concerned about its own survival and
was persuaded that it could maximize that survival by buying
time with concessions of territorial space, the sacrifice of white
Rhodesia (to be followed by Namibia) became a logical option.

Pragmatic after many years of ideological tilting, the government of Prime Minister B. Johannes Vorster determined that waging war in Rhodesia for Rhodesians was more dangerous than defending its own frontiers, and that a new multiracial or black government in Rhodesia could be manipulated and influenced without too much short-term anxiety for South Africa. Helping to ensure a reasoned and gradual transfer of power in Rhodesia would, South Africa realized, enhance the likelihood of peace and stability in southern Africa. Without that peace and stability, South Africa could not hope for the kind of respite, perhaps five or ten years, that it required to begin to reorganize its own internal affairs. Without such an era of good neighborly relations, hostilities would be far more likely, and Mozambique, which shared a border on the KwaZulu homeland, would be very much more threatening.

After the coup in Portugal and the agreement that Mozambique should gain its independence in 1975, Zambian and South African policy regarding the short-term future of southern Africa became congruent for the first time. Like South Africa, Zambia desperately required stability in southern Africa. It sought a surcease from tension in order to attend fully to its own maturing developmental objectives. Moreover, the end of Portuguese imperialism coincided with a precipitous decline in the world price of copper, Zambia's economic mainstay, and exacerbated anxieties about the routes employed to export copper overseas. Even with the completion of the railway from Zambia to Tanzania in 1975, the port of Dar es Salaam would remain congested and inefficient. With civil war in Angola, the tortuous rail route to the port of Lobito would become hazardous, if not unusable. The export of copper (apparently begun covertly in November 1975 to Lourenço Marques) and the import of consumer goods and machinery through Rhodesia therefore held a renewed attraction. Equally compelling, the end of the guerrilla war in Rhodesia could relieve Zambia of its role as an increasingly uncomfortable host to strong military forces capable of supporting division within Zambia. The prospect of small but well-trained private armies contending in Zambia and, conceivably, employing their energies on behalf of one or another competitor for power, worried Kaunda and his United National Independence Party. With a halt to warfare in Rhodesia, too, Zambia could cease devoting a comparatively large proportion of its national budget to the kind of expensive weaponry that was primarily designed to defend its territory from Rhodesian or South African aggression.

Attempts at a Settlement

The changes in Portugal and their impact upon southern Africa thus led to a much heralded conference at the Victoria Falls in 1975. Unusually, the major, if unacknowledged, sponsors of the meeting were South Africa and Zambia. But any chance that the conference might have had to ensure a smooth transition to majority rule in Rhodesia foundered on the rocks of white Rhodesian intransigence and ZANU anxiety. The South Africans could compel Smith to talk, but not to agree. ZANU, for its part, had demonstrated a consistent ability to infiltrate armed groups into the Rhodesian northeast, where its guerrillas had harrassed white settlers. Escalating violence seemed to ZANU the surest, swiftest, and most honorable way to ensure the triumph of black rule in Rhodesia. The ease and precision of Frelimo's takeover of Mozambique strengthened that argument. ZANU saw no reason to lose the initiative. Moreover, it feared that South Africa and Zambia intended the meeting at the Victoria Falls to transfer power in stages specifically to Nkomo. Kaunda was known to be be partial to Nkomo on historical, ideological, and personal grounds. For these reasons ZANU was as difficult as was Smith at the meeting.

One result of the breakdown of negotiations at the Victoria Falls was a tightening of the logistical noose by Mozambique. In early 1976 it cut the rail lines from its ports of Maputo and Beira to Rhodesia. Exporting and importing thus became more expensive for Smith's government. Rhodesia hastily had to construct a single-line link from Rutenga, near Bulawayo, to Beitbridge and the Transvaal. Rhodesia also had to rely on increasingly dangerous road transport ties to South Africa. The old rail line through Botswana to Mafeking remained open, but not for the goods of war, since Botswana began more strictly to enforce its prohibitions against the transport of materiel and of fuel.

In 1976 there was another major attempt to reach a resolution of the Rhodesian conflict. United States Secretary of State Henry Kissinger had in 1975 tried ineptly to avert the coming to power in Angola of a Soviet-backed and Cuban-assisted Marxist party, the Movement for the Popular Liberation of Angola (MPLA), led by Dr. Agostinho Neto. Kissinger, presumably cooperating with South Africa and Zaire, had backed two non-Marxist parties with arms and funds. He had also welcomed the abortive South African invasion of Angola in the second half of the year. However, the United States Senate eventually curtailed the effectiveness of his clandestine assistance. With Angola passing into the hands of the MPLA in 1976 and with a presidential election scheduled for the autumn in the United States, Kissinger made two trips to Africa. His speeches signaled a major attempt to recoup the ground that the United States had lost. So did his actions. With the help of Vorster, and after some perhaps purposely ambiguous conversations with Nyerere and Kaunda, Kissinger persuaded Smith to come to Pretoria. There, in September 1976, Smith—who had frequently said that Rhodesia would never suffer majority rule in his lifetime—agreed that the time had indeed come to transform Rhodesia into a multiracial, ultimately black-ruled state. This announcement was greeted with horror by many Rhodesian whites and with skepticism by blacks. Smith, after all, had deftly avoided being compelled to end his own and white power for a decade. Were American promises and South African pressure sufficient to make him change?

The proof was supposed to come in Geneva, where an all-party conference convened in October 1976 under a British chairman. Smith was there. So were Nkomo and ZAPU, Mugabe and ZANU, Muzorewa and the African National Council, Sithole and his rump ZANU, and James Chikerema and the Front for the Liberation of Zimbabwe (FROLIZI). But the will or the motive to come to closure was not. Once Jimmy Carter was elected president in the United States and Kissinger began moving out of public life, Smith had fewer incentives to negotiate his own demise. Likewise, despite the fact that Kaunda and Nyerere had insisted that ZAPU and ZANU go to Geneva as a newly cobbled-together Patriotic Front, Mugabe and Nkomo still distrusted each other, and their own lieutenants and military advisers were, if anything, more hostile. At that point, too, Nkomo had virtually no guerrillas ready for combat. Mugabe and Tongogara commanded about 5,000 trained soldiers, and were thus unwilling to see their field advantages dissipated at the negotiating table. The other African groups were weak and splintered. The result was booty for the innkeepers of Geneva, frustration in the West and in the capitals of the front-line states (Zambia, Tanzania, Angola, Mozambique, and Botswana), and increased cynicism on the part of black and white Rhodesians. When the Geneva talks recessed for Christmas, it was clear that almost nothing had been accomplished and, depending upon one's point of view, either Smith had again escaped or the Africans had failed to grasp the nettle decisively. The talks never reconvened.

The Patriotic Front

After Geneva the guerrillas redoubled their war effort. ZANU maintained its strength. In 1977, when it had about 1,000 soldiers in the field, another 2,000 to 3,000 in camps in Mozambique, and a further 3,000 to 4,000 in training in Tanzania, ZANU's operations were raising the cost of Rhodesian defenses to high levels and severely threatening white morale. By mid-year, ZANU had demonstrated a satisfactory ability to hinder Rhodesian control of the isolated eastern and northeastern sectors of the colony. It was receiving a steady flow of materiel from and through Mozambique and Tanzania. Thanks to Chinese and some intermittent Soviet and Eastern bloc support, ZANU seemed poised by late in the year to dominate events in a black-ruled Zimbabwe. Whites were leaving the country in large numbers. Casualties were growing on both sides, and even Rhodesian preemptive strikes into Mozambique seemed to halt the attacks only temporarily.

In both the political and the military fields, ZAPU began a remarkable renaissance in 1977. In 1976 ZAPU's military arm could claim no more than a total of 1,000 soldiers. Stout Soviet support, the fresh backing of Kaunda, and a renewed determination on Nkomo's own part proved significant. By mid-1977 ZAPU's soldiers had become more proficient and more numerous. Small squads began to penetrate northwestern Rhodesia from Zambia and shoot their way with relative ease toward the Tuli block area of east central Botswana. Several hundred were in the field at any one time, several thousand were in the final stages of readiness for combat in camps in Zambia (where Cuban advisors joined them), and another 6,000, by late 1977, were undergoing various stages of training. There was a celebrated exodus of young black Rhodesians out of the colony, into Botswana, and on to Zambia for training by ZAPU. The airlifting of these putative freedom fighters continued on a daily basis well into 1978 (paradoxically, in Rhodesian-owned aircraft leased to a South African cover firm and then to Air Botswana, and flown by Botswana-hired South African pilots). By 1978, for the first time in the battle against Rhodesia, ZAPU could legitimately claim that it was not only participating in the military struggle but also — and the Rhodesian army feared it — opening up a credible second front to harass the white defenders.

By the beginning of 1978, the Patriotic Front had achieved a modicum of cohesion. At least Nkomo and Mugabe, despite their personal differences, were publicly cooperative and, whether in New York, Lusaka, or London, personally warm. Yet well into 1979 the Patriotic Front still had no headquarters or officers, except the two cochairmen, no bureaucracy — in short, no existence except as a negotiating construct or alliance of convenience. The old cleavages persisted as well.

Ethnicity deepened the underlying differences between them. Although ethnic distinctions had meant little in Rhodesian politics twenty years before, in 1979, as the spoils of a new Zimbabwe grew closer and more inviting, so the vision of power being parceled out according to tribal affiliation became more and more real. Ethnic antagonism flows, in Zimbabwe, as elsewhere, from the pursuit of power. It provides a means of controlling and utilizing power, and thus of mobilizing adherents and, when the time comes, voters.

The personality differences between the leaders go back to the 1960s. ZANU adherents doubt if Nkomo can be trusted. Even if Mugabe is prepared to cooperate, many of his younger adherents remain suspicious. Supported by Kaunda, they wonder if

Nkomo will sell out Mugabe for a special deal with Muzorewa. Certainly, Nkomo's private conversations with Smith in early 1976, and again in mid-1978, revived the old worries about Nkomo's steadfastness of character.

Ideologically, the two wings of the Patriotic Front are still divided. Tongogara, Mutuuswa, and the Karanga intellectuals (many of whom were trained in the United States), who have emerged only occasionally from Mozambique, still espouse rather doctrinaire Marxist ideas about the desirability of a fully planned, centrally directed economy in accord with Mozambiquan rhetoric. But just as President Samora Machel of Mozambique has acted pragmatically, so there is likely to be a heavy dose of realism lurking behind ZANU's enunciated principles. Certainly Mugabe, whose speeches in China and often-expressed antagonism to special privileges for whites have given little comfort to supporters of free enterprise (notably Sir Seretse Khama, president of Botswana), is much more pragmatic than he usually appears. In 1977 he privately expressed his horror at what Machel had done to the economy of Mozambique. Mugabe lived in Ghana under President Kwame Nkrumah and would not be the first to seek the destruction of the modern economy and infrastructure that provides the basis of Zimbabwe's wealth. But, given some scenarios of future independence, Mugabe may not be free to lead his country according to his own assessment of the ways best to attain desired goals.

Politicians, especially those who have over the years only occasionally espied the promised land through narrow keyholes, may be forgiven for altering their ideologies to suit circumstances and patrons. Mugabe may have shifted his views more than is assumed. But it is even harder to credit the fervent espousal of state socialism that has been uttered in recent months by Nkomo. A sometime businessman who has almost always enjoyed the backing of liberal commercial interests in Rhodesia (and, for a time, in South Africa), Nkomo is an unreconstructed capitalist who is almost certain to disappoint the ideological hopes of his Soviet backers. True, some of Nkomo's key lieutenants have been close to the Soviets for more than a decade, but one suspects a pragmatic streak not far below the surface of their rhetoric. Moreover, others among Nkomo's inner circle include virulent, out-spoken proponents of liberal capitalism and, more precisely, of the kind of personal liberties that are not common in Marxist-governed states. In 1977, in Guyana, Nkomo told Ambassador Andrew Young that he wanted whites to continue to play a significant role in Zimbabwe. He is certain to be much more favorably inclined toward foreign investment and white-directed multinational involvement in Zimbabwe than Mugabe or Mugabe's followers.

Nkomo has never been known to be doctrinaire. In this respect his probable stance, and the stance of nearly all of his immediate lieutenants, promises to differ little from that of Muzorewa, Sithole, or their followers. All want to assume control of a thriving, black, Western-oriented economy. They have no interest in the destruction of what has been achieved, and Mugabe would agree. Nkomo and Muzorewa (possibly not Mugabe) believe that social justice can be obtained within the framework of a prosperous economy. Their approach is, furthermore, not known to be incompatible with the present thinking of ordinary Zimbabwean blacks, whose standard of living and of aspiration has long been much higher than that of Africans in Mozambique or Angola.

Nkomo and Mugabe broke with Muzorewa and Sithole in 1975. Thereafter neither Muzorewa nor Sithole could muster much support among exiles or among the leaders of the frontline states. Only a return home was capable of bringing about a reversal of their political eclipses. As a result, Muzorewa went back in 1976 and Sithole in 1977, both presumably encouraged to fill the internal African political vacuum by Smith's promises of a positive reception. Conceivably, too, there were South African hints of material support. Most of all, Muzorewa and Sithole appear to have been enticed home by their desire to recoup their political losses. They thought that they could do so by joining Smith's substitution of black for white leadership of the government of Rhodesia. The third black actor in what became known as the internal settlement was Chief Jeremiah Chirau, an appointed chief who created the government-backed Zimbabwe United People's Organization (ZUPO) in 1976.

The Internal Settlement

In March 1978, these three black leaders joined Smith to form an executive council; their black followers were given positions as joint heads (with white followers of Smith) of cabinet departments. Although the white-dominated Rhodesian parliament remained legislatively supreme, for the next year the executive council effectively ruled Rhodesia, with the blacks exercising noticeably little influence over the country's political destiny. Chirau and Smith attempted in August 1978 to bring Nkomo into the so-called interim government—a strategy blessed by Nigeria, Zambia, and South Africa—but their scheme was scuttled when its existence was discovered and denounced by Mugabe, Nyerere, and Sithole. Aside from this manuever, however, Smith and his black cohorts assiduously positioned themselves for an attempt to convert the interim, internal settlement into a lasting, black-led, white-backed successor government that could hope for international recognition and an end to Rhodesia's outlaw status.

Toward that goal the executive council began dismantling the legal underpinnings of segregation. It voided the Land Apportionment Act, ended school separation (because of fee requirements, many previously white schools nevertheless remained primarily filled by white pupils), established a minimum wage, and approved a new, white-devised constitution. The constitution, a document of 151 pages, which was submitted to and approved by only white voters in 1979, gave blacks 72 of 100 seats in a new lower house of parliament and 20 of 30 seats in a new upper house, or Senate. But it retained 28 seats for whites (3.5 percent of the total population), and—controversially—specified that between 1979 and 1989 amendments to the constitution could be passed only if 78 percent of the legislature (all the blacks and 6 of the whites) voted favorably.

This limitation on the exercise of black sovereignty was but one of several incorporated into the constitution. In order to ensure continued white control of security, foreign affairs, the judiciary, and the civil service, the constitution transferred day-to-day jurisdiction and all promotion of personnel in those areas to new, white-dominated commissions of "experts." As a whole, the constitutional blueprint for a new Rhodesia was cleverly designed to convey only limited, carefully circumscribed power in defined, fully demarcated spheres of jurisdiction. Moreover, in addition to the protection offered by the commissions, seats in the nineteen-man cabinet were to be allotted to blacks and whites according to the proportion of the vote received by their parties; for at least five years whites would be represented in the cabinet by 25 percent of its total membership. Several key ministries would therefore continue to be guided by whites, not blacks.

The 1979 Elections

Elections under the new constitution were held in April 1979. The main balloting, for the black seats, was held over four days, using mobile polling booths guarded by army patrols. Press censorship limited the spread of dissent; political meetings could not be held freely, and full-scale campaigning was impossible; especially for ZANU and ZAPU, both of which had been banned in 1978. Their exiled leaders urged a boycott, but a total of 1.85 million black Rhodesians cast ballots. That number was about 65 percent of the preelection forecast total of potential voters; but since the Rhodesians had not registered voters and had established no basis for their estimates, the percentage who voted may — in reality — have been either much lower or much higher than the percentage triumphantly reported by white authorities. The movement of the polling booths and military protection in most areas effectively deterred guerrillas of the Patriotic Front, which had promised to disrupt the elections. Yet many outlying rural areas reported very low polls, with high turnouts being listed for the urban and peri-urban black areas. (Two peri-urban polling areas in Central Mashonaland reported turnouts in excess of 100 percent, thus casting doubt on overall percentages and helpfully balancing the low turnouts in rural areas presumably penetrated by guerrillas.)

Whatever the percentage, Muzorewa's United African National Congress (UANC) attracted 67 percent of the black vote, giving him 51 seats. Sithole's rump ZANU obtained 12 seats; Ndebele Chief Kayisa Ndiweni's United National Federal Party,

a possible covert surrogate for ZAPU, won 10 seats; and Chirau's
ZUPO, none. All of the white seats, voted on in separate elections, were held by Smith's Rhodesian Front. In the cabinet,
therefore, Muzorewa controlled ten places, Smith five, and Sithole and Ndiweni two each; for almost a month Sithole and his
fellow elected legislators refused to take their seats either in the
legislature or in the cabinet, calling the massive support for
Muzorewa an indication of the irregularities in the polling procedure. (Before the colony officially adopted its new name of Zimbabwe Rhodesia on June 1, 1979 — it expected to become plain
Zimbabwe in 1980 — and began an era of limited majority rule,
eight of Sithole's supporters were arrested and detained without
trial.) A few weeks before Sithole decided to lead his supporters
back into parliament, Chikerema and six other prominent members of the UANC left Muzorewa's party and took separate seats
on the opposition side of the assembly. This walkout deprived
Muzorewa of his legislative majority, compelling him to rely more
closely than before on the whites, loyal to Ian Smith. Chikerema
claimed that Muzorewa, in his cabinet choices and his other actions, had shown partiality to Manyika; Chikerema and the other
six defectors were all Zezeru.

Muzorewa's Government

In the cabinet, Prime Minister Muzorewa kept the ministries
of defense and combined operations for himself, appointed Francis Zindoga of the UANC as minister of law and order (in charge
of the police), and gave Smith, who had wanted to become minister of defense or combined operations, the title of minister without portfolio. As deputy prime minister, Muzorewa chose a little-
known physician, Silas Mundawarara, who was also appointed
minister of information; Ernest Bulle was appointed minister of
commerce and industry; David Mukome, minister of foreign affairs; George Nyandoro, minister of lands; Walter Mtimkulu,
minister of local government; and Edward Mazaiwana, minister
of education (all six were members of the UANC). Ndiweni and a
supporter received minor cabinet positions, and of the whites,
David Smith became minister of finance; William Irvine, minister of agriculture; and P. K. van der Byl, the most dogmatically

conservative member of the outgoing white cabinet, became minister of justice.

The Rhodesian elections were monitored by groups of unofficial observers from West Germany, Britain, and the United States (the House of Representatives had vetoed a Senate proposal to send official observers). Most of the unofficial observers backed the process and reported favorably on its conduct. As a result Britain's Conservative government, elected in early May, and United States President Carter came under increasing pressure (in the United States, in the form of a Senate resolution) to end sanctions and, finally and once and for all, recognize Rhodesia. Carter's advisors were concerned, however, that any such initiative would widen the existing war and, instead of helping to halt the spread of communism in Africa (the claim of many British and American supporters of the new Rhodesia) would paradoxically remove the last barrier — the American alliance with the front-line states — to the inevitable escalation of Soviet and Cuban influence in southern Africa.

Carter's advisors in the State Department continued to advocate a settlement that would permit the voters of Zimbabwe to choose between Muzorewa or Nkomo and Mugabe — that is, one that would transfer full power to blacks elected unquestionably by the majority in a poll validated by some form of international supervision. To the advisors, and to the front-line states, the 1979 Rhodesian constitution, with its built-in minority veto, was a less than positive contribution to the long-standing Zimbabwean dilemma. Most of all, neither the constitution nor the election of a black government visibly dependent upon whites provided a means conclusively to end the war and bring peace to Zimbabwe. (As Smith passed the premiership to Muzorewa on June 1, he told the press that even the tightly constrained form of majority government that had been empowered under the Zimbabwe Rhodesia constitution had come too soon. Implying that the white bloc in the new cabinet and new parliament would police the Muzorewa administration carefully, he promised to ensure that the colony did not "develop into a banana republic.")[1] Muzorewa's

---

1. Quoted in *New York Times,* June 1, 1979.

victory promised to escalate the war and further involve the Soviet Union and Cuba in its outcome. In the eyes of Africa the Muzorewa victory gave added legitimacy to the martial efforts of the Patriotic Front.

The Continuing Civil War

Nothing Muzorewa or his external backers did during the first days of the new government improved their chances of promoting a cease fire. The Rhodesian army and air force had carried out massive preemptive strikes throughout 1978 and the first nine months of 1979 against guerrilla camps in Mozambique, Angola, and Zambia (including an audacious attack on Nkomo's own house in Lusaka); nonetheless, the guerrillas were still strong and confident of an ultimate victory. The death toll of combatants and civilians since 1972 had reached 14,000 in mid-1979, 5,000 of whom had lost their lives during the first six months of 1979 alone—mute testimony to the increasing intensity of the war. During the year before the elections, the rural areas of Rhodesia had become less and less safe. For example, 1,500 schools had been shut because of war. By early 1979, 90 percent of the country had been put under martial law. In September 1979 martial law was extended to the entire country except for Salisbury and Bulawayo. The cities were unsafe, the outlying regions were perilous, and both whites and Africans had to travel throughout the country in the daytime in convoy. Travel on the roads at night was foolhardy. Journalists filed stories of farmers driving with guns cocked and of elaborate security precautions on white-owned estates and even in the cities. "Almost all white motorists and their passengers carry submachine guns or pistols, while some car owners have fixed monstrous rockets on the car roof. No roads are immune from attack, while on some particularly vulnerable roads, where there is dense vegetation to give the guerrillas cover, there are ambushes every day."[2]

After Nkomo's men used a heat-seeking Soviet SAM-7 ground-to-air missile to shoot down two internal flights of Air Rhodesia in 1978 and 1979, killing a total of 107 passengers,

2. Richard West, "Besieged White Africans," *New York Times*, January 31, 1979.

white panic and anxiety grew to previously unimaginable heights. Most telling of all was the growing cost of the war. Direct expenditures in both 1978 and 1979 were about $1.5 million a day. For a once-prosperous but rapidly deteriorating economy, this was a price that could not be paid—even with South African assistance—indefinitely. Nor could the country's fragile economy endure a war that kept nearly half of its white labor force on patrol and away from their economic pursuits most of the time. In 1978, at least 13,700 whites left Rhodesia. Another 8,061 departed during the first six months of 1979.

Although the government army, with continued South African support in the form of munitions and fuel (and absent a mutiny of its black cadres), could probably have withstood guerrilla incursions for years, the level of combat in 1979 could not sustain high net emigration rates indefinitely. Nor could the economy of Zimbabwe endure the burden of large-scale call-ups and the frequent absence of productive managers and workers. Many observers talk of an outside limit of three years before Muzorewa's Zimbabwe—given 1979's level of combat—would have been compelled to sue for peace.

Prospects for the Future

There are no sure answers, but only a gambler would predict the ability of whites in alliance with Muzorewa to sustain their rebellion for more than a few years. The longer they can, the more surely they will erode the forces of moderation; a Patriotic Front government that gains power as a result of battlefield victory is apt to be far more committed to authoritarianism and, even if Nkomo is then still a leader, to radical rearrangements of the economy. (By that time, too, the economy may have been weakened beyond easy repair.) No established foreign enterprise, much less South Africa and the powers of the West (or even Zambia), would welcome a power that emerged from the barrel of a gun. Even if such a government would probably return in the medium term to the path of economic pragmatism, confiscation of existing extractive industries would receive high priority in the short term. It could be worse, too, for the leaders of tomorrow's military would be far more uncompromising than today's politicians. Beholden to their distant patrons, they would be anxious to demonstrate ideological purity and commitment.

The question remained: What would become of Zimbabwe? If hostilities continued to the bitter end and Cuban and Soviet intervention occurred, destruction and grief might prevent a smooth shift of Rhodesia's highly developed industrial, agricultural, and infrastructural foundations from white to broadly based, internationally recognized, black control. A transformation brought about by guns could plunge Zimbabwe into chaos, causing even more massive white flight than in 1979, and an immediate postindependence breakdown on the Angolan and Mozambiquan models.

There is no easy way to predict the outcome of a further, internationally valid election. If black and white opportunities for coercion were limited, victory would probably go to that group that best combined organizational ability, ethnic mobilization, and personal appeal. In 1979 it was still true that Nkomo's ZAPU had maintained the most extensive national organization within the country. Nkomo's appeal to the masses cannot be discounted; it extends beyond and encompasses his ethnic appeal. Others in his entourage would have an appeal to particular constituencies. It is reasonable to assume that Nkomo could do almost as well on a national basis as Muzorewa, with his appeal to the central Shona, and perhaps to the middle class throughout the country. Mugabe and his followers could be sure only of the Karanga vote. The sum might be enough for a victory of the Nkomo-Mugabe coalition upon which they now count. If so, each would vie with his armed or formerly armed supporters for hegemony. Alternatively, a Nkomo-Muzorewa alliance would arouse the enmity of the Karanga and the then ex-guerrillas. Either result, indeed almost any combination, is a recipe for further civil war or a series of *coups d'état* if no mechanism can be devised definitively to disarm all of the guerrillas and/or maintain the peace after independence.

Thatcher's Initiative

A method that had the virtue of providing for a peaceful devolution of power was unexpectedly suggested in mid-1979 by

Prime Minister Margaret Thatcher of Britain. Although her government, which came to power in May, had been thought to favor the Muzorewa-Smith approach, she spoke vigorously at a meeting of the Commonwealth heads of government in August 1979 of the imperative need for another attempt to negotiate a cease-fire and a scheme for testing the rival claims of Muzorewa and Mugabe-Nkomo in the voting booth rather than on the battlefield.

Taking advice from prime ministers Malcolm Fraser of Australia and Michael Manley of Jamaica, Thatcher demanded that Muzorewa and Nkomo and Mugabe should confer with her in September. Hesitantly, and despite heightened levels of verbal aggression, both sides came. The front-line states had pushed the leaders of the Patriotic Front toward the conference table; Muzorewa, with little choice, given his and South Africa's previous praise for the Thatcher government, also arrived, together with Ian Smith, Sithole, and other white and internal black supporters.

The outlines of the British Commonwealth plan were simple: after a cease-fire and the drastic revision of the 1979 constitution to reduce the residue of white power, elections would be held in order to ascertain whether Muzorewa or the Patriotic Front had the most popular support. Britain would maintain security before and during the elections. The electoral victor would organize a government, sanctions would be lifted, and Zimbabwe would be recognized internationally. The two hardest parts of the proposal were Thatcher's request that Muzorewa make his a real black government (she offered to show him how it could be done) and her determination to preside over full and fair elections, thereby casting considerable doubt upon the acceptability of the April poll.

Thatcher's initiative contended with two different perceptions. First, Muzorewa believed that time was on his side — that the British Parliament would refuse to renew sanctions and that recognition would automatically follow. He also assumed that his white-led troops, backed by South Africa, could withstand guerrilla attack indefinitely, and would not in the near future be inhibited by shortages of liquid fuel. Second, the Patriotic Front,

with 12,000 troops inside Zimbabwe, also believed that time favored its war; negotiations were therefore a waste of verbal effort
unless they were merely to dictate the terms of victory.

A third perception was also relevant in shaping the Thatcher
government's approach to what, because of Zimbabwe's lingering
colonial position, was still Her Majesty's responsibility. Thatcher
and her advisors believed that the Muzorewa government had
grown weak. Losing a crucial segment of his internal following
when Chikerema's group defected, and depending openly on
whites, Muzorewa could do little to avoid the label of "stooge."

The conference ran for more than three months. To the surprise of those who had known Zimbabwean intransigence before,
Lord Carrington, Britain's foreign minister, managed by determination and gifted gamesmanship to compel both the Muzorewa
government and the Patriotic Front to grasp the nettle of compromise in a new and decisive manner. Carrington first persuaded Muzorewa to break with Smith and to accept a new constitution severely limiting white power; whites would henceforth
hold twenty, not twenty-eight, parliamentary seats, would exercise no ten-year veto over constitutional amendments, and would
give up their control of the different "expert" commissions. Next
Carrington set out a transition plan which he effectively gave
both sides no option but to accept. It transferred authority from
Muzorewa to a British governor. All executive, legislative, and
military power was to be given to the governor, who would organize and oversee new elections. It was rather more difficult obtaining agreement on the composition of the electoral supervisory
force, the Front wanting a large, armed detachment. Carrington
preferred a small, unarmed group of observers. The Front also
insisted that its guerrillas be accorded the same status during the
transition period as the soldiers of the official army.

These latter differences bedeviled the final weeks of the conference. But as persistent as Mugabe and Nkomo remained, so
Carrington remained unmoved. In thus concentrating the collective mind of the Front, which understandably did not want to lose
whatever advantages it might already have gained on the battlefield, and, if it gave up its arms, feared having its cadres impris-

oned or otherwise restricted when the polls were about to open, Carrington was mightily assisted by devastating attacks on Zambia by the air force and army of Zimbabwe. In a series of preemptive strikes in October and November, troops loyal to Muzorewa cut rail and road bridges, thus isolating Zambia except to the south. Copper exports could still leave Zambia along that one remaining route, but maize imports vital to the Zambians were held up. Zambia was thus compelled to add its voice to those who were counseling the Front to negotiate. Yet as Zambia itself needed economic relief, so the Front worried about the introduction into the war of a new, dangerous factor: by October it was apparent that the South Africans had reentered the conflict on the side of the Muzorewa government. The Front wanted Carrington to ensure the removal of South Africans from Zimbabwe at the time of a ceasefire. Otherwise, the Front feared a final, inglorious trap.

Carrington's diplomacy brought the possibility of peace to Zimbabwe for the first time since 1965. He promised that the British governor, who arrived in Salisbury in December, would permit neither South African military forces nor the Zimbabwean air force to function after the cease-fire. As a result, Britain and the United States lifted sanctions; 1,200 troops arrived from Britain, Kenya, Australia, New Zealand, and Fiji; a cease-fire was brought about in early 1980; and an election was scheduled for late February, with internationally recognized independence to follow.

Despite the promise of the cease-fire and elections, lasting peace is likely to be unusually difficult to achieve in Zimbabwe. If internationally supervised elections produce no clear-cut victory, the contenders could readily compete for hegemony in conditions less than conducive to ordered development. Indeed, an internally divided government could, given existing ethnic cleavages, lead after a period of a year or two to renewed civil war. Damage to the existing infrastructure and economic deterioration would follow.

Southern
Africa

11 | Evolution or Revolution: The Choices

NO MORE TRYING TEST of policymaking wisdom has been devised than the future of South Africa and its neighbors. The ultimate goals are hardly in dispute. All southern Africans, and most foreigners — whatever their particular persuasion — want to ensure a stable, harmonious, prosperous future for the societies of the region. In countries where confrontation has developed into unimaginably bloody real wars or episodes of equally bloody near war, there is a common yearning for peace — for the absence of conflict, for freedom from the fear of renewed violence, and for days, weeks, and months without the harsh reminders of combat. Everyone, whether black or white, wants at least to achieve the mundane — to be able to enjoy an orderly life without unusual strife. Southern Africans prefer, as do most peoples, to live in an atmosphere marked by stability and prosperity, where harmony, perhaps founded on a common national commitment to particular norms, is a shared aspiration. Few wish to achieve order and stability, however, if it is guaranteed solely by arbitrary, intolerant, governance. Arbitrary governance is almost always inherently unstable, and dangerous for future generations if not for those élites who may benefit during periods of privation forced upon others.

There will be a consensus, even in southern Africa, favoring such general ambitions. But southern Africans less and less in recent decades have agreed among themselves upon their precise definitions. For the long-dominant white minorities, the perpetuation of white hegemony has been equated with the acquisition of stability and prosperity. Given what seemed like a choice between achieving their societal goals by retaining power and sharing it, they choose the first as the best and possibly the only guarantor of continued societal stability. But the retention of power, initially accomplished with ease, little cost, and hardly any shame and guilt, has in recent decades become increasingly expensive, increasingly a subject of international concern and therefore of psychic as well as economic expense, and increasingly unlikely to serve the cause of the societal harmony originally desired.

Whites in Zimbabwe and Namibia have made the kinds of concessions that were anathema a few years ago. Whereas the three societies examined in this book studiously avoided the kinds of power sharing that could, in bygone days, have developed common norms and a value system that cut across the color line, now new methods are being devised to accommodate pressures that have begun faster and faster and more and more threateningly to percolate from below. A key question is whether these maneuvers to associate aspirations that may be diverging faster than they are converging, and any one or more imaginative structural rearrangements, can suffice in the years to come.

The Ingredients of Change

Analyses of South Africa usually reject any model that suggests the present domination of a large majority by a small, if disciplined, minority can or is likely to be perpetuated for more than a few years in the future; precise timetables are purposely left vague. There is agreement that the government of South Africa is strong, its leaders determined and calculating, and its machine of repression and internal control well oiled and well practiced. The fears and motives of Afrikanerdom are not underestimated. Nor is its ruthlessness — its odds-defying hubris and its carefully practiced refusal to respond to external outbursts of condemnation and postures of threat. Afrikanerdom has insulated itself from shame, and subordinated guilt — and almost everything else — to maintaining power in white hands in both the long and the short term. But most analyses nevertheless assume that the status quo cannot last — that the forces of historical determinism will sooner or later overwhelm an unequal, unjust, inhumane system of minority rule. The powerless Prometheus will rise up, break his chains, and — by numerical preponderance and by drawing unbounded energy from the decades of repression — overwhelm whites by one or another form of militancy.

This is an attractive, if unreal, picture. It avoids a counting of those too-numerous societies in the world that have endured repression and authoritarianism — the assault of majorities by minorities, usually elites — for decades and centuries. None still has color as its marker, and that is a qualification that makes of South Africa a distinctly special case. But to assert that the black inhabitants of South Africa shall with certainty and success someday rise up and regain their freedom is to misunderstand how and why the peoples of the Third World have achieved their independence since World War II; it is also to argue from a misreading of that accomplishment to an inevitability that substitutes aspiration for argument, and simple solutions for the complex ones that are appropriate for South Africa's enduring problems.

This is not to suggest that the status quo is apt to endure in any shape rigidly resembling that of the present. A fallacy equal to that of positing — for South Africa — the working of an immutable law of historical determinism is to describe South Africa as a static society that will explode before it shifts. In fact, as earlier chapters have attempted to demonstrate, South Africa has always responded to changing internal and external environments. At times so glacial as to be difficult to discern, there has nevertheless always been movement. In particular, there has been movement that is better designated as maneuvering. Innumerable attempts have been made to redefine and relabel the government's determination to perpetuate Afrikaner power. Those attempts thus to deflect hostile criticism, or to narrow white South Africa as a target of attack from within and without, have offered temporary, expedient relief. None has done or can do more than promise delay. But they have occasioned change, regular redefinitions of the status quo, in recent years a variety of social and economic improvements for some among the majority, and the rethinking and modernization of the axioms of Afrikaner rule. These are all events that indicate official eddying, drifting, shifting, swirling, though without compromise on the key premise of power, and add up to movement or, better yet, a sliding status quo. South Africa in 1980 is not the South Africa of 1970 or 1960.

To reject the status quo as a framework of analysis for South Africa in the 1980s is not to reject the other two alternatives: revolution and evolution. Studies of revolution have shown that the cumulation of crises that usually leads to the cataclysmic overturning of an existing order most often follows a period of liberalization that lifts aspirations and puts a better future almost within grasp. Frustration on its own is insufficient. So are repression and privation, denial and injustice. What seems necessary is the meaningfulness of hope (the sense that dreams are capable of being realized), the development and dissatisfaction of a disgruntled, yet ambitious middle class, the legitimation of the use of violence against rulers, and the conversion to that view of, and then the neutralization or subversion of, the military arm of the government.

By such criteria South Africa may be judged unready for revolution, particularly since the mass of people can never hope to convert to their cause the lesser ranks of the army (most of whom are not black) or gain arms from black police sufficient to hold off the army and air force. The weight of sheer numbers is also more likely to contribute to success if the weapons of combat are roughly equal. But, unlike the underprivileged in the French, American, Russian, and Iranian revolutions, parity cannot be obtained, nor a time in the near future assumed by which the majority of South Africans will have amassed more than sticks, stones, primitive home-made bombs, and an arsenal of similar weapons.

There are small arms in black South Africa, but is there an era ahead when the accumulation of those arms from outside will be sufficient to balance the firepower of the state? The smuggling of massive supplies of arms from outside (and into whose hands?) is difficult to envisage given the character of governmental control of the towns and the countryside. So is the amassing of funds for such a purpose, and the development of the network necessary to ensure the satisfactory distribution of arms prior to a national uprising. The military might of South Africa is awesome, especially in Third World terms. It is better adapted to repressing a massive assault than guerrilla sniping, and it would be assisted by the way in which Africans have been grouped into easily surrounded urban locations and, by and large, kept distant from ports, airfields, and (except for migrant miners) most other strategic sites.

There is a further ingredient: leadership. Non-African outsiders may be unaware of the quality and quantity of black leadership long since driven underground and/or compelled to flee the country. Others, legitimated by the nature of their struggle or the length of their incarceration, are imprisoned, otherwise restricted, banned (and under surveillance), or dead. As quickly as the young, who fueled the fury of Soweto in 1976, or others accept new leaders, they, too, are detained. Aboveground are urban men and women of stature who cannot preach and probably do not want Armageddon to consume South Africa. They speak of the inevitability of revolution if the government fails in time to respond to calls for change. Even rurally based leaders foresee doom if change is delayed, without knowing precisely how to persuade the government to avert the combination of events that they believe will result before too long in revolution. Men and women unseen — ayatollahs hitherto unsuspected — may surely arise to lead their people toward revolution, as may guerrillas infiltrating from outside and fomenting disorder. But the balance of power, or of terror, and the need for so many ingredients to be mixed in precisely the correct order within a context of sophisticated societal control, makes inherently unlikely — as well as merely unpredictable — the likelihood that South Africa's salvation will come by means of a revolution, at least in the 1980s.

To discuss the ways in which South Africa may evolve, since the status quo and revolutionary change are neither realistic nor logical alternatives, is to write not in optimism, but in despair. For successful evolution is no more likely, given what we know of Afrikaner-run South Africa, than a cataclysmic upheaval. Admittedly, evolutionary answers may come in a variety of forms. They may be, indeed are, likely to consist of a series of loosely linked responses that, over time, approximate a solution. They will certainly result less from altruism and sensitivity than from pressure, threats, strikes, uprisings, and combinations of violence that may approach that which is revolutionary without ever quite causing upheaval. Thus, to presume an evolutionary rather than a revolutionary solution to the problems of South Africa is not necessarily to foresee an absence of violence. Diminutions of white hegemony in Africa and in southern Africa, especially in Zimbabwe and Namibia, have distinctly depended upon demonstrations of black power. The flexing of black muscle has enabled white governments to perceive their own self-interest with greater and greater clarity. The gradual transformation of the Smith government into the Muzorewa government is a dramatic case in point, with an escalating guerrilla war the obvious primary motivating force.

For South Africa, evolution could be announced, arranged, and planned for by the ruling oligarchy. It has that power. By boldly charting a future, it could ensure the triumph of an evolutionary solution. But to do so the South African government would have to begin behaving in ways that would be new, and that would mean the massive modification, if not the total abandonment, of the ideological superstructure of apartheid. In some form or other it would necessitate granting blacks the right of political participation and representation — rights that separately and together are anathema to Afrikaners. The sharing of them thoroughly threatens the perpetuation of Afrikaner hegemony. Yet the perpetuation of an Afrikaner stake in an altered South Africa may, in fact, someday mean making just those kinds of concessions. By then they may even seem less heinous and less worrying than other, more bitter, alternatives. The fear is always that by the time Afrikaners are prepared to concede Africans a stake in the country and a share in its government, Africans may be dissatisfied with so little.

The Mechanisms of Compromise

There are an array of potential compromises that could fulfill the requirements of an evolutionary mandate. The use of various kinds of franchise, the qualifications and thresholds of which diminish over (perhaps lengthy) time, would permit political power to be shared slowly, but definitely. The political potential of a black majority could also be realized gradually by the employment of one or another kind of vote weighting, possibly combined with proportional representation. The slogan "one man, one vote" does not always imply "one man, one vote, one value." The latter is the pattern in the West but need not initially be the model for a South Africa undergoing transformation.

These ways of at first diminishing African or enhancing white voting strength could also be linked to methods of rearranging the geographical and therefore the political bases of South African society. Federal forms are often suggested. The present collection of provinces and homelands could be rescrambled (on some kind of Nigerian model?) and larger and smaller states, some with black, some with white majorities, could be linked under loose or strong federal bonds to a racially mixed central tier of government. The reception given to such a scheme would depend upon whether future access to the resources of the whole federation were assured equally for all — whether the mineral wealth and the arable lands of the federation were apportioned roughly along lines judged to be fair. It would also depend upon the manner in which responsibility was proposed to be shared between the central and state governments — whether, in a word, there was a real reallocation of power from the prefederal status quo.

Federal schemes of as yet unspecified kinds have a great appeal to South Africans who want desperately to avoid bloodshed and to find some means of reconciling the opposing sides and posing the least obvious threat to those who are dominant today, and who would be compelled to give up their power. But spokesmen for the disadvantaged increasingly disdain compromises that preserve too much white power and that forever prevent Africans from deciding the destiny of the larger South Africa. That is why Africans emphasize the need for any compromises to be negotiated by blacks and whites meeting together in what is often called a national convention. If an evolutionary solution is imposed, they say, it will be rejected. So will anything that expands from the base of separate development — from the existing homeland model — and that is seen (rightly or wrongly) to be a sly, conceivably cooptive, continuation of past practices.

Africans seek a break with the past that is radical without,

necessarily, being harsh for whites. They are aware of the need
for compromise and conciliation. They prefer an integrated, unified South Africa, but will in the short term doubtless settle for
less, if it is advanced sincerely and is reasonable and just. But
what might prove reasonable in the short term could — that is the
fear — seem less and less reasonable in the medium and flatly unacceptable in the long term.

The federal solution shades in some circles into and encapsu-
lates consociationalism. Based on Dutch and other political models, consociationalism could operate within a federal system, and
within the subordinate states, or in a unified state divided internally into communities. In a consociational state the communities would decide communal questions, but would share with a
central government power over defense, foreign affairs, and so
on. The leading advocate of consociational solutions has offered
a rough blueprint.[1] But his disciples in South Africa have several
adaptations in mind, all of which are intended to preserve a modicum of white privilege or to give Africans the perquisites of power — but within a sphere that is by definition limited. Consociationalism alone, or consociationalism and federalism together,
therefore provide a framework within which the nature of the
prevailing debate in South Africa might be altered and, conceivably — given good will and sincerity, and a bold government — a
solution negotiated. Neither consociationalism nor federalism
can be ordained or imposed by fiat. They will represent organic
growth, and arise out of initiatives that result in negotiation, or
they will not arise at all.

The end product of a compromise that comes too late, and
that results from unacceptable demands on both sides coupled
with unacceptable levels of violence, may prove to be some kind
of partition. A federation gone sour is partition. Alternatively,
partition imposed or freely agreed to is, at an early stage, an innovative method of avoiding irreconcilable demands and escalating hostilities. But South Africa is no Cyprus. Its resources are not
evenly distributed. The population ratios are too unequal. To divide the wealth of the country in roughly fair portions would try

1. Arend Lijphart, "Federal, Confederal, and Consociational Options for the South
African Plural Society," in Robert I. Rotberg and John Barratt (eds.), *Conflict and Compromise in South Africa* (Lexington, Mass., 1980), 51-76.

Solomon and result in scattered white and black pockets, which would make as much nonsense of partition as fragmented home-lands make of separate development. Or it would necessitate vast population transfers. According to the simplest solution, whites would abandon the gold and other mineral deposits and retreat to the western Cape, taking up a life of agrarian and commercial self-sufficiency. But would the largest part of a bi-, tri-, or quad-ri-furcated South Africa be content to lose control of Cape Town? Would whites really abandon their interior cities, their mines, and their farms? The realities of partition would please no one, since a unified or federated South Africa provides so many more advantages for all. A systematic review of the question of parti-tion rejects it as a realistic alternative unless and until a division of the country becomes the only way of putting an end to a civil war.[2]

These possibilities do not exhaust the intermediate or final forms of one or more evolutionary initiatives. There are many others, not the least of which is the simplest to explain: the gov-ernment of South Africa could, however gradually or grudgingly, return the municipal, provincial, and ultimately the national franchise in the Cape to Coloureds and Africans; it could then ex-tend the franchise (initially in the dilute forms already discussed) throughout the country. The Progressive Federal party wrote a minority veto into its 1978 platform; something similar could be incorporated into a negotiated agreement between minorities and the majority.

There are two "official" evolutionary varieties now being promoted. First, the government of South Africa spent much of the 1960s and 1970s creating self-governing and so-called inde-pendent homelands out of the old reserves. These ministates were rural, largely impoverished and overcrowded, and for the most part without significant resources. The plan was to empty white-dominated South Africa of Africans with claims to citizenship. They could all be treated as foreign guest workers in the "white" areas or confined to their mostly distant, barely urbanized, desig-nated homelands. Someday, white cabinet members proposed,

2. Gavin Maasdorp, "Forms of Partition," in Rotberg and Barratt, *Conflict and Compromise*, 107-146.

the homelands would be linked federally with the white giant
state, and a joint central government would provide a framework
for the political participation of all the citizens of the original
South Africa. But by mid-1979, this scheme was beginning to
seem unreal even to members of the National party. It, and separate development, had confused few, and provided no sure way of
escaping criticism or gaining the cooperation of blacks. The position of blacks in the urban areas was becoming more secure. It
was widely acknowledged that whites would always be outnumbered, even in the cities (by four to one in the year 2000); whites
had in their own self-interest begun to cope with this fact as a
reality that could not be wished away.

Second, in 1978 the government proposed and in 1979
started to modify its attempt to associate Coloureds and Asians,
but not Africans, with whites in a new form of central government — a kind of narrow consociationalism. But whites were allotted predominant power, and Coloureds and Asians were given
— according to the first plan — only limited powers of self-government and little opportunity to influence the central or top tier
of government, which would clearly remain in white hands. If
African political participation could be ensured by this means,
or something similar, and if the substance of power were shared
(either federally, cantonally, or through consociation) then, and
only then, would such a new framework offer any method of
changing the South African equation. Even so, Africans might
well continue to insist that only a freely negotiated rearrange-
ment would have a chance of attracting their support.

To describe one or more evolutionary alternatives is neither
to advocate nor to anticipate that any, their clones or their cous-
ins, will in fact provide a solution. For it is not yet evident empiri-
cally that the ruling oligarchy is sufficiently desperate or fright-
ened to perceive that survival and self-interest ordain a selection
of and then a movement toward specific evolutionary goals. Until
confidence in the efficacy of mere manipulations of contemporary modalities erodes or is eroded, it is difficult to predict the
precise ways in which South Africa will evolve politically. In the
late 1970s the National party believed that tinkering with what
was called separate development and the cooptation of rural and

some urban élites would disperse unrest and quiet critics. But the Soweto riots and the loss of the oligarchy's moral leadership as a consequence of the Muldergate scandal (especially the forced resignation of President B. Johannes Vorster) compelled a reevaluation by the thinkers of Afrikanerdom of the best ways in which to maximize their own self-interest as whites.

In mid-1979, Crossroads and Alexandra (two black communities threatened with destruction) were left undisturbed. The minister of cooperation and development (African affairs) formed committees to discuss the future of Africans outside the homelands and began consulting with urban African leaders, some of whom had been jailed for their presumed militancy in 1977. He also talked of enlarging the existing homeland boundaries and of transferring white-run towns to some of the homelands. At the same time, the government accepted the general thrust of the radical reports of two official commissions, one on black labor and the other on living arrangements of blacks in towns. These were significant indications of an awareness of the need to find new answers and new ways of arriving at answers for South Africa.

Later, as part of Botha's dramatic new initiative to win the hearts and minds of Africans, his government sanctioned the formation of black trade unions and the inclusion within them of migrant and commuter as well as stabilized urban Africans. Botha also criticized the existence of legal barriers to transracial sexual relations and marriage, urged that Africans be treated without discrimination, and promised to dismantle the scaffolding of social and economic apartheid. With the consultation of both his military and his economic advisors, Botha became the first prime minister publicly to urge the end of color bars in the work place. If South Africa were both to avoid a revolution and to experience real growth, Botha said, Africans must be given the opportunity to advance in the work place and the freedom to prosper in commerce.

Botha maintained this strikingly fresh position despite the loss of white electoral support. His stance, however, was largely rhetorical, with implementing legislation, if any, to come. Furthermore, he made it completely clear that he contemplated no political alterations: he intended to engage in no negotiations with Africans over sharing power and no response to the oft-repeated black cry for a national convention. Short of pressures from within or from without, at the end of 1979 it was not clear that the ruling oligarchy was prepared to begin making the kinds of political concessions—and they would be seen as concessions—that would permit peaceful solutions to the fundamental problem of South Africa.

The Role of the West

It is often asserted that the South African government does not respond to pressure. But an examination of the events of the last thirty years shows the reverse: time lags there have been, but even the National party and its leadership have reshaped their ideological rationale and their political, social, and economic programs as a result of perceived threats. The understanding that exclusive white domination cannot continue indefinitely in its present form may encourage the ruling oligarchy to embark upon the path of evolutionism. But it is more likely that such an embarkation will be encouraged by renewed urban unrest, by labor discontent and strikes sufficient to threaten the economy, by guerrilla assaults, or by the combination of all three, possibly linked more by coincidence than design to some natural disaster or crisis. Resistance and overreaction could conceivably result in revolution rather than an acceleration of evolution; the great revolutions of the past were punctuated by accidents and idiosyncratic tumults more than they were by designed escalations of violence.

Outside pressure may prove crucial in encouraging evolutionary responses. But the timing of the intervention of outsiders is critical: outside pressure generally proves more efficacious if it supplements internal forces, especially at times when the state is distracted and losing legitimacy. Short of invasion or the launching of full-scale air or sea attacks—all far-fetched possibilities—outsiders would be most likely to seek to induce South Africa to alter its policies by raising the costs of apartheid. If crude oil is made either unavailable or extremely expensive, the character of white life can be compelled to change for the worse, as it was in

1979. The denial of other imports, and boycotts of exports (but who would boycott gold, manganese, chrome, platinum, and other crucial metals?) can add further to the price of privilege. But it has not yet been demonstrated that there is a direct relationship between unacceptable levels of cost and shifts in policy dramatic enough to satisfy the United Nations and other foreigners. Isolating and punishing South Africa may have its own rewards, especially in the West, but if economic weapons are used, with but limited results, they are forfeited for the future. That is one reason why disinvestment, simply conceived, might or might not prove tactically appropriate.

The departure of existing transnational corporations might in fact prove temporarily advantageous, for there would be marginally important new inflows of capital. The process that legally must be employed when corporations wish to disinvest, and repatriate even a portion of their assets, is tortuous and complicated. The usual result is for a local or another foreign concern to purchase the divested assets; foreign corporations are unable to repatriate their physical assets or to do something similar that would have the result of undermining South Africa's productive capacity.

For the reasons discussed earlier, the departure of individual American (or other) enterprises would have no important lasting economic impact on South Africa. However, it is argued that the flight of a group of American (or British, or German) companies would have a psychological and therefore a policy impact beneficial to Africans. Unhappily for the argument, there are no precedents for such a conclusion and many indications that point in another direction. Substantially different is official action. If by the denial of tax credits, or some other mechanism, all American corporations were compelled by law to cease operating in South Africa immediately or over five years, then there would be a greater likelihood of policy responses that would assist an evolutionary perspective. If such actions on the part of the United States were matched by Germany, France, and Britain (the most important single investing nation), then South Africa would be unable to ignore the psychological as well as the potential economic harm of such concerted arrangements.

No one who wants to promote some form of evolutionary change in South Africa should tie his aspirations to the notion that American, British, French, or German legislators will promote so drastic a departure from normal commercial practices. The United States is not eager, because of the principle and of Israel primarily, to encourage boycotts. Nor does the posture of the Senate during 1979 provide assurances as to the attitudes of the United States Congress toward the shutting off of investment in South Africa.

A much more fruitful employment of economic leverage may exist with regard to new investment. South Africa requires injections of foreign capital in order to maintain even minimal growth. American and other governments have in recent years begun discouraging investment in and lending to South Africa. Concern on the part of university and other stockholders has had an adverse impact, especially on large banking institutions. Most of all, the parlous state of the South African economy in 1976-1978 provided a disincentive for corporate investing and term lending.

Capital inflow will continue to be limited so long as South Africa is politically unstable. South Africa has a distinct economic incentive: the more it demonstrates a willingness to evolve rather than confront, the greater the likely desire of investors to look anew at South Africa, and the easier it will be for South Africa to borrow on favorable terms. Governments can enhance bargaining potentials in this sphere.

Short, again, of invasion and economic aggression that would amount to a form of war, governments can do little more to twist the South African arm. They, the United States foremost, can continue to hinder South Africa militarily by denying it American-manufactured strategic weapons, including computers. But the French and the British have never been so chaste. The West can police the petroleum bazaars, but such behavior would provide questionable precedents. (In any case, it is argued, OPEC ought to monitor the shipments of its own members.) If a blockade of South Africa could be limited to tankers, and if cutting off South Africa's crude-oil imports would be sure to result in a major shift in official policy, then that kind of blockade might prove a useful option. But South Africa's strategic petroleum reserves permit consumption at reduced levels for at least a year. Could the West sustain a blockade for a year? Could it do so if it meant either denying Botswana, Swaziland, and Lesotho normal supplies or airlifting refined products there? What about the precedent for Israel, or for other nations disliked by OPEC?

A blockade would arouse some countervailing tendencies. If gold were still fetching top prices, South Africa could — at least temporarily — forego the sale of manganese, vanadium, chrome, and platinum — all minerals vital to United States industry and obtainable elsewhere only at a premium and with the dislocations (particularly for Europe) discussed in an earlier chapter. This is not to say that South Africa has leverage equal in potential to that of the West. Rather, it is not without a few economic weapons, as well as the ability to hold neighboring states (Zambia, and Zaire, too) hostage.

Short of a strategy of confrontation, the West can isolate South Africa, again without assurances or expectations that such methods will result in appropriate responses. To isolate is to lose further opportunities to influence a nation on a day-to-day basis. Realistically, coolness may be preferred to a rupture of relations as a bargaining posture; the West would retain its maneuverability, as would South Africa. From 1977 to 1979, on the issues of Namibia and, to some extent, Zimbabwe, diplomacy that veered from frigidity to the holding out of real incentives brought results. Especially for Americans, the package of incentives may prove much more helpful than a bundle of punishments. For example, South Africa wants the Koeberg reactors to be fueled in the 1980s in accord with an American contract; the United States wants South Africa to adhere to the Nuclear Non-Proliferation Treaty. But there may be room for additional bargaining for other goals. The United States and the West, to take the nuclear example, may be able to provide incentives for South African behavior of an evolutionary kind. It may be able to add its weight, at the right moment, to those within South Africa who are accelerating the progress of any evolutionary tendencies.

These are, alas, tactical suggestions. For those who would prefer to destroy apartheid in one fell swoop, with one grand simplistic gesture, this book and this chapter can give but cold comfort. There is no panacea. Instead, for outsiders, the cure must be the combination of remedies that gives influence and is essentially reactive without being supportive.

The West needs South Africa as presently governed for no strategic purpose and for no economic purpose beyond those already described. Those who see a white minority regime as a barrier to communism little understand what has happened in Africa since the 1950s, the conservative and Western-oriented inclination of South African blacks (at least so far), and the fact that it is the very persistence of white rule that destabilizes much of Southern Africa and provides the greatest reason, and the only excuse, for Soviet involvement.

Indeed, W. E. B. Du Bois may have been more prophetic than he realized. If the color line can be eliminated in South Africa — if it can be smudged or erased as a social taint and a political determinant — then, and probably only then, will South Africa take its rightful place as the economic powerhouse and political leader of black Africa. Neither the constellation of nations envisaged by Prime Minister Pieter W. Botha nor any similar coprosperity sphere can survive if the leaders of South Africa fail to devise a lasting, workable compromise within their own domain. Only then can they harness all South Africans to the wheel of prosperity and growth. The task of Western statesmen is to nudge, cajole, and otherwise make possible the development within South Africa of political systems that deliver full participation to blacks without submerging whites. That is a tall order, and one that no one should suppose can be fulfilled quickly or — depending upon the boldness of South Africa's leadership — without episodes of great societal pain.

Afrikaners have compromised before, and will recognize once again that their self-interest is obtainable only by carefully calculated retreat. The laager is too simple and sweeping a metaphor. Yet none should underestimate their grit in adversity, their obstinacy, or their stamina. There are some checkpoints. The first two focus upon Namibia and Zimbabwe. If and when South Africa returns to an earlier decision to shed control over its periphery, then the wars for those territories will end and black majority rule begin in earnest. For South Africa is decisive in both territories. If it sees its distant defense perimeter breached by guerrillas or its already high costs of control increased too much, or if it is increasingly denied supplies of crude oil, then South Africa will cease defending its satrapies. By so doing it might also signal a willingness to begin rearranging its own future. It can expect support from the West for both decisions, and renewed cooperation as the peripheral territories go their own ways and South Africa begins to prepare itself for a long process of evolutionary change.

There are no guarantees of such a process. Evolutionary beginnings may be delayed too long. Like the dinosaur, South Africa as we know it today may not be able to adapt to an altered environment. Then violence will become increasingly common; the chasm between the races will grow; the labor on which white lives depend may become scarce; and a managed transition may become less and less a real possibility. Neither Babylon nor Rome fell in a day, but the longer the dimensions of the threat remain unappreciated, the longer the demographic realities (especially in the urban areas) and their political consequences are denied, the more destructive may be the combat and the more devastating the eventual result.

Index